INVASION OF THE MOOCs: THE PROMISES AND
PERILS OF MASSIVE OPEN ONLINE COURSES

INVASION OF THE MOOCS:

THE PROMISES AND PERILS OF

MASSIVE OPEN ONLINE COURSES

Edited by Steven D. Krause and
Charles Lowe

Parlor Press
Anderson, South Carolina
www.parlorpress.com

Printed in the United States of America
S A N: 2 5 4 - 8 8 7 9

Library of Congress Cataloging-in-Publication Data

Invasion of the MOOCS : the promises and perils of massive open online courses / edited by Steven D. Krause and Charles Lowe.
    pages cm
  Includes bibliographical references and index.
  ISBN 978-1-60235-533-0 (pbk. : alk. paper) -- ISBN 978-1-60235-534-7 (hard : alk. paper) -- ISBN (invalid) 978-1-60235-535-4 (adobe ebook) -- ISBN 978-1-60235-536-1 (epub) -- ISBN 978-1-60235-537-8 (ibook) -- ISBN 978-1-60235-538-5 (kindle)
  1. MOOCs (Web-based instruction) 2. Web-based instruction. 3. Education, Higher--Computer-assisted instruction. 4. Distance education I. Krause, Steven D. II. Lowe, Charles.
  LB1044.87.I68 2014
  371.33'44678--dc23
                        2014017050

              2 3 4 5

Photograph of Steven D. Krause by Mike Andaloro. Used by permission. Photograph of Charles Lowe by Daniel Royer. Used by permission.
Cover Image Alien in a Flying Saucer. ID 24796944 © 2012 by Candonyc, Dreamstime.com. Use by permission.
Cover design by Charles Lowe

This book is printed on acid-free paper.

Parlor Press, LLC is an independent publisher of scholarly and trade titles in print and multimedia formats. This book is available in paper, cloth and eBook formats from Parlor Press on the World Wide Web at http://www.parlorpress.com or through online and brick-and-mortar bookstores. For submission information or to find out about Parlor Press publications, write to Parlor Press, 3015 Brackenberry Drive, Anderson, South Carolina, 29621, or email editor@parlorpress.com.

Contents

Introduction: Building on the Tradition of CCK08

Charles Lowe

CCK08: Connectivism and Connective Knowledge, a massive open online course (MOOC) with over 2200 students that was created and facilitated by George Siemens and Stephen Downes, is generally considered by many as the MOOC which started the current revolution in online education.* I remember in 2008 reading about Siemens and Downes' plans to host an online class that would have traditional paying students, while also inviting anyone else to read the course materials and participate in the online discussions. It seemed to me a fascinating experiment in online learning that continued a rich tradition of experimentation by educational technology innovators interested in seeing the ways in which the tools of the Internet and electronic discourse could provide alternative—or even better—methods for learning. For instance, in 2002, six years before CCK08, George Siemens proposed what he called a "'non-course course'" in which fifteen participants would use a Yahoo Groups to engage with a facilitator-created set of questions. Siemens was interested in stimulating "an exploratory, community-created knowledge building process," instead of creating a traditional course that required digesting teacher-provided content. The focus of the non-course course was elearning, and the goal was for the discussion participants to generate ideas about the possibilities of learning. Siemens later summarized their discussions into small articles on his elearnspace website, covering topics such as instructional design and facilitating learning in groups.

In retrospect, Siemens' non-course course doesn't seem as exciting or as novel as it did to me then because thousands of educators have since experimented with different modes of online learning. This is not to discount the value of such early experimentation, but instead to recognize that most educators now know many people who have successfully used Internet platforms such as discussion boards, wikis, blogs, social networking sites, and virtual reality software to create virtual learning spaces that are as integral to their course as the syllabus the teacher hands out at the beginning of the semester. These days, it would be rare to find a post-secondary teacher in western countries and other developed nations who had not used at least one of these tools themselves multiple times. The early experimentation of Siemens and many others like him were important first steps in establishing best practices for integrating electronic discourse into the classroom, and such experimentation and knowledge formation about its pedagogical uses is an ongoing process as new Internet discussion mediums became available.

At the same time that Siemens was experimenting with his non-course, 2002 was also the year of a very important event: MIT's establishment of their OpenCourseWare initiative. The MIT faculty had voted to share their entire course content online, creating an example for the importance of creating and sharing educational resources for the rest of education to follow. This was a huge boost for those of us who had already been advocating the sharing of classroom materials, the need for open access to scholarly works, and the use of open source software in education, and it spurred a UNESCO discussion forum about opencourseware in the same year where the term open educational resources (OER) was coined. While fundamentally, open educational resources are defined as course materials (and software) that can be freely shared, OER has further meaning as a movement that was discussed at that UNESCO Forum. At its core, OER has an idealistic vision of creating freely available educational opportunities for anyone with Internet access, educational opportunities equivalent to the traditional classroom which would particularly help those in developing areas of the world. MOOCs, to me, seem a logical progression toward this goal from what was begun with open course ware. Certainly, institutional repositories like MIT's are important to the

OER movement for making courses materials available online that can potentially be used by teachers for designing their own classes, or for self-learners engaging with the material to suit their own objectives. Yet, without the context provided by daily classroom interactions, lectures, and individual teacher feedback, a visit to any open course ware class repository is a step into empty classrooms that allows the Internet user to see the content of each course after it has happened, but without participating or even viewing the course in progress. Compare this to MOOCs, which open the door for anyone to join in the course from the beginning as a student in the class. This is a richer educational experience, and there is ample evidence that the vision discussed for OER at that UNESCO forum is closer to being met, with people around the world joining in the educational experience of MOOCs, all thanks to the experiment which was CCK08.

Now that it is several years since CCK08, MOOCs have invaded higher education—for better or worse. There are MOOCs that have tens of thousands—if not hundreds of thousands—more students than CCK08. Millions of dollars of grants have funded many experiments with a variety of MOOC based on different theretical principles and using different inteactive tools. Elite colleges are creating MOOCs to enhance their own reputation, although ironically not offering college credit for the courses themselves. Politicians, looking for yet another route to cheap education, are pushing MOOCs upon public institutions, with commercial entities determined to monetize the MOOC equally prodding the debate in favor of MOOCs for higher ed. If that isn't enough, mainstream media tends to already treat MOOCs as accepted valid substitutions for traditional college courses; after all, cheap education is always attractive to the public. It sells news.

And yet in opposition to all the momentum that MOOCs have gained from outside higher education, the majority of educators continue to question whether or not MOOCs can offer an equivalent college learning experience deserving of college credit. There has been extensive debate in the blogosphere and in publications such as *The Chronicle of Higher Education* and *Inside Higher Ed,* and education is far from a consensus in support of offering college credit. It is reasonable to question the amount of learning happening in MOOCs since the teacher's role has been greatly reduced compared to the traditional classroom, mostly to that of a course instructional designer who administrates the class in progress. Not surprising, since it is impossible for the teacher to have individual interaction with even a small percentage of students in MOOCs numbering in the thousands, much less tens of thousands. What is lost without these student-teacher connections? That's the question that has yet to be answered.

In this collection, you'll find various educators discussing their position on this issue and sharing their pedagogical experiences as instructional designers, teachers, and students of MOOCs. Glenna Decker leads off the collection with an essay on the history of MOOCs to set the context for the rest of the collection. And my fellow co-editor, Steven Krause, ties everything up at the end with some final reflection drawn from the essays themselves and their authors.

Within the book, there are some strong arguments presented against MOOCs. James Porter reflects on what a MOOC is and how it compares to the traditional writing classroom, in the end surmising that "a well-designed MOOC" might be superior to how composition is taught in some classes, but that an effective writing teacher with a good course design will always trump the MOOC because of the individual attention students get. Recounting his experience taking an xMOOC, Aaron Barlow yearns for more self-directed learning, and he discusses the post-colonial assumptions behind the pedagogy that seeks to offer this free education to all. In his essay, Bob Samuels argues that the current push for these massive classes where the teacher is more of a "guide" is exactly the opposite of what education needs, that small, interactive classes should be the goal instead.

Other essays ask us to reflect on what a MOOC is or comment on recent MOOC discourse. Steven Krause asks us to consider the MOOC as more of an interactive textbook than a course, and he explores the implications of that perspective. Jeffrey Grabill, in the context of describing why Michigan State University is considering a writing MOOC, points out the value of MOOCs as sites for pedagogical research. Jeff Rice wants us to understand how many of the conversations about MOOCs also apply to traditional modes of education, that only the "large number of students" has evolved. Nick Carbone cautions against the pitfall of seeing MOOCs as a solution to providing cheap education, and he talks about some instances where MOOCs are suitable for some learners.

Many essays in this collection are written by faculty in my field of writing studies, and so several of the essays address the issue of feedback on writing in MOOCs. Alexander Reid begins by pointing out the unsuitability of machine-based grading for evaluating writing, and then discusses potential challenges of developing MOOCS for learning to write. Bill Hart-Davidson explains the value of deliberate practice supported by feedback from peer networks for learning to write and leaves us with the observation that while MOOCs are not there yet, they very well could be reconceived to achieve those objectives. Drawing upon his experience in helping to design the Duke University composition MOOC, Edward White explores how student assessment of student writing can be used to facilitate learning in the absence of teacher feedback.

From faculty who have taught MOOCs, there are essays that could help to improve teaching in MOOCs and in the traditional classroom. For instance, Karen Head reflects on some of the unanticipated issues with MOOCs that resulted from her experience teaching "First-Year Composition 2.0" at Georgia Tech University. Teachers of the ED-CMOOC at the University of Edinburgh—Jeremy Knox, Jen Ross, Christine Sinclair, Hamish Macleod, and Siân Bayne—make the case for the importance of drawing on participant feedback for continuing to refine MOOC design. Denise Comer shares her daily experiences as a teacher of the Duke University writing MOOC, providing an insightful narrative in the life of a MOOC teacher. The "Rhetorical Composing" MOOC faculty team at Ohio State University—Kay Halasek, Ben McCorkle, Cynthia L. Selfe, Scott Lloyd DeWitt, Susan Delagrange, Jennifer Michaels, and Kaitlin Clinnin—relate how their experiences with teaching in a MOOC has caused them to question some basic assumptions about the teaching of writing. And finally, Alan Levine, an instructor of the "Digital Storytelling" ds106 MOOC, implores readers to understand the importance of openness in MOOCs.

Other essays include people who have participated as students in MOOCs. While each is either a graduate student or faculty member trained in pedagogy, and certainly their observations may not reflect the experience of the individual leaner from outside education, their insights are invaluable nonetheless. Laura Gibbs points out potential problems she observed with the Coursera MOOC software platform for supporting learning on a large scale, and she offers some suggestions for improvement. Jacqueline Kauza describes the loss she felt from the lack of human interaction in comparison to a face-to-face class. Melissa Syapin reflects on how MOOCs did not fit her general sense of an educational experience. Elizabeth Woodworth explores the valuable connections she made as a leaner with other students using social media in a MOOC. And Heather Noel Young provides insight into her sometimes difficult user experience as a student with MOOC course materials.

Hopefully, you will find these essays as interesting and informative as I did, and I am thankful to the contributors of this collection for that experience. Most important, I hope you will see these essays as posing additional important questions about MOOCS, continuing the grande experiment started by CCK08. For whether or not the MOOC has a place as a credit bearing course in college, I have no doubt that there is much education can learn from the continued offering and exploration of MOOCs.

WORKS CITED

Siemens, George. "Elearning Course." *Elearnspace. Elearnspace.* 8 Aug. 2002. Web. 20 Jan. 2014.

INVASION OF THE MOOCS

MOOCology 1.0

Glenna L. Decker

The challenge with writing a brief introduction to MOOCs (Massive Open Online Courses) is that the phenomenon is still developing.* This rapidly evolving movement may, or may not, radically alter higher education as we know it. Some refer to MOOCs as a disruptive technology, suggesting that they are the turning point for the business model of higher education, affecting not only the revenue stream from students, but also the role of faculty, the need for brick and mortar, and the way degrees are constructed. Others suggest that MOOCs are another educational fad that are receiving a great deal of attention now, but expect that the interest and excitement will wind down. However you look at it, the conversation is still unfolding, and it is one we cannot simply ignore. To get us started, I will present a few basics that include an explanation of what they are with an overview of the history, and will highlight some of the main points and the questions they raise in the ongoing dialog.

MOOC is an acronym for *Massive Open Online Course*. *Massive* refers to the potential of extremely large enrollments; thousands of students register from all over the globe. *Open* can mean a few things, such as open enrollment to anyone who has Internet access regardless of their prior learning. It can also mean that, at least initially, courses were free to anyone interested in registering. Some hold that open should refer to the concept of open access, meaning that the content is not only free and available to all, but holds at most a Creative Commons licensing status so that the content can be downloaded, saved,

---

and even adapted for one's own purposes (with credit to the developer). *Online* is the means of content delivery, and *Course* implies that there is some traditional convention of how a course operates, such as requiring enrollment, a start and end date, instructor-developed content delivered to the learner, and some means of assessment.

Those who are loyal to the original MOOC in 2008 will bifurcate the name into types of MOOCs; cMOOC is based on distributed learning and connectivism, a theory of learning, whereas xMOOCs, such as those we hear about the most, lean towards Behaviorism and use more conventional instructor-centered delivery methods with objective assessment and automated grading. George Siemens, one of the original MOOC facilitators, describes them, "cMOOCs focus on knowledge creation and generation whereas xMOOCs focus on knowledge duplication" (Siemens).

The proliferation of MOOCs is worth noting, but mostly in context of who is involved. Online courses have been widely offered by higher education institutions since the 1990s. Independent courses for credit evolved into online degrees, and then into for-profit institutions. The Ivy Leagues didn't embrace online learning, other than to offer some non-credit courses (e.g. AllLearn, a consortium of Oxford, Yale, and Stanford), until in 2002 when MIT launched OpenCourseWare, a movement to put all of their undergraduate and graduate course content online, freely available to anyone (MIT OpenCourseWare). Other elite institutions joined in, clearly stating that they offered content alone with no credit available; it was an act designed for the public good. The Ivy Leagues set the standard, and many other colleges and universities followed suit by putting course content online.

The term MOOC is credited to Dave Cormier who coined it following the first massively enrolled course—in 2008 George Siemens' and Stephen Downes' course on Connectivism and Connected Knowledge had 25-tuition paying students taking it for credit, and an additional 2,300 students who took it at no cost and without earning credit. Siemens and Downes, both of whom hold strong philosophies towards the open education movement, instead credit David Wiley and Alec Couros, each of whom developed their own wiki-based free courses in 2007. Several free online courses followed in the next few years, but wider fascination began in 2011 with media attention over a course on artificial intelligence.

THE BIG THREE

In 2011, Sebastian Thrun, then a professor at Stanford University, was inspired to take his course on artificial intelligence, put it online, and freely open it to anyone who wanted to enroll. He had an international enrollment of 160,000 students, and of those, 28,000 students completed the course. Thrun's course gained a lot of attention from others in elite institutions, and launched the still emerging movement. Thrun left Stanford to start *Udacity*, a for-profit company that continues to offer free online courses in the Science, Technology, Engineering, and Math (STEM) disciplines, often taught by faculty on leave from other elite higher education institutions. Inspired by Thrun, two other Stanford faculty members, Andrew Ng and Daphne Koller, started their own for-profit MOOC provider called *Coursera*, and Stanford now partners with 33 high caliber universities, collectively offering nearly 400 free courses (currently), taught by faculty from these distinguished partner institutions. Although there are others offering MOOCs, of note is the not-for-profit consortium *edX*, a partnership originally between Harvard and MIT, then joined by Berkeley and the University of Texas system, and now with over two-dozen national and international higher education institutions. This list continues to evolve with many others entering the fold.

Continuing this trend, we are now seeing the development of MOOC providers globally, drawing in regional partnerships. The Open University in the United Kingdom is using their distance education expertise to provide the platform FutureLearn. Launching in 2013, at least 26 UK Universities have signed on (as of this writing). Also in 2013, Open Universities Australia launched Open2Study, another platform with a mix of academic, vocational/technical, and professional/industry institutions providing courses. The next to launch courses in September 2013 is from the European Union. OpenupEd is still forming partnerships, with an inaugural 12 institutions representing 11 different countries, and as many more on the horizon to join. OpenupEd courses vary in discipline and in the language in which they are offered.

HIGHER EDUCATION PROGRESSION OR A PASSING TREND?

Education has a history of jumping onto trends, constantly seeking ways to improve teaching and learning. Technology exacerbates the opportunities to discover the next new thing that may solve all of our problems. Why, then, is it relevant to talk about MOOCs? It is possible that in time we will look back and realize that MOOCs were another fad. Even if they will not single-handedly change the nature of how we do what we do in higher education, I think that there are reasons to pause and consider their potential impact.

We first recognize that the nation's most elite institutions drive this movement. The response from those at other institutions is to keep up with the Ivy League—so much so that it temporarily cost the President of University of Virginia her job. Dr. Theresa Sullivan did not appear to be aligning her university with MOOC start-ups quickly enough, prompting the Board of Visitors (BOV) to request her resignation. Two years into her presidency, with a satisfactory job performance and an overall positive relationship with faculty, the sudden and unexplained move was met with outrage from faculty and students. Email trails between members of the Board, and at least one email communication with a donor revealed that the impetus was a growing fear that Dr. Sullivan was not responsive to a shifting culture towards online teaching and learning. Specifically, the institution was falling behind the initiatives of elite institutions such as Stanford and Harvard (Rice; Schwartzman et al.). U-Va had not joined a MOOC consortium. The negative press and a call from Virginia's Governor resulted in her rehiring two weeks later. Unbeknownst to the BOV, she had already begun talks with faculty about MOOCs.

As stated earlier, top tier institutions did not embrace offering credit for online courses in their own degree programs, yet we know that many others did. How is this different? I suggest that a primary purpose in moving courses online is for student access, to reach those at a distance from the institution or for flexible scheduling to continue learning in the context of busy lives. It is a useful recruitment and retention strategy. The Ivy League institutions never needed to do this, and still do not. For them, it is not about access to their own students; it is about access to the rest of the masses. They will lead because they can. If anything, the widespread enrollment of MOOCs emphasizes their brand and keeps them held high above the rest. To underpin this, Coursera's own contract states that they will offer courses only from institutions that are members of the Association of American Universities, and from outside North America, only those institutions that are considered in the top five (Rivard). The top tier faculty teach the MOOCs, and in so doing, the faculty member becomes famous beyond those in a specific discipline; in essence, they become academic rock stars. The average (or below average) person from anywhere in the world can now learn from the academic rock stars. David Wills, a professor at Amherst, stated to Nathan Heller at *The New Yorker*, "It's like higher education has discovered the megachurch," (Heller).

We should not overlook the potential for what we can learn about learning through research available through MOOCs. With tens of thousands of students in a single course, harnessing available data can provide a great deal of insight into human learning behavior that can inform educators using any delivery method. EdX plans to use the opportunity; Piotr Mitros, edX's chief scientist, stated "It's a live laboratory for studying how people learn, how the mind works, and how to improve education, both residential and online" (as quoted by Parry).

As it is, however, there is great concern that MOOCs are moving ahead too quickly without any empirical research to support their effectiveness. The literature on MOOCs is culled through myriad news articles, blogs, and higher education RSS feeds. There has been little evaluation into the actual design and delivery of most MOOCs to determine if they meet acceptable standards for online course delivery, and it is probably a fair assumption that they do not given the importance of student to faculty interaction expected in a quality online course. The course content is likely exemplary given the pedigree of the developer. Still, complaints from MOOC participants include that other than taped lectures, students do not interact with the "rock star" faculty. In some courses, students may interact with one of several teaching assistants, but more likely, it will be with fellow learners, or at best, someone with enough experience to volunteer for group leadership. If learners have questions about the content, they can post them and may receive a potentially accurate response from another, or if other students vote on the value of the question, it might be promoted to the top of a list—then maybe the faculty member will see it and respond. Or maybe not. Engaged peer learning is an essential and valuable contributor to the learning process. Can it serve as a substitute for faculty presence? (For more information, see https://coi.athabascau.ca/ or http://communitiesofinquiry.com/.)

The extremely high attrition rate of MOOCs could be evidence that it does not. Using Class Central, an online MOOC aggregator, educational researcher Katy Jordan compiled available data on MOOCs offered between October 2011 and April 2013 to determine completion rates. The average completion rate for MOOCs that relied on any peer grading was only 5.3%, and those that relied on automated grading was 9.2% (Jordan). (Please note that this is only reporting percentages and not actual numbers.) To date, a majority of participants are from outside of the United States, and co-founder of Coursera Daphne Koller reports that many of the students have already earned degrees. They are dropping in for interest, curiosity, and lifelong learning. Perhaps she is not as concerned about retention.

At What Cost, and to Whom?

Students who successfully complete a MOOC may have nothing to show for it except their own learned knowledge. Some MOOCs offer certificates of completion and some offer badges, and the current trend is for MOOC courses to be considered for college credit. The American Council on Education (ACE) recently evaluated five MOOCs and determined that they are credit worthy. Students successfully completing any of those courses may apply for transfer credit into a degree-granting institution. It is up to the institution as to whether they will accept such credit. As of press time, the progress is slow for adoption of transfer credits from a completed MOOC.

Colleges and universities may need an evolving plan to manage MOOC related inquiries and requests for credit. Given that the for-profit MOOC companies such as Udacity and Coursera produced no business plan for sustainability, there is only speculation as to how they will create revenue. The development of a MOOC is costly and can entail production costs as well as faculty time. Faculty report spending 100-plus hours on course development, and another eight to ten hours weekly while teaching, often at the expense of their regular institution responsibilities. While initially well funded (through venture capitalists in the cases of Udacity and Coursera, and for edX, Harvard and MIT each contributed $30 million), there will be a need for the companies to make money.

Speculation has included the potential that students may have to pay to receive a certificate of completion or pay to take assessments, typically at a local proctoring site. Some may begin charging nominal fees to students. Other means that have risen to the top include employee recruitment, per-fee tutoring or assignment feedback, and offering a fee-based service to match successful student's resumes with industry. Coursera is developing relationships with universities to provide course content, selling licensing rights to the institution to embed the course into the curriculum, or use the content in a flipped-classroom model. The deals allow the university (currently, several state systems) to pay Coursera a base fee for course development, and additionally a tiered per-enrolled-student fee. Coursera's point is that if the university charges their standard tuition rates and enrolls more students because of the MOOC, they can recoup and exceed their initial investment. Udacity and San Jose State University are now collaborating to offer a MOOC alternative for five courses and for a fee of $150, students can earn between 3 – 5 SJSU credits. Although put on hold while further reviewing the research, the President and the Provost of SJSU report their commitment to working with Udacity (Lopes Harris). Udacity claims to also be reviewing the data and addressing concerns. It seems as though both entities still anticipate a for-credit possibility for students. As a member of the Western Association of Schools and Colleges, there is little reason to doubt the transferability of these credits to another institution.

The question remains, is this MOOC movement a threat to higher education as we know it? The conversations around this question include concerns that eventually the traditional business model will need to shift to accommodate the existence of MOOCs and credits. In the United States particularly, one fear is that they will drive down the cost of higher education. Many perceive this to be a benefit, but will it also mean the demise of smaller liberal arts and state colleges and universities who cannot financially compete? The trend of states providing substantially less funding to higher education, along with the conversations in Washington D.C. about the extent to which the federal government will support students through grants and loans, poses huge threats. The costs passed along to students are already prohibitive for many.

What if a student did not have to pay tuition, or paid a very nominal fee for a course? Will they take it whether or not the course meets the same quality standards and faculty contact? The fear is that students will if they can, affecting enrollment in traditional public funded institutions. An inevitable outcome is a further divide between those who can afford traditional college tuition, and those who cannot—an extension of the digital divide, bifurcating opportunities based on educational access.

One way to save money is to cut the payroll, and faculty and staff may face redundancy. For institutions who contract with the MOOC providers to use their content, there is concern that remaining faculty may be relegated to an enhanced Teaching Assistant role, there to support the elite content provided by the rock star academic. Not only does this assume that Ivy League faculty can hold a monopoly over the discipline's content, I worry that it could potentially lead to collective singular thinking. One value of a college education is exposure to many perspectives, insights, experiences, and diverse thinking. My worst-case scenario is global groupthink. If a majority of the world's higher education seeking learners were exposed primarily to only one person's thinking in any given discipline, the eventual and inevitable results are unfathomable.

The conversations and speculations occurring in response to the emergence and proliferation of MOOCs are very important, valuable, and completely necessary. Colleges and universities should be, and are, talking about the costs and value of higher education. This movement pushes the conversation to ask better questions and to seek and act upon viable answers. Discussions that initially emerged when it became apparent that MOOCs were becoming a phenomenon centered around the potential impact on traditional higher education, and listed benchmarks to determine when to be *concerned*. In a very short period, those benchmarks are being realized. In the same news cycle that we read about Amherst turning down the opportunity to jump on the MOOC bandwagon, and that Harvard is getting backlash from faculty about how decisions were made and what impact edX will have on Harvard, we also read about the giant leaps forward by MOOC providers. Mentioned earlier, ACE evaluated and approved five MOOCs as creditworthy, more are on the way. California lawmakers are pushing through legislation to require state institutions to accept approved MOOC credit in response to the number of students' waitlisted and unable to take required courses. Most threatening, however, comes from the state of Georgia. Along with other institutions, such as California State University and Colorado State University, Georgia State University passed a policy to accept MOOC transfer credits. That

wasn't enough for Georgia Tech. On May 14, 2013, they officially announced the first MOOC degree program with a matriculation date of
Fall 2014 ("Online Master of Science"). In partnership with Udacity
and AT&T, Georgia Tech will offer a Master of Science in Computer
Science through the MOOC platform, for less than $7000. As is typi-
cal for a MOOC, anyone can sign-up and take any of the courses, but
those pursuing the Master's degree will pay, albeit only around 20%
of what the traditional students will pay. Georgia Tech asserts that the
program will have the same content and rigor as their existing and
highly ranked program, and that the MOOC students who are degree
seeking will need to meet the same criteria for acceptance.

If nothing else wakes us up, this announcement should. The very
brief history of MOOCs demonstrates a domino effect. If this is one
more domino along the path, there will surely be more to follow.

MOOCs as a Public Good

Before we assume that it is all impending doom, I would like to take a
moment to consider how valuable it is to millions of people around the
globe to have access to content that has previously been only available
to the privileged. Educators strive to spark in their students the desire
for lifelong learning. Although access to technology remains a barrier
for many, there still exist significant numbers of people who can now
participate, to whatever degree they choose, in formal and semi-formal
learning. This is a very good thing. Stephen Downes, who first distinguished the types of MOOCs by their pedagogy, and co-facilitated
the "first" MOOC, writes as part of his vision statement on his website, "This to me is a society where knowledge and learning are public
goods, freely created and shared, not hoarded or withheld in order to
extract wealth or influence" (Downes).

Conclusion

It seems also fair to reiterate the possibilities of what we can learn from
MOOCs. If the collaborating universities, most well known for their
contributions to research, take advantage of the excitement around
MOOCs and are able to use them as a laboratory, there is a great deal
that we can learn. It will be very useful to have additional insight into

such questions such as, how do we learn in this environment? How do we navigate in the online environment? How do we form and operate in online learning communities? What happens when a class populates with learners from nearly every country in the world? I am certain that there are myriad other questions that can be addressed better on a scale the size of a MOOC than in a traditional-sized college course.

In whatever approach we take in response, it seems clear that we cannot ignore the MOOC phenomenon. During the rise of online courses, many worried that the format would eliminate the need for faculty, and university administrators would view them as a panacea to cure financial woes. Those fears went unrealized, and we continued with our business, adapting to the changes and learning how to take advantage with new pedagogies and opportunities. Here we are nearly two decades later facing a new obstacle or opportunity. As with online courses, it may not be the MOOC in its current form that changes higher education, and the movement as it exists may lose some of its current momentum. But undoubtedly, we will look back and recognize this turning point for whatever does come next. MOOCs are a disruptive technology, and higher education is most certainly going to evolve as a result. Those who simply try to ignore what is coming or to deny the impact, will likely fail and fold.

Works Cited

Downes, Stephen. "Vision Statement." *Stephen's Web*. Ed. Stephen Downes. N.p., 2010. Web. 29 May 2013. <http://www.downes.ca/index.html>.

Heller, Nathan. "Laptop U." *The Innovator's Issue*. Spec. issue of *The New Yorker* 20 May 2013: n. pag. *The New Yorker*. Web. 10 May 2013. <http://www.newyorker.com/reporting/2013/05/20/130520fa_fact_heller>.

Jordan, Katy. "Synthesising MOOC Completion Rates." *MoocMoocher*. N.p., 13 Feb. 2013. Web. 25 May 2013. <http://moocmoocher.wordpress.com/2013/02/13/synthesising-mooc-completion-rates/>.

Lopes Harris, Pat. "Update: Online Initiatives." *SJSU Today*. San Jose State University, 22 July 2013. Web. 5 Sept. 2013. <http://blogs.sjsu.edu/today/2013/update-sjsuudacity/>.

MIT Opencourseware. Massachusetts Institute of Technology, n.d. Web. 5 Sept. 2013. <http://ocw.mit.edu/index.htm>.

"Online Master of Science in Computer Science." *Georgia College of Tech Computing.* Georgia Institute of Technology, n.d. Web. 5 Sept. 2013. <http://www.omscs.gatech.edu/#np-855>.

Parry, Marc. "5 Ways That edX Could Change Education." *The Chronicle of Higher Education* 1 Oct. 2012, Online Learning: n. pag. *The Chronicle of Higher Education.* Web. 5 Sept. 2013. <http://chronicle.com/article/5-Ways-That-edX-Could-Change/134672>.

Rice, Andrew. "How Not to Fire a President." *The New York Times Magazine* 16 Sept. 2012: 56+. *ProQuest Newsstand.* Web. 5 Sept. 2013.

Rivard, Ry. "Coursera's Contractual Elitism." *Inside Higher Ed* 22 Mar. 2013: n. pag. Web. 25 May 2013. <http://www.insidehigh-ered.com/news/2013/03/22/coursera-commits-admitting-on-ly-elite-universities>.

Schwartzman, Paul, et al. "U-Va. Upheaval: 18 Days of Leadership Crisis." *The Washington Post* 30 June 2012: n. pag. *Education.* Web. 5 Sept. 2013. <http://www.washingtonpost.com/local/education/u-va-upheaval-18-days-of-leadership-crisis/2012/06/30/gJQA-VXEgEW_story.html>.

Siemens, George. "MOOCs Are Really a Platform." *eLearnspace.* eLearnspace, 25 July 2012. Web. 3 June 2013. <http://www.elearnspace.org/blog/2012/07/25/moocs-are-really-a-platform/>.

Framing Questions about MOOCs and Writing Courses

James E. Porter

Of course you can "teach writing" in a MOOC—at least as well as you can "teach writing" via a textbook or a YouTube video or a PowerPoint presentation or a writing center tutorial consultation.* All those genres, presentations, and interactions (both online and face-to-face) are ways that composition instructors teach writing. All those approaches are potentially effective ways to help student writers—depending, of course, on (1) the knowledge, expertise, and commitment of the instructor and (2) on the integrity of the instructional design, which is to say, on the quality of the presentation, on its appropriateness to its intended learner audience, and on the goals it sets (and whether it successfully achieves those goals).

We don't need to be afraid of MOOCs—although I think it is legitimate to distrust the hype that surrounds MOOCs. We should willingly embrace the idea that MOOCs can be a valuable addition to the toolbox of methods that writing teachers use to help writers. And the MOOC has the distinct advantage of expanding composition teachers' reach and impact, providing access to a much broader audience than simply campus-resident students who come to us in relatively small classes (<25) or via 1-on-1 tutorial consultations. In other words, the MOOC can be a good and potentially great way to teach writing and help writers.

---

* This work is licensed under the Creative Commons Attribution-Noncommercial-ShareAlike 3.0 United States License. To view a copy of this license, visit http://creativecommons.org/licenses/by-nc-sa/3.0/us/ or send a letter to Creative Commons, 171 Second Street, Suite 300, San Francisco, California, 94105, USA. For any other use permissions, contact the original author.

But—and here's the question researchers and teachers in composition had better be prepared to answer—can a MOOC ever be an adequate substitute for, and achieve comparable learning outcomes as, the first-year composition course? Here I am thinking of the standard 3-credit, first-year composition course that most universities offer (actually, most *require*) as a way to prepare students for college-level writing and to assess their level of competency and preparedness. In other words, English 101. FYC. The bread and butter course for the field of rhetoric/composition. **Could a writing MOOC—taught on a student-teacher ratio of hundreds or maybe even thousands to one—do that just as well?**

This is a vitally important question for composition researchers and teachers to answer because there are powerful agents—state legislators, higher education boards, boards of trustees, upper administrators—who have quickly grasped the economic implications of the MOOC for higher education, and who are desperately looking for ways to cut college costs. If the answer to the question is, "Yes, a MOOC can achieve comparable outcomes," then there will no longer be an argument for the standard composition course model that has been in place at least since the end of World War II—one composition instructor in a classroom of approximately 20 first-year students—and writing teachers will very quickly and dramatically have to change their fundamental thinking about teaching composition at the college level.

This is a well-defined, researchable question, and several prominent composition scholars are already addressing it, offering writing MOOCs and assessing the learning outcomes.[1] I eagerly look forward to seeing their results. In this essay, though, I want to reflect on two conceptual subquestions that are methodologically important to answering the larger question.

1.   Is the MOOC a course—or is it more like courseware?
2.   What are we comparing MOOCs to?

Before we evaluate the efficacy of the MOOC vis-à-vis the conventional first-year composition course, it would be a good idea to reflect on and critically address some key questions: What objects of analysis are we studying and comparing, and why? What should be our frame (or frames) for the analysis of MOOCs?[2]

1. Is the MOOC a *Course*—or *Courseware*?

The MOOC acronym hit the popular press in 2012, but the MOOC idea evolved out of several earlier projects that made instructional materials widely available online. In 2002 MIT launched its OpenCourseWare project, which provides online instructional materials for free under a Creative Commons open access license. Currently the program archives course materials for 2,150 courses (http://ocw. mit.edu/about/). In 2008 Andrew Ng, co-founder of Coursera along with Daphne Koller, started the Stanford Engineering Everywhere program, which offered online course materials for several Stanford engineering courses (also under a Creative Commons open access license). In fall 2011 Ng's online course on Applied Machine Learning at Stanford University enrolled over 100,000 students. That course was probably the unofficial birth of the MOOC, the moment that first caught everybody's attention.

These early MOOCs (though they were not yet called that) operated under an open-access principle. MIT's OpenCourseWare project licenses its available course materials under a Creative Commons open access license that allows students to share, redistribute, and remix the course materials any way they like, as long as they credit the source and license the new materials they create with the same kind of license. The Open Yale Courses project, which began in 2007, currently offers 42 online courses using the same license.

What is interesting about these open-access courseware projects is that they publish free "course materials," or "courseware," but often label the materials as "courses." Now there is a troubling elision, and one that lies at the core of MOOCs. Does "the course" = "the materials for the course"? Not entirely, no, unless you happen to think that the textbook = the course, and very few would make that mistake. Let's think about all those elements of any course that are not embodied in "the course materials," such as the delivery, the performance, class discussions, the instructor, the students, the students' contributions (including writing)—the unfolding action of a course in time. That simple, careless elision ("course" = "course materials"), a now common one, has significant implications for teaching and for the future of higher education.

This elision is by no means new. In taking a Udacity course on Introduction to Statistics, Audrey Watters notes that the experience was not unlike a previous experience of hers, twenty years earlier, taking a distance education course via US mail. That earlier distance education course consisted of "a textbook, a package of worksheets, and a box of 20 some-odd videotapes" (Watters 2013). When I open my print copy of *The New York Review of Books,* I can find an ad for "The Great Courses" (http://www.thegreatcourses.com/), a company that has been in existence since 1990. The company publishes lectures on a wide variety of academic topics, delivered by "award-winning" professors with "profound insights in their respective fields," and available in a variety of formats (CD, DVD, or digital audio or video). It is important to notice: These things are advertised as "Great Courses," not "Great Lectures." Here again we see the synechdochic substitution of "all for some," a common logical fallacy of generalization. MOOCs are being framed in a comparable way, and very effectively, in a way that erodes the full meaning of "course"—and in a way, I fear, that diminishes the value added of the faculty member. Instead of challenging the frame, instead of insisting on a more nuanced and complex notion and range of meanings for "course," many universities have not only accepted the frame but, ironically or sadly, are reinforcing it.

Any college course obviously consists of a variety of course materials. But it also includes a delivery, a performance, an enactment, and, of course, interaction with students. Too many discussions these days, particularly in the popular press, accept the frame that "the course" is a commodity, an object, to be bought and sold as if it were a textbook. In too many discussions, the course is assumed to be no more than a kind of multimedia textbook of content—with the instructor as the perhaps expendable conveyor of that content. I have no doubt that some college courses run this way: that is, as the primarily one-way delivery of content from instructor and/or textbook to the student, conceived of as an empty vessel (or nearly so). In the MOOC world, this thing is called, pejoratively, an xMOOC. It is based on what Freire calls the banking model of education, and it certainly exists; it may even be a useful model for some kinds of knowledge at some stages of learning.

This model obscures a vital point about the value of higher education. The value of many college courses is not primarily *the delivered content.* Rather, the real value added is *the interactive performance:* the social exchange, the enactment, the interaction that happens between content, instructor, and students, and that results, ideally, in learning. The value added by the university is perhaps mainly the service and ecology (Benkler 2008), not the content alone—that is, the entire learning environment that universities promote, that supports faculty development and delivery of courses, whether those courses are face-to-face or online.

An online college course perhaps should be treated as resource or service, not as a commodity to be bought and sold as an object (Vaidhyanathan 2002). Many courses, and perhaps most composition courses, function more like extemporaneous performances, and audience-participation performances at that. The course might have a script (a plan, a set of established materials), but the course itself unfolds in time as performance involving the instructor interacting with students and involving the creation of a fair amount of unplanned, unorchestrated content.

Let's remember that students can be course content creators, too. The assumption of the cMOOC (or "connectivist MOOC") is that students themselves create knowledge and promote learning in their activities and interaction in a course. While an xMOOC might operate more like a textbook, a Frierean, one-way information transfer model, a cMOOC is designed to make use of the communal aspects of social media and to maximize student interaction, remixing, and social dialogue. The assumption of connectivism is that learning happens not only in the one-way transfer of content from instructor to student/s, but more importantly in the networked, crowdsourced collaborative interaction between participants and in participants' active contributions to and remixing of course content (see Ravenscroft 2011; Siemens 2005). Indeed there is an even stronger claim at play here (one not unlike the assumptions of Socratic dialectic): that the interaction between participants potentially creates new knowledge and course content.

This is not a new or unfamiliar idea composition teachers. Composition teachers have been teaching cMOOCishly for a long time. Back in the 1980s we referred to this as a social contructivist approach to learning or knowledge development, or as epistemic rhetoric. Even earlier still Plato called it dialectic. Now it is known as connectivism. Well, OK.

Here is an added complexity: For most composition courses—and you have to understand that colleagues in other disciplines do not always appreciate this—the primary course content does not pre-exist the course; it is, rather, *the students' own writing*, which emerges through the course. Granted, the composition instructor develops or imports much course content in the form of the overall frame/plan for the course, readings, textbooks, the writing assignments, the rhetorical principles, the exercises and activities, the handouts and slides, etc. But the students themselves contribute a good amount of the content themselves (e.g., when their own writing itself become the primary content for a class discussion about a certain rhetorical approach or technique)—and a good chunk of the composition course consists of *the instructor commenting on and interacting with that writing, on an individual level.* Can a MOOC, even a dynamically designed, social media-based cMOOC, replicate that?

Composition textbooks are pretty massive things, some of them running over 500 pages long. But when did composition teachers ever confuse the textbook with the "course"? Is a MOOC a "course" or should it be framed as a MOOMT ... Massive Open Online Multimedia Textbook? Michael Feldstein and Chris Wolverton, among others, have raised this question and have speculated that the MOOC will eventually come to compete with the textbook market moreso than with the university course market. Perhaps they are right, but MOOC marketing is headed in a different direction. For the immediate future we have to identify and challenge a number of related some-for-all substitutions that synecdochically threaten to diminish what a university education is supposed to mean: Course = course materials. Course = lectures. Course = content. A university education = a collection of courses. In all of these equations what is getting overlooked, or deliberately obscured, is the question of the value added of the instructor. What value do instructors contribute? For many, the answer to that question is very simply *lectures*—and lectures can easily be captured, archived, and scaled up via video. But what if the answer to that question for many courses, like college composition, is not lecture but rather *engaged interaction?*

I am the co-author of an online textbook, *Professional Writing Online,* along with Patricia Sullivan and Johndan Johnson-Eilola. When we originally developed the idea for *Professional Writing Online,* at Purdue University in the mid 1990s, we had in mind not so much an online textbook as a set of online course materials that would provide an interactive social space for students and teachers to interact online within the text itself. We imagined asynchronous discussion boards and synchronous chat forums within the textbook, and we even imagined that the textbook would expand through contributions from both teachers and students. (For example, we wanted to set up the textbook so that teachers could upload their own assignments, so that students could contribute samples.) Our idea was that the three co-authors would serve almost as editors and curators for contributed material, that we would enter the textbook at scheduled times for synchronous chat with instructors and students, that the textbook would be an organic, growing entity.

This idea scared publishers to death, who saw in this model nothing but security and copyright nightmares, and as a threat to the prevailing business model. ("Who would own the copyright for the discussions?" one publisher asked us.) In 1996-1997, we started conversations with three major composition textbook publishers. All three were nervous about the idea of a purely online textbook, much less an online social media textbook. The "innovative" publishing model in place at that time, barely, was that you would publish a print textbook with a "companion web site" (which did not strike us as very bold or innovative). We ended up going with the one publisher (Allyn & Bacon) who was at least willing to commit to the idea of an online textbook. But the publisher insisted on there being a companion print guidebook along with it. And so the first edition of *Professional Writing Online* appeared in late 2000 with a companion print guidebook. The online textbook had many external hyperlinks to publicly accessible web resources, and so was a Web 1.0 online textbook. But it was not at all the kind of collaborative Web 2.0 kind of social space that we had envisioned.

So what if we think about MOOCs as if they were online social media textbooks, multimedia textbooks that provide video lectures, much like the "Great Courses" program that has been around since 1990, but that also support online interaction around and within the textbook (much like the original idea for *Professional Writing Online)?* Within this frame—MOOC = MIT (multimedia interactive textbook)—the value of the MOOC becomes more apparent, I feel. It's a great *textbook*, a community-based textbook! It might even provide a great course plan or syllabus. But it should not ever be mistaken for or misrepresented as a *course*.

Siva Vaidhyanathan (2002) points out the problem of universities defining themselves as "content providers," as so many are wont to do. When they do that, universities position their faculty as an unnecessary and grossly expensive delivery mechanism of dubious value. Why do we need to pay 20, 40, or 80 lesser composition instructors to develop content for composition courses, if we can have the One Master Composition Instructor do it in a MOOC?

But let's flip the frame. What if the significant value that universities provide is not *content* but rather *interaction and ecology*? In a given course the student is given the opportunity to engage and interact with a smart disciplinary expert; and, further, that disciplinary expert passes a judgment on that student's proficiency; and further that students gets to interact with other comparably smart and talented people in a classroom. Over the entirety of a student's college education, this typically happens 43 times in the space of four years (128 credit hours for graduation/3 = 42.7). The student engages 43 different disciplinary experts across a range of disciplines, and receives a grade on his/her performance in each exchange. This means something.

Now, let's inspect the previous claim more closely. How much engagement and interaction actually happens, particularly in lecture classes of 80, 200, or 400 students? Admittedly not very much. But in the composition classroom of ~20 students, yes, it is supposed to happen: the system is designed for the instructor to engage and interact closely and frequently with each student's writing, providing feedback, suggestions, and advice for improvement. This is supposed to mean something, too.

In regards to our understanding of "course," we need to be wary of the some-for-all fallacy, of the *reductio ad absurdum* fallacy, of the slippery slope (Porter 2013). A course is *not* a course (of course of course). A course should not be reduced to any one of its isolated components— whether content, or course materials, or the Great Professor, or the students, or the design, or the technology. None of these things is itself the course per se, and even the conglomerate of these things is not the course. The course consists of the interaction of all these elements, and in the spaces of those interactions lie *surprises,* which are an important part of learning (Whithaus and Neff 2006). Of far greater importance to assessing course effectiveness are results, outcomes, learning: What have students demonstrated that they have learned or gained from a course? And yet we have to be cautious even of that: Do the results of a course always reveal themselves by the end of the course, or do the really significant results actually appear farther down the road?

2. What Do We Compare MOOCs to?

When composition researchers study the effectiveness of writing MOOCs, what are they comparing it to, methodologically? Yes, they are comparing it to "the conventional first-year composition course"—but which course where, and taught by whom? My colleagues and I at Miami University engaged this question in our study of online composition, a study (based on data collected in 2012 from four on-line composition classes) aimed at determining whether a fully online composition class could be just as effective as a traditional, brick-and-mortar composition class taught in a physical classroom (Cummings et al. 2013). Please note: We were not studying *a writing MOOC* but are rather were focusing on a *fully online composition course* with relatively low enrollment (<20).

Our preliminary results indicate that first-year composition students can learn writing and develop as writers just as effectively in an online composition class as in a traditional composition class meeting in a physical classroom—or at least we have determined that the outcomes are comparable. Yes, it is possible to teach composition very effectively online. *Depending on context.* Ah, here is where we need to closely examine the local conditions of instruction: Who designed the curriculum and who taught the course, with what level of interaction and engagement, to what number of students possessing what level of commitment and technical literacy? The devil, or angel, does indeed lie in these details.

There were six key contextual factors that shaped our results. For the three composition sections we studied in Summer 2012 we had (1) knowledgeable, experienced, engaged, and committed composition instructors (doctoral students in rhetoric/composition) who were (2) teaching only one section of composition each (3) using a well-developed, tested, and revised composition curriculum (4) to highly motivated students who took the course electively, (5) taking only one class, and (6) in much smaller-than-typical classes (~13 per class). In other words, these three composition classes were not at all typical: in the six respects listed, the teaching conditions were certainly ideal.

Two clear findings did emerge from our findings, one that did not surprise us and one that did. The students reported that the two elements of greatest value to them in the course were (1) the engagement with the instructor (that did not surprise us) and (2) the instructor's video lectures (that did). What made the course effective, from the students' viewpoint, was the presence, interaction, and concerted engagement with the instructor—and the instructor in each of these composition classrooms was an experienced and knowledgeable teacher with expertise in the field of rhetoric/composition, teaching only one section of writing at that time. In other words, this was a completely a-typical context for composition instruction.

The vast majority of college composition courses offered at US universities are staffed, offered, and delivered in a very different manner. Mostly the first-year composition course is staffed by overworked and underpaid part-time instructors, as in our study, but how frequently do these instructors have the level of expertise—not to mention the time or institutional support—that was afforded the instructors in our study?

There is a large body of scholarship on the history of the first-year composition course that explains why institutions of higher education think that students can achieve the necessary level of writing competency by taking (or, more frequently, testing out of) one required first-year composition course (or maybe two), usually taught by overworked adjunct faculty and/or teaching assistants, who typically—and in this regard unlike every other discipline at the university—have very little if any subject matter expertise in the area in which they are hired to teach. This system is held in place by several troubling assumptions—e.g., teaching composition does not require subject matter expertise; composition is a remedial proficiency that students should have when they arrive; and that college-level faculty shouldn't be required to teach—that too often composition instructors and administrators themselves promote, or at least tolerate. I include myself in that last criticism.

Composition instructors and administrators work themselves to death trying to design, administer, and teach the first-year composition course in a way that will make a difference to students. Doing so is often framed as "sacrifice," as a worthy commitment, and I do believe it is that. But I also believe that in doing this composition teachers and administrators participate in the illusion that a "course," or at best two, can accomplish the task of teaching college students to write effectively. Enter the MOOC, which (like its partner in crime, the AP exam) threatens to collapse this illusory structure. Maybe we should be rooting for the MOOC to collapse it.

So here's my working hypothesis about the MOOC as a potential substitute for the required first-year composition course (or courses):

- No MOOC can be as effective as a good composition course, as taught by a knowledgeable, committed, and engaged instructor who has the time to commit to close, frequent, one-on-one interaction with students.

- No MOOC can meet the writing needs or promote the writing development of the majority of college students. Like composition textbooks MOOCs do not scale *down* very well, and so they are not likely to meet the needs of individual students, at least not without the presence of an engaged instructor to tailor the instruction.

- A well-designed MOOC might be at least as effective as, maybe even better than, most composition courses as currently taught at US universities; at scale they might well achieve better outcomes than the typical status quo. In our studies we have to make sure that we are comparing MOOCs to the "typical status quo," rather than to an idealized version of it.

Practically speaking and on the level of scale, how effective are first-year college composition courses anyway? A good MOOC might achieve better results than a badly taught, undersupported composition course, taught by overworked and underpaid part-time instructor—and it could *certainly* do better than the AP Composition exam, which for many students is standing in for the first-year composition course.

I doubt that a given MOOC will achieve better results than a well-designed composition course taught by a knowledgeable, engaged, and committed instructor—but how many of our first-year composition courses actually meet that standard? Too many composition courses are taught by MOAFs (massively overworked adjunct faculty) and by MOAUTAs (massively overworked and underprepared teaching assistants whose area of expertise is not even composition). I am looking forward to seeing the research results that address this question.

Of course my colleagues keep reminding me. Be wary of generalizing about MOOCs, there are different kinds MOOCs! Sure, I agree, but one denominator common to all of them is the M, massive; they are designed to be taught on a student-teacher ratio of thousands to one. No matter how brilliant the instructor or instructional team, no matter how careful and thoughtful the integrity of the design, is it possible to do on that scale? Again, the question is not, Can we teach writing effectively in a MOOC? The question in front of composition teachers and administrators is much more specific than that: **Can we design a MOOC that will replace the first-year composition course (or any college writing course)?** In this regard we should heed the warning of the SUNY Council of Writing, in their *Resolution on Massive Open Online Courses and the Teaching of Writing* (July 2013): The Council's statement "opposes the prospect that MOOCs—or any other form of massive-scale instruction—might be accepted for credit in writing … . Completion of the Writing requirement should always involve close work with a faculty member who can provide students mentorship, careful assessment and a genuine sense of a human audience."

CONCLUSION

This past year I completed two online course programs, the Quality Matters program and the Sloan Certificate program, both designed to certify faculty to design and teach online courses. The strength of these programs, in my view, is that they focus very intently on the integrity of instructional design, focusing on the coherence and the appropriateness of the relationship between course content, course outcomes, and online course design—and that is a useful, if incomplete, focus.

What the programs both neglect, in my view, is the importance of instructional *context*. "The course" is imagined from a formalist frame as a well-made urn, an aesthetic object that can be evaluated, like a well-made essay, apart from its particular context, abstracted from the both rhetor (the instructor) and audience (particular students). In short, just like the current traditional composition paradigm, these programs fail to account adequately for audience, for the messiness of context, for the specific (and peculiar) needs of particular students at particular institutions. That is the generous reading of the neglect. The more paranoid conspiracy version is that these programs imagine courses as detachable from instructors. The course is an independent object that is transferable from instructor to instructor and that really does not even require the instructor as an advanced content expert—a model well-suited to for-profit educational institutions. Yes, you do need the instructor as a course curator and manager. But you don't need the instructor as a disciplinary expert or researcher/scholar. And you don't need the instructor as the intellectual presence who engages students' content knowledge or intellectual development on an individual basis. That's an expensive model of dubious value.

What value does the instructor provide? Why do we need researchers/scholars to do college-level teaching? The MOOC "is forcing us to begin to articulate the value instructors add" (Feldstein 2013). In terms of our disciplinary focus, does the composition instructor provide value, essential value for promoting composition proficiency?

I come back to the two criteria that I referenced at the opening of this essay. A "good course" is based on (1) the knowledge, expertise, and commitment of the instructor and (2) on the integrity of the instructional design, which is to say, on the quality of the presentation, on its appropriateness to its intended learner audience, and on the goals it sets (and whether it successfully achieves those goals). That second factor is a contextual factor: Does the course meet the needs of its intended audience? Does it scale down well to a variety of learners in a variety of locations? Here is where the smaller local course has the advantage over the MOOC: In the hands of the knowledgeable, expert, committed, and engaged instructor, it can scale down, and very effectively. And composition administrators have long used this argument to support smaller class enrollments for composition courses—in the range of 15 to 25, typically—because that enables the instructor's deep interaction with and response to each student's writing.

Or at least that is the assumption. How much research evidence do we actually have that this is the case? Is it the case in most, some, all, or very few of first-year composition classes? In the age of MOOCs, this is a research question not only worth pursuing, but it is one that we need to answer immediately. Because the MOOC is here, standing ready to replace the first-year composition course.

NOTES

1. In Spring 2013 composition instructors and researchers were offering MOOCs, and studying their outcomes, at Duke University, Georgia Tech University, Ohio State University, and Mt. San Jacinto College. All four of these MOOCs were funded, at least in part, by a grant from the Bill & Melinda Gates Foundation.

2. Here I am calling upon Erving Goffman's and George Lakoff's approaches to frame analysis. An excellent example of frame analysis applied to MOOCs is Aaron Brady's May 2013 essay "The MOOC Moment and the End of Reform."

WORKS CITED

Benkler, Yochai. "The University in the Networked Economy and Society: Challenges and Opportunities." *The Tower and the Cloud: Higher Education in the Age of Cloud Computing.* Ed. Richard N. Katz. EDUCAUSE, 2008. 51-61.

Brady, Aaron. "The MOOC Moment and the End of Reform." *The New Inquiry,* 15 May 2013. http://thenewinquiry.com/blogs/zunguzungu/the-mooc-moment-and-the-end-of-reform/

Cummings, Lance, Renea Frey, Ryan Ireland, Caitlin Martin, Heidi McKee, Jason Palmeri, and James E. Porter. "Kairotic Design: Building Flexible Networks for Online Composition." 2013. Unpublished manuscript.

Feldstein, Michael. "MOOCs, Courseware, and the Course as Artifact." *e-Literate* [blog], 12 April 2013. http://mfeldstein.com/moocs-courseware-and-the-course-as-an-artifact/

Goffman, Erving. *Frame Analysis: An Essay on the Organization of Experience.* New York: Harper & Row, 1974.

Lakoff, George, and Mark Johnson. *Metaphors We Live By.* Chicago: U of Chicago P, 1980.

Porter, James E. "MOOCs, 'Courses,' and the Question of Faculty and Student Copyrights." *The CCCC-IP Annual: Top Intellectual Property Developments of 2012.* Ed. Clancy Ratliff. The Intellectual Property Caucus of the CCCC, March 2013. 2-18. http://www.ncte.org/cccc/committees/ip/2012developments

Porter, James E., Patricia Sullivan, and Johndan Johnson-Eilola. *Professional Writing Online.* 3rd ed. Boston: Longman/Allyn & Bacon, 2008. http://www.ablongman.com/pwo

Ravenscroft, Andrew. "Dialogue and Connectivism: A New Approach to Understanding and Promoting Dialogue-Rich Networked Learning." *International Review of Research in Open and Distance Learning* 12.3 (2011): 139-160.

Siemens, George. "Connectivism: A Learning Theory for a Digital Age." *International Journal of Instructional Technology and Distance Learning* 2.1 (2005): 3-10.

SUNY Council on Writing. *Resolution on Massively Open Online Courses and the Teaching of Writing.* July 2013. http://www.ipetitions.com/petition/suny-cow

Vaidhyanathan, Siva. "The Content-Provider Paradox: Universities in the Information Ecosystem." *Academe* 88.5 (2002): 34-37.

Watters, Audrey. "The Early Days of Videotaped Lectures." *Hybrid Pedagogy,* 10 April 2013. http://www.hybridpedagogy.com/Journal/files/Early_Days_of_Videotaped_Lectures.html

Whithaus, Carl, and Joyce Magnotto Neff. "Contact and Interactivity: Social Constructionist Pedagogy in a Video-Based, Management Writing Course." *Technical Communication Quarterly* 15.4 (2006): 431-456.

Wolverton, Chris. "Are MOOCs Textbooks Masquerading as Courses?" *Gravitropic* [blog], 8 April 2013. http://www.gravitropic.net/2013/04/are-moocs-textbooks-masquerading-as-courses/

ACKNOWLEDGMENTS

I would like to thank the co-editors and several collection participants for their very helpful comments and suggestions on earlier drafts of this essay, including Kay Halasek, Steve Krause, Charlie Lowe, Cindy Selfe, and Heather Young.

A MOOC or Not a MOOC: ds106 Questions the Form

Alan Levine

By Any Other Name

My undergraduate and graduate studies were in Geology, a field rampant with classification schemes.* The words of my petrology professor at the University of Delaware have always come to mind when we talk about categories of almost anything. "Doc" Allan Thompson said, "In the world of classifications, there are those who are lumpers and then those that are splitters."

With a new classification term like "MOOC," we encounter conveniences and shortcomings by characterizing all examples that fall under that term. Even splitting them into cMOOC and xMOOC varieties produces generalizations that lose significance of what lies within, or between.

This essay includes my experiences at all levels with an open course that defies classification with the ongoing MOOC discussions. Digital Storytelling, a.k.a. ds106 (ds106.us), is the open course started at the University of Mary Washington (UMW) by Jim Groom and first offered openly in January 2011. My association with ds106 has been as an open participant and later, as a teacher of the class both in person and online.

Influenced by the original Connectivism and Connective Knowledge course (CCK08) that spawned the acronym, as well as the open teaching strategies of David Wiley and Alec Couros, when first released, ds106 self-identified as a MOOC. Its design followed the lead of these first experiments in being a networked structure of online sites authored by participants, both registered UMW students and open participants in their own digital spaces, aggregated at the course level.

Because of all of the attention around Sebastian Thurn's AI MOOC at Stanford—the first "super-sized" MOOC—I've felt like I had to make it clear the ways ds106 diverges from what was being touted in the media. For a time, the front entrance of the class site bore the throw down statement "ds106 is not a silly MOOC."

With two and a half years of online activity, more than 500 for credit students at UMW and other schools mixed with a dynamic open community of equal size (or larger, in total the site has aggregated at least 2600 sites), the question of being a MOOC or not is irrelevant. In this essay, I outline the elements of ds106 that differentiate it from most of what mainstream media lumps into the MOOC terminology:

- A syndicated network architecture that might potentially be, but not necessarily, **Massive** by mimicking the design of the Internet itself
- **Openness** in all facets—the methods, tools, and all content—plus a foundation built on open source software
- **Online** in not just where it lives, but Internet culture is woven into the course itself as an ethos
- A structure where the **Course** experience for registered credit-seeking students need not be the same as that of open participants taking it for their own interests, yet the boundaries between these groups disappear, making it as much community as course.

What we have created is not a one magic button software solution for teaching online, but the strategies and structures are offered freely (and openly) for others to model. Some may explain away what looks like "the fun class" (a design assignment to create ds106 propaganda posters was called "over-branding" by Stephen Downes) suggesting the methods do not apply to other academic areas. But that is mistaking the external appearance for the ideas beneath.

My ds106 experiences have run a full spectrum—brainstorming ideas for the original open course, participating as an open online participant, teaching a section at UMW in person (Spring 2012), and online (Summer 2012, Fall 2012, Spring 2013), and building/contributing to the programming of the platform itself, including an experimental "headless" version in Fall 2013 just for open participants. Experiencing it in this detail makes it impossible for me to "lump" ds106 in with nearly anything else.

The Story of a Course About Storytelling

The ds106 class at UMW breaks a few conventions of a typical course. It requires no textbook and there are no quizzes or exams. And on the books, ds106 does not exist-- if you explore the UMW catalog, you will find no such course. Officially the course is listed as Digital Storytelling, CPSC 106, an undergraduate computer science class that counts as a creative elective:

> People have been telling stories since the beginning of time, but how is storytelling evolving in the digital age? This course explores how computers are being used to tell stories. We'll study text-based technologies—blogging, the web—and how those models have changed the way we publish and disseminate narratives. We'll also study the roles of audio, video, and images in narrative: computer animation, the ethics of altering digital images, and the Story Corps project. Students will use technology including blogs, virtual worlds, and computer games to create and tell their own stories. No previous computer experience is necessary.

This class has been taught in the past and recently as a traditional lecture and textbook based class. When UMW Instructional Technologist Jim Groom taught a section for Spring 2010, he crafted a basic tenet of ds106 by requiring all students to publish their work and write about ideas behind it in their own blog space. The course itself used RSS syndication technology to aggregate individual student work to the class site. Groom leveraged the university's experience of running an institutional wide blogging platform UMW Blogs. Based on Gardner Campbell's conceptualization of a personal cyberinfrastucture, students were tasked with registering their own web domains and managing their own installations of the WordPress platform. Rather than students using a resource that belonged to the institution, they would learn to assert their own digital identity openly in a form they could own, manage, and take with them.

Having followed the class from the outside, I was very intrigued in December 2010 when Groom announced he would open up the Spring 2011 UMW course to allow open participation in ds106. Along with colleagues Tom Woodward (Henrico County public schools) and Martha Burtis (UMW), we brainstormed with Groom the ideas that fed into the first open iteration of the course. What was most interesting is that before the official UMW course started in mid-January, through word of blog and Twitter, people (including me) started registering their blogs with the ds106 site and began free form media creation—exploring animated GIFs well before they resurged as a popular Internet meme—and even launching an Internet radio station (see below).

The Spring 2011 ds106 course was an explosion of creativity as open participants followed the syllabus and interacted with the registered UMW students, with several hundred individual blogs joining the ecosystem. The idea of an open assignment bank emerged as a participant contributed source of creative tasks—rather than having one set of required assignments for a unit—students and open participants are able to choose from a collection of more than 600 ones in areas such as Visual, Design, Audio, Video, Mashup, etc. These are ones that ds106 participants have added to the site, each with a crowd-sourced difficulty rating (1-5 stars). Assignments have unique tags, so when a participant published on their own site their work on an assignment, if their site is connected to the ds106 site, the assignment bank site can automatically add their example to a specific assignment listing.

Another emergent component to ds106 is its own Internet radio station. The idea of ds106 Radio arose as a desire for a more open and community focused synchronous platform than typical slide dominated environments such as Blackboard Collaborate and Adobe Connect. Harkening back to the powerful genre of radio storytelling, ds106 Radio is a free form broadcasting platform to bring in guest speakers, publish student audio work, and explore mobile tools for audio storytelling/performance. It became the focus of group projects to write and produce a full radio show that would then be premiered live on the radio station.

Further iterations of the course as fully online ones saw experimentations with a class as performance act (2011 Summer of Oblivion, 2012 Camp Magic MacGuffin, 2013 The ds106 Zone), expansions to allow similar classes at other institutions to join the infrastructure, and development of components such as The Daily Create and the Assignment Remix Machine.

MASSIVE: SCALE LIKE THE INTERNET DOES

The MOOCs you read about in *The New York Times* grow to tens to hundreds of thousands of students, by replication: the same experience, the same schedule for all and very often distancing the instructor from student. What scales is the teaching of open course, what can be repeated en masse via video lectures and automated assessments. As a network model, it would map as a star shaped pattern, where central is the superstar professor and the platform provider.

The Internet itself provides a more effective model of scaling, one where the network is distributed, and ds106 achieves this using what we refer to as the "syndication bus"- the subscription of a course site to ones managed by its participants, where updates are communicated via RSS feeds. Whether participants are registered students at UMW (and elsewhere) or general interested open participants, we are able to aggregate on one site the work of anyone who elects to connect their site to ds106.

Yet there is another level of this distributed network that we can aggregate many sources together and yet re-organize them again in meaningful groupings. Since that first open version of ds106, educators at other institutions teaching similar, but not exactly the same, courses (i.e. York College, Kansas State University, Kennesaw State University, University of Michigan, Temple University Japan, SUNY Cortland, Jacksonville State University) have joined ds106 and have had their students blogs also brought into the community site. Because of the way we set up the registration on the site, we are able to split out views of the contributions from these groups to their own unique slices of the ds106 site or view them in one massive flow of content.

When someone not affiliated with one of these designated classes signs up for ds106, they are free to follow a current running class, explore the assignments available—there is no set syllabus or path for open online participants. Their level of activity is driven by their own interests and schedule, and thus we bypass any notion of "dropout"— or in ds106 parlance, anyone who joins is "#4life."

Thus, there is actually no single ds106 course- what we have are multiple courses running on overlapping schedules, and people choose to do portions in the spaces between. While this overall structure appears perhaps more fragmented and unorganized—as much as the Internet itself, it is not organized neatly into folders and categories; ds106 unfolds and is emergent, serendipitous as the web itself.

While this approach of growth may not achieve the 100,000 MOOC level of registered participants, it does offer a more customizable, flexible approach for both teachers interested in using the ds106 resources and for learners to choose their own levels of participation. Because of the way we syndicate content into ds106 (a local copy is made in the ds106 site, but links always point back to the source), since January 2011 we have aggregated over 30,000 distributed blog posts from some 2600 unique participants. The main site itself has attracted 25,000 unique visitors since the start of the 2013 year (as measured with Google Analytics).

OPEN IN THE WIDEST POSSIBLE SENSE

For the majority of MOOCs, the first "O" indicates open for entry, but often course materials and activity are hidden behind logins and passwords. Every bit of ds106, from content, to the tools we use, are open for viewing and re-use.

In our teaching of ds106 at UMW, the media that students create are not the full end goal; we ask them as well to document in their blog the thinking behind their work, the influences, and the details of how they made it. We ask them to explore issues of creativity, copyright, and Internet culture as they engage in work that builds off of others.

The ds106 platform is built on open source software—all of the course sites run on WordPress, and the aggregation is achieved via a free plugin (Feed WordPress http://feedwordpress.radgeek.com/). While UMW students are required to use their own hosted version of WordPress for their own sites, open participants can use any platform, self hosted or on services such as Blogger, WordPress.com, Tumblr, as long as it produces an RSS feed. The ds106 radio station is built on the open source Airtime software. Participants are encouraged (but not required) to post their media on available free social media sites- flickr for images, Soundcloud for audio, and YouTube or vimeo for video.

Note also that ds106 lacks a reliance on discussion forums for participant communication. Again, the openness of ds106 is shown in the use of Twitter as the main vehicle of communication (the #ds106 hash tag). Others connect in a Google+ Community. Participants ask and answer questions, share work and resources in the open spaces of the web itself.

Who joins in this type of environment? We have seen higher education practitioners from around the world, K-12 educators exploring it for professional development, elementary school teachers modifying assignments for use with 3rd graders, professional photographers/videographers, java programmers, retired artists, researchers at large corporations, traveling musicians—all find parts of ds106 that trigger their creative interests. In the Fall of 2013, a group at 3M is participating in ds106 activities but from within their intranet.

ONLINE IS MORE THAN WHERE TO FIND IT

By definition, a massive open course online can potentially be accessed by anyone with access to the Internet. In most MOOCs, the online component is a place to publish content- lectures, readings, etc.

But ds106 is more than just a means to put content online, it actively functions to help participants be part of the creation of web content, weaving the very fabric of the web. They do this not only by creating media, but also publishing their ideas and sharing tutorials, lessons, and adding challenges for others to do.

And Internet culture itself becomes raw material for parts of the course, with assignments based on Internet memes, and fostering the idea that storytelling is not only something that can be published on the web, but can also be told within the web itself (see the Web Stories and Fan Fiction types in the ds106 Assignment Bank).

Invariably while working on remix and mashup assignments, participants encounter issues of copyright as their work often gets flagged on YouTube or SoundCloud—this is the opportunity for them to explore the question of what should be available for them to use as media if they are creating something new. One of the goals for the ds106 experience is for students and participants to ponder the question of ownership of their own content, the value of sharing via Creative Commons licensing, and how they can assert their own digital presence in a way that does not rely on the vagaries of third party providers which may take away services once provided free for individuals (e.g. Posterous, Google Reader).

And sometimes without any prompting or direction, some people use ds106 as a way to explore the nature of character and online identity by creating online personas, such as the fictitious Dr Oblivion, a character created and later destroyed by Jim Groom in teaching of the Summer 2011 ds106 class. Other characters have appeared such as Ol Hatchet Jack based on the frozen mountain man from the movie *Jeremiah Johnson*, or the Talking Tina doll from a Twilight Zone episode.

COURSE OR COMMUNITY?

A course is finite in time and space; ds106 goes beyond those boundaries more as an open community of creativity. Some participants are just interested in using the openness of ds106 radio to share music, live action, and real time communication. Others tap into low threshold creative challenges of the Daily Create. Others use ds106 in Twitter as a reference to a much broader mode of storytelling and media creation.

What has emerged through ds106 is a space for it to be both, and yet the course parts are not rigidly bounded. They are course and community permeable in the way open participants can be part of an existing course, or contribute by offering feedback and resources for registered students. Again, a ds106 course is not a slice of the Internet sectioned off to a closed corner, it exists as part of the open connected network itself.

At the time of writing this article in August 2013, there is no currently running ds106 course at UMW. Yet people continue to do work on their own, and reflect and feed off of the work of others who are exploring assignments or taking up other creative challenges (e.g. a July Daily Create challenge).

We have seen an interesting set of related spinoffs of ds106 such as the book club reading group organized by open participant K-12 Educator Ben Rimes. Another educator in Scotland, John Johnston, has been inspired by his ds106 activities to develop new tools such as flickrsounds, a tool that matches images and audio from social media sites. This expansive capability becomes possible in an open community space.

WHERE DOES THE DS106 STORY GO NEXT?

While courses have completion dates, a really good story should never end. As an experiment, in the Fall 2013, we will run a version of the course specifically for open participants (re-using a syllabus from the Spring 2013 UMW course) that will not be lead by any teacher, but facilitated by participants themselves—this has become known as the "Headless ds106."

Other open courses have used similar approaches to ds106, including the open photography course phonar at the University of Coventry, the Educational Technology and Media MOOC (ETMOOC) and the Making Learning Connected MOOC

And given much interest in the ds106 structure, there are possible plans to develop portions of it as more generalizable WordPress templates, so you could create a site like the Assignment Bank or the Daily Create for use in other areas.

Whether ds106 is a MOOC or not actually matters little. What is more important is using openness in the ways best exemplified by the greatest experiment and implementation on massive scaling—the Internet itself.

WORKS CITED

Airtime. Web. 21 Oct 2013. <http://www.sourcefabric.org/en/airtime/>.

Campell, Gardner. "A Personal Cyberinfrastructure", *EDUCAUSE Review*, vol. 44, no. 5 (September/October 2009): 58–59.

ds106 assignment bank. Web. 21 Oct 2013. <http://assignments.ds106.us/>.

ds106 Assignment Remix Machine. Web. 21 Oct 2013. <http://remix.ds106.us/>.

ds106 Book Club. Web. 21 Oct 2013. <https://sites.google.com/site/bookclub106/>.

ds106 Daily Create. Web. 21 Oct 2013. <http://tdc.ds106.us/>.

ds106radio. Web. 21 Oct 2013. <http://ds106.us/ds106-radio/>.

Educational Technology and Media MOOC (ETMOOC). Web. 21 Oct 2013. <http://etmooc.org/>.

Headless ds106. Web. 21 Oct 2013. <http://ds106.us/2013/07/21/coming-soon-the-headless-ds106-course/>.

I am Talky Tina. Web. 21 Oct 2013. 2013. <http://iamtalkytina.com/>.

Johnston, John. *flickrsounds.* Web. 21 Oct 2013. <http://johnjohnston.info/flickrSounds/index.php>.

July 2013 Daily Create challenge. Web. 21 Oct 2013. <http://www.youtube.com/watch?v=ubHn4xEnRP8>.

Making Learning Connected MOOC. Web. 21 Oct 2013. <http://blog.nwp.org/clmooc/>.

Ol' Hatchet Jack. Web. 21 Oct 2013. 2013. <http://olhatchetjack.wordpress.com/>.

phonar, Coventry University. Web. 21 Oct 2013. <http://phonar.org/>.

UMW Blogs, University of Mary Washington. Web. 21 Oct 2013. <http://UMWblogs.org>.

Why We Are Thinking About MOOCs

Jeffrey T. Grabill

In September of 2009, I posted a thought piece on the Writing in Digital Environments (WIDE) website on the value of writing programs.* It got me in some trouble with my colleagues because they saw me as questioning the value of our writing program. I *was* asking us to question the value of all writing programs, and so while we were implicated in my question, the local trouble was instructive—asking questions about a core mission is always dangerous. Still, I take the view that such questioning ultimately leads to better programs.

In that piece, I speculated about cost and value decisions—not by university administrators and faculty but by parents and students. Students have to make cost and value decisions all the time with respect to education. What can they afford? What is the value of a degree, institution, or class? With respect to first year writing, most students see it as a low value class, something that they must take and that they would much rather manage at the lowest cost possible: testing out, using AP credit, and so on. This is why we must have a compelling answer to the question of value. We must be able to show convincingly what we do better than anyone else, particularly our lower cost competitors and partners, and how we enhance education on our own campus. This is why the question of value is the single most important question that a writing program must answer. I realize that these value and cost dynamics are also variable with regard to writing programs themselves. Michigan State, for instance, will never again be inexpensive. We must therefore be valuable.

Finally, I articulated categories of work that I associate with a high value writing program, categories that will be familiar to this audience: a research focus, new ways to engage writing across the curriculum and/or writing in the disciplines initiatives, and a focus on life-long learning in writing. While familiar, these categories, if taken seriously, disrupt the commonplace and often assumed notion that a writing program = first year writing and push us toward new models.

At the time I wrote that blog post, we were experiencing significant economic stress driven by the "great recession" of 2007-2008, and it was clear to me (though vaguely clear) that this recession broke something in higher education. We can debate this claim about what might be broken and when it broke. (For a quick, thoughtful take, read Bryan Alexander's blog post 'Late Night Thoughts on Higher Education Finance": http://bryanalexander.org/2013/07/27/late-night-thoughts-on-higher-education-finance/.)[1] My point for now is simply this: the "great recession" of 2007-2008 is the origin point for why we were thinking about MOOCs at Michigan State in 2012.[2]

Writing programs and departments must be valuable, and this likely requires new ways to understand ourselves, how we deliver writing instruction, and how we understand our relationship with our college and university. How we choose to think differently will vary most particularly by institution type and within institution types. At a research institution like MSU where research expectations have visibly increased during my time here, we might think about ideas such as these (this list is not intended as exhaustive, and it isn't innocent either):

- That the value of the writing program is located in the fact that it is a research program that produces research and forms of intellectual property that have value
- That the value of the writing program is located in its ability to provide evidence-based instruction in writing
- That the value of the writing program is a function of the fact that it can be flexibly deployed to meet the needs of learners and programs when and where they need it, both in the curriculum and across the lifespan
- And that, finally, a writing program must think about where it can best impact the learning of writing on any given campus

and focus its talent and resources on those key moments and places

A decision to think about MOOCs is consistent with the ideas in that list. With regard to MOOCs in particular, it might be worth asking a question like "why now?" That is, why MOOCs now? There are a number of inputs, of course, but a few seem most salient. In addition to tight economic pressures and growing dissatisfaction with outcomes, learning technologies are improving at a rapid pace. I see a bit of this in my role in an educational technology startup, and it is true that technologies for learning are getting better, becoming more focused and theory driven, and becoming less expensive.[3] The smartest people I have met in educational technology are focused on providing better education at lower costs. I take them seriously. For me, then, the current moment invites creativity and innovation, and while I am pretty sure that MOOCs as they are currently designed and implemented will not persist, I am confident we will see a number of innovations that will persist that have their origins in this moment.

And this brings me to perhaps the most important reason that we are thinking seriously about MOOCs. We are a research institution. Core to our mission is the mandate to produce high quality research with impact. A writing program at a research institution should be a research program. The primary value that we provide to the institution, to the discipline, and to the world at large is research. And so, at a research institution, a writing program should produce knowledge that transforms how we understand writing, the teaching of writing, and the ways that individuals and groups develop into more effective writers. Understanding our value in this way means that we are not a teaching program that does some research, but a research program that helps students develop as writers. It means that the program must identify some strategic goals for research, support certain research programs over time, and collaborate and coordinate work among and across faculty and students.

MOOCs are therefore of primary interest to us because of our research focus, and they are perhaps most curious to us because of their research scale. MOOCs are attractive with regard to scale because there's a lot more data that can be "mined" in one MOOC than there typically would be in a year's worth of an entire first year writing program. In addition, while a typical writing program might have dozens of different sections and instructors, the MOOC is a single common experience, making the data more comparable. We are interested in learning and improvement in student writing, and the focus and scale of a MOOC allows us to test and build theory.

At the same time, a MOOC allows us to test, again at scale, new innovations in pedagogy and technology. It should be possible to learn writing at MSU in a number of ways, and right now that is not true. Most students are limited to our fifteen week face to face experience from 8-5. Even our current online options fail to reach significantly beyond this model. If MSU has a vision to make it possible to learn writing anytime and anywhere and to learn it across an individual's lifespan (and this is not yet our shared vision), then we must innovate while growing the value of what we offer. MOOCs are a platform for experimentation, and our goal is to make the most of this moment.

Finally, a word about access. Access has been a persistent concern of mine during my career. One of the primary ethical arguments from MOOC providers is grounded in the claim that MOOCs provide education for populations without access. It is easy to be cynical about such claims. Indeed, cynicism might be a job requirement for faculty in the humanities. But I am hopeful (not necessarily optimistic, but hopeful). Can the MOOC moment produce models and technologies that significantly grow access to high quality educational opportunities? We don't know, of course, but we should try to find out. Higher education is not a stranger to innovation and change—the land grant institution is a magnificent example.

As I write, we have just completed our own MOOC, and so it is too early to write about outcomes. We tried to create an course that helps participants think like a writer and to experience the basic moves of writing. It is designed as an inductive experience. There was very little didactic instruction, for instance, and so our hope and expectation is that learning is a function of participants moving through a set of scaffolded experiences. The most fundamental experience is a write, review, revision planning, and revision sequence. This will likely seem familiar to most writing teachers, but we are attempting to facilitate particular kinds of review practices from writers and to strongly encourage and facilitate revision planning. We see revision planning in particular as the most likely place where learning will occur. As a moment of intervention, revision is essential. As the research literature has long made clear, revision is (perhaps) the key practice that distinguishes expert from novice writers (beginning with the fact of revision, then the quality of the revision). Of course, all of this was done with an eye on writing instruction at scale, and the complexities of scale put tremendous pressure on how we designed the experience. Our research, therefore, focuses on how participants experience the course (e.g., variables that contribute to learning; those that do not), how they review (e.g., alignment with criteria), and what they learned.

We have learned a few things already. There are a surprising number of MOOC enthusiasts out there, and ours was understood as "different" by those participants. They wondered why we didn't have video lectures, some were surprised by all the writing that they had to do, and these enthusiasts noted how we differ from Coursera (some liked the differences, some didn't, some thought we were "weird.").[4] We have learned that in a global context, there is no shared understanding of what a writing course is and does, little familiarity with North American writing pedagogy, and no understanding of what the "developmental writing" or the "first year writing course" are. In some ways, we have been naively US-centric. Still, we believe that we have inherited a mission to make education accessible and transformative. This is our land-grant legacy. We have engaged this MOOC moment because of our identity as a research institution and also as part of a larger and multi-faceted effort to understand our value to others.

Notes

1. This essay is too small to get into the details, but higher education institutions are increasingly highly leveraged operations via students and their loans, state and institutional debt, and so on. Large systems are capable of existing for a long time as highly leveraged enterprises (e.g., the Soviet Union, Detroit, or Japan). Eventually, however, either the model changes or the operation fails.

2. I have played fast and loose with "we" so far in this essay. I'm going to continue to do so. I'm clearly using it as a form of identification (I want you with me!). I'm also referring to others at MSU. I want to be clear, however, that "we" doesn't refer to everyone at MSU. There is (and will be) some disagreement at MSU about what I write in this essay.

3. I helped start an educational technology company called Drawbridge (http://opendrawbridge.com/). Our first technology is Eli, a software service for writing instruction (http://www.elireview.

com/). In my role with this company, I have spoken with hundreds of teachers, administrators, investors, and others who are associated with technology startups. I have learned much from these conversations. Perhaps most importantly, I have learned how to see education from the outside. I have also seen a large number of compelling learning technologies.

4. With regard to differences in technology, we used a combination of Canvas as our LMS, Eli as our service for feedback, revision, and peer interactions around writing, Twitter, and Facebook. We also had to host some video content via services other than YouTube to get around firewalls in certain parts of the world.

The Hidden Costs of MOOCs

Karen Head

In my early twenties, I collected college sweatshirts.* I had over thirty of them, including ones from Yale, Princeton, Berkeley, as well as the Sorbonne and the London School of Economics. Owning these shirts provided me with some false comfort because, for a variety of personal and economic reasons, I had not yet gone to college. I felt more important when I wore one. Occasionally, someone would point to my shirt and give me the thumbs up. I liked this. One day a man engaged me in the grocery store check out line. That day the shirt was from Harvard. "Don't you love it there?" he asked gleefully. "Yes, um, it's great." I stammered. The moment I said it I felt the weight of the lie. "And the campus is so lovely, which dorm are you in?" Cornered, I quickly "remembered" something I'd forgotten and left the line. I stopped wearing the shirts except at home, but it took me a few years and two earned degrees to donate them all to the local thrift shop.

FREE ISN'T FREE

When I finally did go to college, I was fortunate to have some financial assistance, but nine years post-doctorate, I still make a monthly student loan payment. Consequently, the idea of providing useful educational information in a free and open way is appealing to me.

When I was first approached about teaching a Massive Open Online Course, I was eager to consider how I might be able to reach out to

* This work is licensed under the Creative Commons Attribution-Noncommercial-ShareAlike 3.0 United States License. To view a copy of this license, visit http://creativecommons.org/licenses/by-nc-sa/3.0/us/ or send a letter to Creative Commons, 171 Second Street, Suite 300, San Francisco, California, 94105, USA. For any other use permissions, contact the original author.

people who couldn't gain access to educational materials in traditional in-class or limited-access online/distance learning environments. As a poet who began exploring the possibilities of digital augmentation and dissemination when I arrived at Georgia Tech, I was interested to know how this technology might, as it had with my poetry, allow me to consider new approaches. I think many people who first engaged in the idea of MOOCs felt the same way about exploring the new possibilities.

The humanitarian benefits of MOOCs were at the forefront of the early rhetoric used to tout these courses. By the time I seriously entered the conversation (in September 2012), the language was already shifting to include words like "value" and "monetization" and "credit-bearing." Coursera is the company with which I am most familiar because it is the learning platform (the mechanism by which course content is marketed and delivered to students) I had to use. As a start-up company eager to market its potential, Coursera has positioned itself from the beginning as something of an extraordinary value—aligning itself with only the most elite institutions. A person could take a course and get a certificate of completion with a prestigious university logo. In some cases (we opted out for our course), students can pay Coursera for a course certification called Signature Track. Cost for this certification ranges between $30-$100 per course. Since this certification is not the same as official course credit, might these certificates be the newest form of sweatshirt deception—for a price similar to the cost of a sweatshirt?

Rarely is anything of value truly free and open. There are costs, even if they are not immediately apparent. A new industry must evolve to support the production and delivery of MOOCs. Production costs for videography and course design specific to Coursera (what I have previously called the "Coursera-ification" of the course) for our MOOC was approximately $32,000, covered in our case by a grant from the Bill & Melinda Gates Foundation. The balance of our funding ($18,000 from the grant, plus another $10,000 of internal funding from Georgia Tech) was divided between the postdoctoral fellows who worked on the project. Neither myself, nor my Co-PI, Dr. Rebecca Burnett, received any additional pay for our work—something that wouldn't be acceptable to some faculty, especially given the huge time commitment. As I reported previously in the *Chronicle of Higher Education*, even if you routinely teach large courses, a MOOC requires far more time to prepare and execute. To prepare the three lectures offered in a single week, our team spent about 20 hours planning and developing content. I spent an additional eight hours rehearsing my lectures. It took just under four hours to record the video for three formal lectures. I cannot speak to the editing process, because another unit at Georgia Tech did that work, but it usually took five to 10 days to receive the edited video and get Coursera approval. Even then there was more work to incorporate any quiz links or other "in-class work" that took place during lecture pauses. Finally there was the "Courserafication" process of uploading and configuring the content for use on the Coursera site. Formatting assignments and other content took still more time. All this work happens before the course begins. Once the course is in session, students expect 24/7 monitoring and quick responses to their queries, questions, and comments. If there is a problem, you really must address it quickly—you do not have the luxury of waiting until the next class meeting like you do in traditional courses. For the eight weeks of our course, I felt as if I was tied to the course. Although, in reality, our entire team felt tied to the course for 9 months.

In addition to the costs of "making a MOOC," students who wish to take these courses must have the means—computer access is a cost to the provider if not the user—and there is always the investment of a person's time. In some places, Internet content downloads or actual access time is capped. Students facing such restrictions may have difficulty meeting course requirements if they cannot afford the costs. In this chapter, I would like to elaborate some of the other hidden costs—as I discovered them during the process of preparing and teaching the Freshman Composition 2.0 MOOC.

THE COST OF PRIVACY

Without question there are some professors who are interested in teaching MOOCs because they imagine a certain kind of fame will accompany the experience: Rock-star professor anyone? Perhaps for some instructors this makes the workload of designing, producing, and delivering a MOOC worth the time and effort, and in some cases worth the lack of remuneration. Fame and teaching are not usually used in the same sentence. Even the Hollywood representations of teachers, often presented as grandiose depictions within the plot (think: Lulu singing "To Sir with Love" or the students atop desks bellowing "My

Captain, My Captain" in *Dead Poets Society*); still, such depictions do not provide audiences with representations of fame. With MOOCs there is a certain kind of fame, but perhaps not what many people imagine.

Another consequence of fame is a loss of privacy. I never considered some the possible implications of being a public figure—the "face of a MOOC" who could have thousands of participants who suddenly think they know you. Now instead of being the "face" in front of twenty-five students, you become, to some, the face of English Composition (or whatever course) at your institution. Additionally, you really have to withhold yourself in ways you do not with a traditional sized class. Even if the sense of fame is merely an illusion—the reality being that you have more than the usual number of students who simply want your attention—you do have practical issues to consider about your privacy.

Some of the practical privacy issues can be serious. As I wrote in an article for the *Chronicle of Higher Education*, a few days before enrollment opened for my course, one of our IT specialists advised me to change my public email address because some students would likely try to contact me outside of the course platform for more personalized attention. Certainly I could understand why a student might want to do this, but I also understood the potential of overloading my inbox, and how this would disrupt my regular correspondence and university duties. This conversation quickly turned to questions about how other public information about me could be misused. Might students overwhelm my voicemail? What if a student decided to make an unannounced visit? In other words, what about my general privacy and my personal safety? While I have never given my personal contact information to students, they have always been able to contact me via email, my office phone, and even during virtual office hours I hold using video-conferencing tools. Like many other problems associated with the idea of "massive," I had never considered how different the faculty-student contact question might be different in a MOOC.

Suddenly this adventure had taken a darker turn. I had a sobering hour-long conversation with Georgia Tech's Chief of Police about how people often show up on campus unannounced and unwelcomed demanding to see students or members of faculty, staff, or administrators. The director of security for my building suggested I temporarily move my office to a more remote and secure location where even Georgia Tech students and staff would have difficulty finding me. I had decided all of this was ridiculous until someone began repeatedly calling my office. This person refused to leave any messages, saying only that the call was in reference to MOOCs. He pressed my staff to give out my personal mobile number. I still do not know who this person is or what he wanted.

Instances like these feel ominous. One question I feel compelled to ask is if university administrators are ever to require faculty members to teach MOOCs, would they be prepared to consider the possible implications of requiring someone to become a public figure? Who would be responsible if an instructor is stalked? What if an instructor is harmed? Even if a university can protect an instructor on campus, what happens when he or she goes home? Certainly one might argue that these dangers exist in the traditional brick and mortar environment. However, we do have a screening process that happens with admission. We have more information about our students; in a MOOC students don't even have to provide their names. In traditional face-to-face classes, we can read non-verbal cues, and we often are aware of issues students have before they join our classes (e.g., they have learning or behavioral challenges that require accommodation). Will a university's security and privacy policies transfer to students enrolled in MOOCs? The cost of security is a dear one—extending to both an institution's ability to provide protection and to the instructor's well-being, should the worst happen. Considering ways to scale up our policies as we scale up our class enrollments is an important administrative responsibility.

QUESTIONS OF OWNERSHIP

Historically, an instructor's course materials have been regarded as part of his or her intellectual property. As TyAnna Herrington explains,

> Possibly the most notable disagreement to arise after the enactment of the Copyright Act of 1976 is that over the survival of the professor (or teacher) exception, which was generally applicable in cases decided under the 1909 act. The professor exception is a judicial creation that excepts the work of academics from work for hire status, despite determinations as to their status as employees under the law. (143)

Herrington further explains why this is significant by citing Lauren Lape's "Ownership of Copyrightable Works of University Professors: The Interplay between the Copyright Act and University Copyright Policies "(1995):

> Section 26 of the Copyright Act of 1909 provides that the work author include the employer within the scope of the employee's duties. Under the language of the 1909 act, the works of professors could have been considered works for hire, but no court found this to be the case. In the two cases where this issue was considered directly, neither court found that professors produced work for hire. (qtd. in Herrington, 143)

The question of who owns your course materials, including your likeness in video form, is an important one, and it seems to be getting more complicated in a world that already struggles to decide ownership in a digital context. Intellectual property lawyers are busy in courts everywhere trying to sort out the new rules regarding property placed in the cloud and on platforms like Google Drive or DropBox with end user license agreements often worded in ways that allow your property to be co-opted in many questionable ways. It remains unclear how platforms like Coursera might make future use of the course materials uploaded to their platform. And, even if Coursera treats materials in a responsible manner, what happens if another company buys them out? The contracts that universities currently have in place may not account for all the possible eventualities.

I have already mentioned the certificates of completion that Coursera provides to students; these are the free certificates that are automatically sent to students who successfully complete all course requirements. During the enrollment period for my course, I received an email from one of our distance education staff members who was helping to coordinate certain materials across all of Georgia Tech's MOOCs with Coursera. He was requesting a high-resolution image of my signature to be placed on all certificates of completion for the Freshman Composition 2.0 course. At first I wondered if I was simply being difficult or overly cautious, but each time I mentioned the request to someone (including several of my colleagues in the College of Computing who specialize in online security issues), the response was always the same: "You didn't give it to them, right?" Upon further investigation, I realized that fifty-one people had administrative access to our course site. I had no idea who most of these people were. I soon discovered that thirty-eight worked for Coursera, twelve worked for various units at Georgia Tech, and then there was me. Any of these people would have access to download my signature. I pushed my question through to our legal department, and they redirected me to the Georgia Tech Research Corporation because our contract with Coursera was under their auspices. I refused to submit my signature until I could be fully informed about any potential liabilities. To date, I still have not heard anything about the legal issues. A week after my course ended, I received a note from a Georgia Tech coordinator working with Coursera saying that I could simply provide a typed version of my name in an italicized font.

If all this sounds confusing, it is. That is part of my point. Because Coursera is a for-profit venture (and because I believe it likely will be purchased by another larger company), I worry about how their assets might be used in the future, including my signature, my likeness, and our course materials. Even though we designed content to be freely available, there is no way I can prevent Coursera (or a future company) from charging for it. More important, I worry that at some point our team could be told that our course materials do not belong to us, and if we would like to use them again, we will need to pay to do so. I haven't signed any additional contracts or received any information about my rights (or our team member's rights) in this regard. What the future holds, I do not know, but I am unsettled by the potential ways our materials might be used.

KNOWING WHAT STUDENTS KNOW

For decades, scholars who specialize in teaching and learning have tried to find more interactive ways to engage students. Instructors have been encouraged to favor student-centered discussion and project-based learning approaches to teaching, rather than traditional lecturing at the front of the classroom. Lecturing is easy if you know the material, but the kind of mentoring necessary in other more engaged teaching models is more demanding. I suppose it was naivety, but when I began taping the lectures for my MOOC, I was immediately unsettled by the realization that I would be unable to check in with my future students. I would probably never have a meaningful conversation with most of them. How could I with such large numbers?

In my traditional classroom, I know the strengths and weaknesses of every student, and this allows me to make just-in-time changes to accommodate their needs. Even in traditional, small-scale distance learning courses, instructors engage regularly with students via forums, chats, video-conferences, emails, and even, in some cases, face-to-face meetings. A pre-taped lecture and a set of discussion forums for tens of thousands of students doesn't allow for very much individual student engagement or accommodation. Also, when students provide feedback about a course component that could be improved to accommodate their needs, making changes mid-course is very difficult. It can be costly and time-consuming proposition to re-tape lectures, redesign and deploy new content. Obviously reflection and revision is necessary and desirable in any course, but I don't have to employ videographers and other technical specialists when I engage in this process for a traditional class.

And, what of evaluation? All our team could do was to prepare students to be the best peer-assessors they could be. I couldn't personally evaluate their work in the way I do with a traditional class. Peer-assessment is a valuable tool, but it is not the same as substantive feedback provided by an expert—a key problem we wanted to explore. That is, we wanted to know how much we could gain with limited, guided peer-review. Even with our peer-review approach, we had to sacrifice some of our preferred strategies. Ideally, students who complete peer-assessments can communicate post-assessment to ask questions about the feedback they have received. This post-assessment connection was unavailable in the Coursera platform.

Another option for assessment is machine grading. For a composition course this would only offer evaluation of the most basic of mechanical considerations (and even these functions are often evaluated incorrectly—hence Les Perlman's results when writing nonsense essays that score high in certain grading systems), evaluating the kinds of things that must be narrowly programmed with constrained prompts and writing types. Currently there are no machine grading interfaces that address higher order concerns like style and logic for any possible writing scenario. For now, peer or machine assessment lacks the individualized and expert attention a student gets in a traditional classroom. Something may be better than nothing, but the hype very early turned to how MOOCs might be a substitute for many traditional class experiences, but in the current format, I do not believe that is possible for a composition course. One example often cited as a successful course is the Modern Poetry course taught by Al Filreis. Filreis eliminated grading completely, choosing instead to have peer feedback only, something I learned when I enrolled in his course to see how he was approaching this and other pedagogical challenges. If we are willing to offer MOOCs only in a non-credit bearing way, then this might be sufficient. However, there are too many conversations about how to grant credit for me to believe this is viable in the long-term.

GIVING IT ALL AWAY

On the surface, providing specialized and free educational content is an attractive idea. As for content access, which is available from many traditional and online sources, it is true that more people might gain access to certain otherwise restricted content on a MOOC; for example, there are many reasons I can't attend Harvard or Stanford to take a class, but I can easily enroll in a MOOC. However, if we are touting a special kind of "classroom" in addition to providing content, then students should understand they might also miss out on many other essential components available only in smaller classrooms and traditional university situations. Content delivery is clearly something that can be done effectively in a MOOC. However, we must consider how it is decided what the content should be and who should deliver it.

Many are the times I've chosen a particular restaurant because of a buy-one-get-one-free offer. And, yes, sometimes I even return to the restaurant if I like the food and the service. I also understand that any business that relies exclusively on such loss-leaders eventually is bound to fail. Perhaps some elite institutions can afford to give away their courses (even accredited ones) for a time. Eventually, if they are the only providers left, they may even recoup any losses once sustained. Certainly such a scenario will represent far more dramatic losses to schools that cannot compete. If at some point a school closes, there will be the obvious loss of employment for everyone associated with the school—from the administrators to the faculty to the support staff. And, if that school is in a small town, the negative economic effects will continue to cascade into the general community. These losses are palpable. More immediately, I am concerned for the graduate students who often teach as a way to finance their education. I can easily imagine those positions disappearing.

Beyond the economic implications, I am specifically interested in the rhetoric surrounding the focus on only elite schools providing MOOCs. Even with the addition of some larger state institutions (already we see Coursera adapting their business model for the best profitability), the rhetoric often still focuses on elitism while simultaneously promoting a kind of egalitarianism. No matter the institution, there is a very plain argument: Some instructor at some school is the best person to teach some subject. People who believe in a "best instructor" model would likely argue that there is no need to have hundreds of different approaches to teaching a given subject. However, this argument does not account for the vast knowledge base available in many subjects. The content in any course is always as much about what is omitted as what is included. If we agree to the precedent of only one course on 20th American Fiction or one course on the Foundations of Psychology or one course on World War II, the information in those singular courses will become the canon. While there may be some curricular points that are universal for any course, there remain many other considerations, examples, experiments, and models that, if chosen for review, offer a variety of student experiences within the basic framework of any course. Recently a professor has encountered stiff criticism for saying he doesn't teach female authors. What if he was the "final word" in a MOOC about literature?

The implications for such a "one size fits all" course approach reach far beyond the classroom. Having a variety of experiences means that when a group of people is working together on a team, perhaps designing a new building, they will more diversely understand the array of possibilities. Limiting content by limiting the number of instructors means limiting possibilities of what students might learn. If we do not consider the loss of a varied curriculum, we will narrow the entire educational experience into what only a small number of people privilege. Even if it were true that a single "best" instructor existed for a course, if he or she wasn't on the faculty of one of the partner schools associated with one of the MOOC platform providers, then that course would never happen or the world would have to settle for second best as a price of elitism. If we seek to offer the best educational opportunities to the world, we will have to open these platforms to anyone interested in teaching—and reward them accordingly. Currently, most MOOCs are offered from schools in the United States. We also face a new form of colonialism if the West continues to dominate the courses offered on MOOC platforms. If we expand MOOCs to anyone at any institution, then we could have a myriad of voices, and that would be a wonderful thing. Here is where we could leverage the advantage of having so many students—along with their differing views and experiences. If we do not do this, we risk a dangerous kind of single-mindedness that could significantly diminish innovation and limit problem solving in every sector of our lives.

POTENTIAL GAINS

Until we begin frank discussions about what "free and open" means, we cannot move toward investigations about how MOOCs might help us improve the work we already do well. There are many interesting conversations we should be having about how technology can enable instructors to do the work that only humans can do. If, while we are investigating the potential uses of technology, we can also provide some general content to supplement whatever educational experience a person has (even if the supplement is the only educational experience), we can turn our arguments to ones about gains rather than about losses. For example, our entire team learned lessons about designing better online resources. We also had students who couldn't participate in traditional courses who sent touching and inspirational emails thanking us for offering the course.

Many of the arguments about MOOCs tend to take a "for" or "against" stance. Rather than focusing either on the dismantling of current educational structures or on leaving things as they are, I would like to see us shift our arguments to ones about strengthening our practices. There are costs no matter our approach, but hopefully we will provide students with something more meaningful than a sweatshirt.

WORKS CITED

Herrington, TyAnna K. "Who Owns My Work? The State of Work for Hire in Academics in Technical Communication." *Journal of Business and Technical Communication*, 13.2 (2 April 1999) 125-153. Print.

Coursera: Fifty Ways to Fix the Software (with apologies to Paul Simon)

Laura Gibbs

Coursera's software hasn't received much detailed attention, although it is a major factor in the Coursera learning experience.* As a Coursera student, I was disappointed by the software while completing the Fantasy-SciFi class (Fall 2012) and ongoing software frustration has since led me to drop other Coursera classes. Surely I am not alone in that regard, although it is impossible to know just how much the software experience, especially the limited social dimension, contributes to Coursera's non-completion rate. Pedagogy and software are closely entwined in online education, especially in MOOCs — and even more so in xMOOCs, like Coursera's classes— where instructors are largely absent, leaving a gap to be filled by technology-mediated learning and/or social interactions with fellow students. In this necessarily brief overview, I will try to show how Coursera's own educational model conflicts with their minimalist software approach and then provide a list of fifty improvements that might help bridge that gap.

COURSERA AND SOFTWARE MINIMALISM

Coursera has taken a minimalist approach to the design of its learning platform, and the result is surprisingly feature-poor compared to other learning management software and social networking platforms. I call this surprising because Coursera's open enrollment strategy requires the software to support massive numbers of highly diverse students, while Coursera's commitment to learning analytics means they must gather as much data as possible about those students. Here are just some of the reasons why Coursera will need to develop a more robust learning platform:

- Coursera's professors may have no prior experience teaching online. That makes them highly dependent on Coursera's software. So too with the students: the diversity of Coursera students — diversity of culture, language, educational background, technology experience, etc. — means that many students will rely on Coursera's software to guide and shape their class participation.
- The massive scale of the courses makes it risky to rely on external tools. For example, Coursera's "Fundamentals of Online Education" (Winter 2013) was cancelled after the professor asked all 40,000 students to enroll in teams using a Google Doc, thus exceeding the capacity of the Google Docs system. At the time of this writing, Coursera's software still does not provide support for team formation.
- Even when professors and students might find ways to network and use tools outside the Coursera platform, that is actually a drawback for Coursera's plans to rely on data-driven artificial intelligence to fill the instructional gap created by the absence of human teachers. To gather the requisite "big data" about how their students learn best, Coursera must maximize the time students spend in spaces monitored by their own software.

It is thus essential that Coursera's software provide a learning environment suitable for both professors and students who might be new to online learning, along with social networking features that can support massive levels of student engagement. What follows, therefore, is a list of suggestions for ways to further develop the platform so that the massive enrollment levels could become the basis for a learning network which would in turn generate rich streams of data for learning analytics. (*Note:* Things happen fast in the world of MOOCs, so some of these features may already have been adopted by Coursera; the list represents my experience as a student in Coursera courses from summer 2012 through spring 2013.)

Fifty Ways to Fix the Software

Discussion Boards

Coursera's discussion boards need major improvement to cope with what should be massive participation levels.

1. Randomized Content. To promote better discovery of discussion board content in boards with hundreds or thousands of threads, there needs to be a sorting option which would bring up discussion board threads at random, instead of only the latest or most-read content. (NovoEd, formerly Venture Lab, successfully implemented this feature in response to massive discussion board activity in their MOOCs.)

2. Sort by Reply. To reduce the number of orphaned discussion board posts with no replies, there needs to be a filter for the number of replies (0-1-2) so that posts with few or no replies can get attention. (Discussion board posts with no replies were one of the biggest problems I noted in all the Couresra classes in which I participated.)

3. Filter by Persons. With a system of friends, cohorts, groups and/or teams (see items #8-11 below), it would be possible to filter the discussion boards for personally relevant activity, so that you could see the discussion threads where your friends are active, where your team members are active, etc.

4. Build Conversations. As people create their own learning sub-networks within a class, they need to be able to alert their fellow learners to relevant discussions, using something like the Twitter @ or Google+ plus sign to notify people that they have been mentioned in a discussion board conversation.

Personal Streams

Rather than using an old-fashioned topic-based discussion board system, Coursera could benefit from features seen at the newer personal-stream-based platorms such as Facebook, Twitter, and Google+.

5. Streams and Sharing. Personal streams facilitate both following and sharing (retweeting at Twitter, repinning at Pinterest, etc.). As people share and re-share posts, the content value of a stream-based system increases, and follower networks provide valuable information for learning analytics and recommender systems. In contrast, upvoting and downvoting discussion threads, while useful for rating fact-based contributions, does not actively spread good content from person to person throughout the network.

6. Streams and Safety. Unlike a discussion board which belongs to everybody/nobody, a person's stream is their own, allowing them to block other users from their stream as needed. Letting students block users from a personal stream is far more effective for creating a safe discussion environment than having staff monitor discussion boards, as Coursera currently attempts to do.

7. Sharing Across Courses. The real networking power of Coursera would increase exponentially if students were able to share a personal stream across classes, taking advantage of the fact that Coursera students can and do enroll in more than one class at a time, creating a powerful network of interconnected classes.

Groups

One of the biggest challenges for MOOC software is to help students in massive classes find ways to connect in smaller groups.

8. Friends. Some kind of friending or following system is needed so that students can form lasting connections that endure for the whole course, and even beyond, rather than one-time encounters.

9. Activity Groups. To make sure that posts are read and replied to, some kind of "quadblogging" tool would be very useful, with students either self-forming their own groups of interconnected blogs or else having their blogs and/or discussion board posts assigned to random respondents.

10. Team Formation. As the aforementioned "Fundamentals of Online Education" course cancellation demonstrates, Coursera needs its own team-formation tools, and they could learn much from looking at the NovoEd MOOC platform and its strategies for team development.

11. Team Tools. Once teams are formed, the teams need communication tools. Again, NovoEd provides a good example with its team blogs: when a team submits an assignment, that assignment is automatically posted to the team blog for further discussion, sharing, and feedback above and beyond the formal grading process.

Online Identity

How people identify themselves (or not) in the Coursera network demands careful scrutiny.

12. Reduce (Eliminate?) Anonymous Posting. In the different Coursera classes I participated in or enrolled in for inspection, anonymous posting was allowed in every discussion board post. If anonymous posting must be allowed, it should not be allowed by default but instead a special option which the professor enables for a specific thread for a specific reason. (The Fantasy-SciFi discussion boards were marred by many rude anonymous posters who made fun of other students in the class or even attacked them; I saw the same thing again when visiting that same class in its second iteration.)

13. Allow Persistent Pseudonyms. As an alternative to anonymous posting, Coursera could allow students to choose unique persistent pseudonyms so that students could then use either their real name or their pseudonym for any given post. This would not necessarily reduce rudeness, but it would minimize the confusion that inevitably results in a conversation with multiple anonymous posters, none of whom can be distinguished from one another. (This confusion was also a problem in the Fantasy-SciFi course.)

14. Better Personal Profiles. For students who do want to connect with others, Coursera needs better personal profile pages. In particular, the profiles need to facilitate person-to-person communication. An optional "comment wall," a feature students could turn on or off as they prefer, would strengthen networking inside the Coursera platform.

15. Course-Specific Profiles. In addition to each student's Coursera-wide profile, there need to be course-specific profile segments where instructors add questions that solicit information specifically relevant to that course.

16. People Search. Being able to search for people within classes and across the platform (by shared interests, by past classes taken, by shared languages, by professional background, etc.) could greatly reduce the feeling of being "lost" that students naturally experience in these massive classes.

Blogs and Portfolios

Blogs and portfolios are essential elements for student learning as well as for the development of a learning network.

17. Course Blogs. The Coursera platform needs a blogging tool, both for class assignments and also for personal sharing and reflection. Compare, for example, the NovoEd platform in which each submitted assignment automatically shows up as a blog entry, allowing for discussion and feedback above and beyond the grading process.

18. Blog Aggregator. Students should also be able to register their external course-related blogs so that the content of those blogs can be aggregated and shared. (In the Fantasy-SciFi class, there was a valiant but doomed effort to do this manually through lists shared at the discussion boards, a solution that was completely inadequate to the massive enrollment.)

19. Blog Stream on Homepage. A blog stream of both internal and external student blogs would provide excellent fresh content for the homepage. To learn more about this strategy, gaze upon the wonder that is "Digital Storytelling 106" at ds106.us and be amazed! (For a "behind-the-scenes" look at DS106, see Alan Levine's contribution to this volume.)

20. Portfolios. Coursera should develop its own portfolio tool so that students can document and share their work during a class, while also allowing the student to export their final portfolio when the course is over.

21. Portfolio Archive. An archive of past student work is a great learning resource; seeing the excellent work of past students can inspire current students to do excellent work of their own. Coursera courses could benefit from an archive of portfolios that persists from one class to the next, allowing students to learn not just from their fellow students but from past students as well.

22. Portfolios and Assessment. In addition to a portfolio tool for use by all students, Coursera could integrate the portfolio tool with its SignatureTrack service. The availability of identity-authenticated portfolios would make it possible for students' written work and other digital creations to be assessed by other institutions as part of a credit-granting system.

Hashtags

The power of hashtags would improve the efficiency of Coursera's own network as well as helping Coursera students to use other social networks effectively.

23. Unique Course Hashtags. Each course needs a unique hashtag whose use is promoted by the professor. (There was no hashtag promotion in the several courses I took, so the students made up their own hashtags, resulting in multiple hashtags that diluted their value.)

24. Hashtag Taxonomy. Courses would also benefit from a taxonomy or folksonomy of additional hashtags for specific course topics and activities. The professor could seed the hashtags which would then be further developed by the students themselves. (The current tagging system in the Coursera discussion boards is completely chaotic and therefore of little value.)

25. Internal Hashtags for Site Search. To extend the extremely limited search features of the Coursera platform (there is, for example, no site-search feature), clickable hashtags could help students find relevant class content.

26. Hashtags at External Sites. For students who want to use other social networking tools, hashtags are essential for finding and connecting with other students at those networks.

27. Harvest External Hashtags. A harvest of hashtag-labeled content from Twitter and other external sites would would feed fresh, relevant content to the course homepage. (Kudos to the Blackboard CourseSites platform for having taken advantage of this Twitter-hashtag strategy in their MOOCs.)

28. Tagging for Curation. Tagging could help both instructors and students to curate resources together. Ideally, Coursera would develop its own curation tool (see #37 below), combining content tagged at external sites and content tagged inside the Coursera platform itself, with students rating the content to increase its value.

Course Homepages

The homepage for a class provides a great opportunity for student engagement, but Coursera's homepages are not highly engaging.

29. Custom Homepage Layout. A widget-driven system would allow instructors to add and arrange their own customized course content more creatively; even better, students could be allowed to customize the page with widgets of their own choice. With more dynamic and personalized homepages, students could find stimulating new content each time that they log in.

30. Custom Homepage Themes. Having a variety of homepage themes would also reduce homogeneity. Standard navigation and standard labeling of tools is useful, but that does not require standardization of all design elements. (Compare traditional textbooks: they have distinctive covers and design features, while still supporting standardized elements such as a table of contents, index, etc.)

31. Visual Engagement. Instructors could benefit from image libraries (CC-licensed images, student-contributed images, etc.) to bring some visual life to the homepages in support of the course's specific content. A random check of various Coursera homepages shows them to be text-heavy without any strong visual elements that explore the course content in visual modes.

32. Community Building. Professors who might not be used to promoting online interaction and community building would benefit from easy-to-use tools to add "meet your fellow student" activities, meme contests, image caption contests, polling, etc. to the course homepage.

Communication

Especially in a massive online course, effective broadcast communication from the professor is essential.

33. Daily Announcements. Even if students are not working on the course every day, daily announcements provide a trail of information for them to pick up at any time while also building a strong instructor presence at very little cost of time for the instructor, especially if the software supports re-use of announcements from one iteration of the course to the next.

34. Homepage Announcements. If students could click a "Hide Contents" or "Keep Open" button on the title bar of each daily announcement, that would allow students to prune the homepage announcements while giving Coursera valuable feedback about announcement reception and student participation.

35. Announcement Notifications. In addition to email notifications and homepage display, Coursera needs additional notification options such as RSS, text messaging and other mobile-friendly notifications, browser-bar notifications, desktop client, mobile apps, etc.

36. Course Progress Dashboard. Students need to be able to see at a glance their progress towards course completion. (In the Fantasy-SciFi class, there was no display of progress or grades without paging through the completed assignments one by one and manually calculating the scores.)

Course Resources

In addition to the required course materials (videos, readings, etc.), there should also be a wide array of course resources for students to explore.

37. Curated Course Resources. Coursera professors are in a position to provide valuable recommendations about online course resources, yet the software does not seem to support a "course library" beyond the assigned videos and readings listed in the syllabus. There needs to be a resource management tool seeded by the professor which could then be curated together with the students, with students rating the resources.

38. Cross-Course Resources. In addition to course-specific content libraries, Coursera could develop valuable libraries of online resources that would be useful across courses in related subject areas, along with general student support (writing support, research support, citation support, etc.).

39. Wiki Integration. Right now, the Coursera wiki tool requires a separate log-in and is completely disconnected from the actual course sites, with all courses sharing one wiki. This primitive wiki implementation needs major improvement to make it more useful.

Videos

Videos are the primary mode of content delivery in many Coursera classes, so maximizing the value of those videos should be a top priority.

40. Video Rating. While some videos include integrated quizzes that students complete for self-assessment, the video player should also allow students to rate videos for content, production values, etc. Without student ratings, how will the professors know which videos are most in need of improvement?

41. Integrated Video Transcript. The video transcripts need to be integrated with the video display so that students can read and annotate the transcript while watching the video. In addition, since videos provide the bulk of a course's learning content, it is essential that the transcripts be searchable.

42. Integrated Note-Taking. An integrated note-taking tool would greatly increase the learning value of the videos, yet the Coursera video player offers no note-taking features. Being able to take notes inside the platform would both help the students and also provide valuable information to Coursera about video effectiveness. (See the VideoNot.es tool for a great example of software that could, and should, be integrated into the Coursera platform itself.)

43. Video Errata. Even when done from scripts, videos naturally contain numerous errors. The videos do not need to be re-shot, but they do need errata lists. (When I checked the second offering of the Fantasy-SciFi class, no errata lists were provided and students were inquiring earnestly about the same errors all over again at the discussion board.)

Student Support

Without the usual level of instructor or institutional support that college students normally receive, Coursera needs to fill that gap with its own user support services.

44. Software Training. There need to be friendly, reassuring tutorials for all aspects of the course software, especially discussion board options, the text editor used for course assignments, features of the video player, use of the course wiki, etc.

45. Other Course Roles. In addition to instructors, staff, TAs, and tutors, there are many more roles that participants could play: discussion forum moderators and summarizers, curation moderators, technology consultants, foreign language experts, etc. Coursera could expand the "tutor" role to include an even wider range of roles, clearly labeled, so that these individuals and their contributions would be easily recognizable.

Student Feedback

Coursera's software needs to continuously collect user feedback, both to improve the classes and also for the development of Coursera's learning analytics.

46. Student Feedback. The more feedback, the better. For example, why not have feedback buttons integrated into course materials and assignments? Instructors can invite students to respond to surveys, but Coursera needs to take the lead in gathering feedback about the software platform itself, and they should also assist the instructors in gathering feedback that comes directly from students as they are using the platform, in addition to survey responses.

47. Activities Opt-Out. Coursera could learn a lot from letting students declare that they are opting out from certain class activities and why. This would allow students to avoid feeling like they are "failing" to get the certificate (they are instead simply choosing to do some activities and not others), and it would give Coursera valuable information about students' interests and goals.

48. Unenroll Button. Coursera asks no questions when a student unenrolls from a class. Especially given the debate surrounding low completion rates for these courses, Coursera needs to solicit specific feedback when students unenroll.

Two Un-Recommendations

Finally, two things to avoid in developing the Coursera platform:

49. Do NOT Robograde Student Writing. Machine-grading of quizzes and exams is obviously important in MOOC assessment strategies, but machine-grading of student writing would be unreliable and inappropriate. For more on this important topic, visit the Human Readers website at humanreaders.org.

50. Do NOT Police Plagiarism with Automated Detection Services. There have been problems with plagiarism in Coursera classes, which demonstrates a need to change the assignments and/ or better educate the students about plagiarism. The use of automated plagiarism detection services would be inappropriate because such services require a human instructor to accurately interpret the results.

CONCLUSION

Based on my experiences as a Coursera student (along with over ten years of teaching fully online courses, non-massive), it seems to me that if Coursera is going to succeed over the long term, they need to devote additional resources to software development in order to make their massive class enrollments into a positive factor rather than a negative one. Coursera software should facilitate and encourage participation by all the students enrolled in a class, not just a small, self-selecting subset of those students, and I hope that this list might be useful to Coursera's software developers as they move forward. In their ambitious plans to gather sufficient "big data" for data analytics that will compensate for the absence of human instruction, Coursera needs to find out much more about just what all those students are doing (or not doing) and learning (or not learning) inside their courses. If they can do that, then Coursera's massive enrollments could work towards their pedagogical success, rather than against it.

ACKNOWLEDGMENTS

Thanks to Kimberly Hayworth, Phil Hill, Steve Krause, Alan Levine, Susan Lieberman, Vahid Masrour, Debbie Morrison, Jonathan Rees, Claudia Scholz, Anderson White, and Edward White for their feedback on earlier versions of this essay.

Being Present in a University Writing Course: A Case Against MOOCs

Bob Samuels

One potentially positive result of the current fascination with MOOCs is that universities and colleges may be forced to define and defend quality education.* This analysis of what we value should help us to present to the public the importance of higher education in a high-tech world. However, the worst thing to do is to equate university education with its least effective forms of instruction, which will in turn open the door for low-quality distance learning models. For instance, one of the most questionable aspects of higher education is the use of large lecture classes. Not only does this type of learning environment tend to focus on students memorizing information for multiple-choice tests, but it can also undermine any real distinction between in-person and online education. As one educational committee at the University of California at Los Angeles argued, we should just move most of our introductory courses online because they are already highly impersonal and ineffective. In opposition to this argument, we need to define and defend high-quality in-person classes. We also should determine whether the use of large lecture classes actually save schools money.

Although some would argue that we should prepare students for the new high-tech world of self-instruction, we still need to teach students how to focus, concentrate, and sustain attention in an in-person-

---

* This work is licensed under the Creative Commons Attribution-Noncommercial-ShareAlike 3.0 United States License. To view a copy of this license, visit http://creativecommons.org/licenses/by-nc-sa/3.0/us/ or send a letter to Creative Commons, 171 Second Street, Suite 300, San Francisco, California, 94105, USA. For any other use permissions, contact the original author.

al social environment. In large classes, where the teacher often does not even know if the students are in attendance, it is hard to get students to stay on task, and many times, these potential learners are simply on their laptops surfing the web or text messaging. In a small writing class, it is often harder for students to be invisible and to "multi-task," and while some may say that it is not the role of university educators to socialize these young adults, it is clear that the current generation of students does need some type of guidance in how they use technology and participate in their own education.

When people multi-task, it often takes them twice as long to complete a task, and they do it half as good. For instance, my students tell me that when they try to write a paper, they are constantly text messaging and surfing the web: the result is that they spend hours writing their essays, and their writing is often disjointed and lacking in coherence. Since they are not focused on a single task, they do not notice that the ideas and sentences in their essays do not flow or cohere. Literally and figuratively, these multi-tasking students are only partially present when they are writing and thinking.

As many higher education teachers have experienced, some students are able to participate in online discussion forums but have a hard time speaking in their small seminars. Once again, students may find it difficult being present in front of others and taking the risk of presenting their own ideas in the presence of others. Some distance educators argue that we can resolve this problem by just moving classes online, but do we really want to train a generation of students who do not know how to communicate to other people in a natural setting?

The Web can also create the illusion that all information is available and accessible to anyone at any time. This common view represses the real disparities of access in our world and also undermines the need for educational experts. After all, if you can get all knowledge from Wikipedia or a Google search, why do you need teachers or even colleges? In response to this attitude, we should re-center higher education away from the learning of isolated facts and theories and concentrate on teaching students how to do things with information. In other words, students need to be taught by expert educators about how to access, analyze, criticize, synthesize, and communicate knowledge from multiple perspectives and disciplines.

While some MOOC advocates argue that the traditional methods of instruction I have been discussing are outdated because they do not take into account the ways the new digital youth learn and think, I would counter that there is still a great need to teach students how to focus, concentrate, and discover how to make sense of the information that surrounds them. Too many online enthusiasts sell the new generation of students short be arguing that they can only learn if they are being entertained or if learning is an exciting, self-paced activity. Yet, we still need to teach people to concentrate and sustain their attention when things may get a little boring or difficult. Not all education should be fast-paced and visually stimulating; rather, people have to learn how to focus and stick with difficult and challenging tasks.

During her Ted Talk on MOOCs and the future of education, Daphne Koller of Coursera stressed the value of breaking course lessons down into twelve- minute chunks because most students can only sustain their attention for this short period of time. Koller also emphasized the need for constant quizzes and tests to see if students were mastering the subject matter. Another presenter argued that all information has to be visually compelling and fast-paced in order to cater to the new generation of students.

In response to the more extreme forms of MOOC hype, we have to ask if in this age of distracted living, where people crash their cars while text messaging and parents ignore their children while multi-tasking, do we really want a generation of students to take college classes on their laptops as they text, play games, and check their Facebook status updates? Isn't there something to value about showing up to a class at the right time and the right place with the proper preparation and motivation? The idea of anytime anyplace education defeats the purpose of having a community of scholars engaged in a shared learning experience. Furthermore, the stress on self-paced learning undermines the value of the social nature of education; the end result is that not only are students studying and bowling alone, but they are being seduced by a libertarian ideology that tells them that only the individual matters, and there is no such thing as a public space anymore.

When students have to be in a class and listen to their teacher and fellow learners, they are forced to turn off their cell phones and focus on a shared experience without the constant need to check their Facebook pages or latest texts. This experience represents one of the only reprieves young people will have from their constantly connected lives. In fact, students have told me that they would hate to take their classes online because they already feel dependent on their technologies.

From their perspective, moving required classes online is like giving free crack to addicts and telling them that it will be good for them.

In order to help my students understand their dependence on technology and their alienation from nature and their own selves, I often bring them out doors and tell them that they cannot use any technology or talk to anyone. This exercise often makes students very anxious, and when I later have students free write about the experience, they write that they are not used to just doing nothing, and they felt an intense need to reach for their phones: this dependence on communication technologies will only be enhanced by moving to distance education.

MOOCs, then, not only add to our culture of distracted multi-tasking, but they also often function to undermine the values of university professors. In the rhetoric of student-centered education, the teacher is reduced to being a "guide on the side," and this downgraded position entails that there is no need to give this facilitator tenure or a stable position; instead, through peer grading and computer assisted assessment, the role of the teachers is being eliminated, and so it is little wonder that colleges operating only online employ most of their faculty off of the tenure track.

MOOCs also tend to separate teaching from research and have basically "debundled" the traditional role of the faculty member. Like the undermining of newspapers by new media, we now have more sources of information but fewer people being paid to do the actual on the ground work of researching and reporting. Also as Wikipedia has turned every amateur into a potential expert, our society is losing the value of expert, credentialed educators. Although some see this as a democratization of instruction and research, it can also be read as a destruction of the academic business model and a move to make people work for free as traditional jobs are downsized and outsourced. At the same time, the MOOCs may move us to a model where there is a handful of superstar professors teachings hundreds of thousands of students, while the vast majority of the faculty are reduced to being teacher assistants.

Many proponents of MOOCs, like Koller of Coursera, proclaim that education is democratized by having students grade each other's work. But isn't this confusion between the roles of the student and the teachers just a way of rationalizing the elimination of the professor? Moreover, the use of computer programs to assess student learning is only possible if people think that education is solely about rote memorization and standardization. Yes. We can use computers to grade students, but only if we think of students as standardized computer programs.

In contrast to massively open online courses, small, in-person classes often force students to encounter new and different perspectives, and the students cannot simply turn off the computer or switch the channel. Unfortunately, too many colleges and universities rely too much on large lecture courses that allow students to tune out during class and then teach themselves the material outside of class. While I am all for flipping the class and having students learn the course content outside of the classroom, we still need to use actual class time to help students to engage in research in a critical and creative fashion.

This push for small interactive classes will be resisted by the claim that it is simply too expensive to teach every student in this type of learning environment. However, in my book *Why Public Higher Education Should be Free,* I show how it is often more expensive to teach students in large lecture classes than in small seminars once you take into account the full cost of having graduate assistants teach the small sections attached to the large classes. Furthermore, the direct cost of hiring faculty to teach courses is often a fraction of the total cost of instruction, and massive savings could be generated if higher education institutions focused on their core missions and not the expensive areas of sponsored research, athletics, administration, and professional education. Being present at the university means that students and teachers are present in their classes and that education is the central presence of the institution.

Works Cited

Koller, Daphne. "What We're Learning from Online Education." TED. Jun. 2012. Web.

Samuels, Robert. *Why Public Higher Education Should Be Free.* New York: Rutgers Press, 2013.

Another Colonialist Tool?

Aaron Barlow

When I tried taking a Coursera xMOOC on Digital Media in the early part of 2013, two related aspects of it seemed distressingly familiar (aspects that are, I might add, specific to the huge xMOOCs of Coursera, Udacity and edX and not necessarily to the cMOOC, which has different structures of expectation and participation).* One of these aspects was familiar to me through my experiences as a Fulbright scholar and Peace Corps Volunteer in West Africa and relates to the problems of third-world development. The other stems from my own childhood experiences with experiments in education.

First, I remember a group of European professors in Burkina Faso who were sure they knew what would work for students at schools even in remote rural communities. They knew the goals and purposes of education, how it had always been done, and were flexible enough to be able to modify the means of reaching their ends. Yet, the teachers from those African schools, at the university for a summer institute, were horrified at the suggestions of the professors. The Dutch physicists at the University of Ouagadougou, well-meaning and extremely amiable, were hurt by the rejection they experienced. They knew that the schools they wanted to help had few resources—no electricity, no running water and only ancient and tattered textbooks (and not enough of them)—and that the need for assistance was great. They wanted to construct physics lessons that use only locally available materials, and they had developed a number of them, all quite ingenious.

When they tried to share them with the actual teachers, however, they were shocked by the negativity their projects elicited. Among other things, the teachers accused the professors of harboring colonialist attitudes; they asked them why they were assuming that African students were only worthy of the second rate, of pale imitations of what the European children were getting. The very offering of these tools, the Burkinabe teachers said, was admission that education in the bush could never equal education in the capitals of the developed world. It was a sign not just of neo-colonialism but of acceptance of the widening gap between rich and poor. The xMOOC I experienced, it seemed to me, was a sign of the same attitudes those well-meaning professors from the Netherlands were carrying.

Second, my emotions in response to the xMOOC were exactly those I had one childhood summer when I was thrown headlong among teaching machines and programmed instruction. Almost immediately bored by what was in front of me, I had to be constantly called back to task. A few years later, behavioral psychologist B. F. Skinner, who had been instrumental in the work on teaching machines, would describe almost exactly how I had felt:

> Though physically present and looking at a teacher or text, the student does not pay attention. He is hysterically deaf. His mind wanders. He daydreams. Incipient forms of escape appear as restlessness. "Mental fatigue" is usually not a state of exhaustion but an uncontrollable disposition to escape.... A child will spend hours absorbed in play or in watching movies or television who cannot sit still in school for more than a few minutes before escape becomes too strong to be denied. (97-98)

I was bored and felt no connection with what was happening, no control. In both the teaching machine and xMOOC situations, the plans and activities confronting the student seemed to have little to do with me, the actual learner.

How do these two, Africa and Cambridge, connect? Quite simply, the student enrolled in an xMOOC, I believe, is in much the same position as both the student before the teaching machine and the colonized individual. She or he is forced to deal with foreign assumptions having little to do with the reality of the learner or the colonized. Attitudes toward both are quite similar to those parodied by Philip K.

Dick in his 1963 science-fiction novel *The Man in the High Castle*. In it, Dick presents a passage from *The Grasshopper Lies Heavy*, a "novel" he "quotes" inside his own. It speaks of shipping an

> almost witlessly noble flood of cheap one-dollar... television kits to every village and backwater.... And when the kit had been assembled by some gaunt, feverish-minded youth in the village, starved for a chance, of that which the generous Americans held out to him, that tinny little instrument with its built-in power supply no large than a marble began to receive. And what did it receive? Crouching before the screen, the youths of the village—and often the elders as well—saw words. Instructions.... Overhead, the American artificial moon wheeled, distributing the signal, carrying it everywhere . . . to the waiting, avid masses. (150)

I have referred to this passage numerous times over the past decade, even using it in one of my books. It is prescient, almost a prediction of the xMOOC today as it has been of other attempts, like Nicholas Negroponte's One Laptop Per Child (OLPC) project, to bring advancement to the needy. Like the attitudes Dick satirizes, those behind both the xMOOCs and OLPC (among other projects) rest on assumptions unquestioned among the rich, powerful and show very little understanding of the situation of the poor, powerless and untutored. As is true even in the best colonial situations, though colonialist intentions can appear to be benign or even positive, their projects as often seem to stem not from the needs of the intended recipients (who most of them really know nothing about) but from those of the creators (themselves).

Looking back, I think the same was true of many of the creators of teaching machines and the theories of programmed instruction—among them my father. My parents' house was always filled with "teaching tools" and "learning tools." Where most kids built toy houses out of Lincoln Logs, I used Cuisenaire rods, little colored blocks that are, I understand, also great for teaching kids basic arithmetical concepts. My father, a behavioral psychologist, was a consultant for Field Enterprises; the company was constantly loading him up with samples and prototypes.

We spent the summer of 1961 in Cambridge, MA while my father did something or other with teaching machines at Harvard—and where I, very patiently (after all, they gave me a quarter after each session), was subjected to a variety of machines that were supposed, I assumed, to somehow increase my knowledge. Or something.

I remember the details of the Harvard Museum much more clearly (it was a wonderful place for a nine-year-old to wander)—along with expeditions to spear (with forks on sticks) half-dead fish in the then-polluted Charles River. I don't even recall the topics of the teaching-machine lessons.

I do remember that I liked the programs and machines when the subjects were trivial and easily mastered. I hated them when I felt I was their captive—and that, unfortunately, was most of the time. Unlike in the museum, where I had complete freedom to explore, I felt coerced—and there was no one I could explain that to. It was worse than the feeling in school where, when bored, I could at least turn to my own fantasies. These machines were so filled with little tasks that I couldn't even find relief in daydreams.

Even Skinner came to understand this, and the place of programmed instruction quickly moved from the center to the side for the classroom: learning cannot be reduced to programs. Most of the other teaching-machine and programmed-instruction people eventually understood this as well... though the public image was that they were training students in the equivalent of Skinner's own "operant chambers." In reality, in their behaviorist "rat labs," the professors were instructing students in "shaping, " teaching through approximation and reward, a process heavy on immediate teacher/student interaction. By the end of the 1960s, almost all of these psychologists were working on the assumption, growing from their experiences with "shaping, " that programmed instruction and teaching machines could only be part of a much greater learning environment. The same, I am sure, should be true of the MOOC—but few MOOC proponents yet seem to recognize that, or how much personal interaction is going to be needed between instructor and student to make a MOOC work.

Sometimes, when I was working a programmed-instruction device on my own, I would give up on the set-out path and take the thing apart. I remember something called the Cyclo-Teacher which had large paper discs and smaller blank ones to be inserted into a device that allowed you to read a question from the large disc and write an answer on the small. You'd turn a knob, and the next question would appear along with the answer to the previous one. Quickly, I abandoned the device and the sequence, simply taking the large discs and reading those parts of them that interested me, forgetting about the program and ignoring the questions. That may be what is going to happen with the MOOCs. Because there is no up-close human interaction, the students will eventually be taking them apart rather than following the prescribed pattern. That is not bad, but it is not the intent.

Also, that is what kids like to do. Like my wanderings in the museum, I could tailor the machines to my own ends. I remember a big machine I sat in front of—well, about all I can remember is the color brown, a chair, and dingy walls. I don't even know what they were putatively trying to teach. I could do nothing but sit and wait for instructions and then do someone else's bidding. Even then, I quickly caught on that my own learning *as an individual* was really just an afterthought.

Compared to that dull room, I recall the museum vividly, its wide staircases, musty smells, dinosaur skeletons, and much more. There, I felt in charge—even in the gift shop where I would often stare, lusting after the wonderful toys and models I could not afford. When I explored the xMOOC, I wished it were more like that.

Perhaps it could be, but that will not happen until the MOOCs, even the xMOOCs, are created from a student perspective and not an administrative one. Not until they include both room for students to explore on their own and for teachers to work individually with the students. Not until they can move away from rigid goals and evaluations.

Like the MOOCs today, the teaching machines of those days weren't wrong for education or improper, they just weren't enough on their own to be the centers of education. They certainly hadn't been developed from specific *student* needs alone but, too often, for the needs of the psychologists (though not Skinner or my father, who both knew better), and students have to be that center if education is to succeed. In Cambridge, I wanted to build and to reach for things others said were beyond my grasp; the machines kept my arms short.

That was my problem: I always wanted more, and wanted to be able to control when I got it and how. That's how I felt about the xMOOC I took as well: it was (like many standard courses, unfortunately) a guided tour, and I felt I could not deviate from the marked path. There's nothing wrong with the xMOOC; it just isn't *enough*. It bored me because it was so meager and even more predictable than a class that does no more than adhere to a textbook.

There are ways of constructing an educational apparatus where the student is given a great deal of control, and the best of the MOOCs might be heading toward that. The danger is, as in colonialism, that the tendency toward centralized control and away from individual initiative and exploration is built into the existing structures of most of them. In other models, such as the Personalized System of Instruction (PSI) model described by behaviorist Fred Keller in his article "Goodbye, Teacher" in the late 1960s, attempts are made to sidestep such traps. In PSI, the teacher becomes something like an architect, while the student is the builder who has an array of tools available for the particular application. One doesn't use a saw, after all, to drive in a nail. Keller envisions a suite instead of a classroom, a suite including a lecture hall, carrels for individual study, a conference room, and areas for small-group work and conferences. Each space would be outfitted with different devices and scheduled for a variety of events, but the student picks and chooses among them according to his or her present needs, working toward mastery of individual modules. In today's world, this would be truly multimedia education, with relevant books, images (both moving and still), sounds and much more available to the student amid constant contact with other students, with what Keller calls "proctors" (more advanced students working for the course), and even with the instructor.

In a way, this sound like the xMOOCs, just in physical space and not electronic. But the xMOOC, when I tried it, was nothing like the varied experience of PSI or even, as I said, of the Harvard museum. It felt more like the teaching machines that Keller was already moving beyond fifty years ago. Why? It is in colonialism that we find the answer.

What is the xMOOC lacking that the PSI suite contains? Both can host lectures, both have facilitators, both have room for individual initiative, both have architects, and the pace of both is controlled by the student. The difference is simple: The xMOOC starts with the institution while PSI starts with the student, *exactly* the problem faced in many colonial and neo-colonial situations where leadership and power come from far away. And the results are likely to be just as disappointing.

Why does that initial focus and source of initiative make such a difference?

Part of it comes from the attitudes of the colonialists/instruction-al-designers, even the best of them. Peter Buffett, son of investor War-ren Buffett, puts it this way, naming what he saw through his work "Philanthropic Colonialism":

> I noticed that a donor had the urge to "save the day" in some fashion. People (including me) who had very little knowledge of a particular place would think that they could solve a local problem. Whether it involved farming methods, education practices, job training or business development, over and over I would hear people discuss transplanting what worked in one setting directly into another with little regard for culture, ge-ography or societal norms.

> Just so, the colonial power is also much more interested in the needs of the home country than in the colony, thinking something resembling what has worked one place will work in another. The instructional designer can fall into the same trap. As a result, as Michael Hechter observes, the "peripheral economy is forced into complementary development to the core, and thus becomes dependent on external markets" (33).

Pleasing the course creator can become more important than any actual learning. That is, everything feeds to the center, the top, eco-nomic and even cultural structures becoming centralized and, even though in a *de facto* fashion, controlled. Walter Rodney uses the ex-ample of African roads and railroads to explain how this works. The roads and railroads built by the colonial powers were useful even to the colonies—but look at their structure:

> These had a clear geographical distribution according to the extent to which particular regions needed to be opened up to import-export activities. Where exports were not available, roads and railways had no place. The only slight exception is that certain roads and railways were built to move troops and make conquest and oppression easier (209).

The assumptions behind this, assumptions that blind people from the metropole from seeing the obvious structural deficiencies of the patterns of development (or of what Rodney terms "underdevelopment"), and assumptions that are quite similar to those behind both the xMOOCs and OLPC, are summed up by Michael Hechter:

> One of the defining characteristics of the colonial situation is that it must involve the interaction of at least two cultures—that of the conquering metropolitan elite (cosmopolitan culture) and of the indigenes (native culture)—and that the former is promulgated by the colonial authorities as being vastly superior for the realization of universal ends. (73)

The structural paternalism of colonialism, generally unrecognized by the colonialist, is no different from that of the formulators of the xMOOCs. They may claim that they are constructing their digital roads and railroads for the "good" of everyone, but it is their own good that gains most and—as we have seen in the aftermath of colonialism, the "good" for the others often turns out to be no good at all.

The centralized decision-making from the metropole, as Buffett intuits, is never going to work well for those at the periphery. The scholars who moved beyond their teaching-machine and programmed-instruction projects recognized this structural deficiency, having learned that they, too, had been focusing on one point only, on their own goals for learning and not on the spot within the student where learning really begins. Just so, effective development in the third world has to start with the local communities and "on the ground, " not in the universities and think tanks of the metropole.

Keller, recognizing that he needed to move from a teacher-centered to a student-centered model, compares standard attitudes of teacher-centered education to how the teacher should be conceived in a PSI environment:

> His public appearances as classroom entertainer, expositor, critic, and debater no longer seem important. His principal job, as Frank Finger (1962) once defined it, is truly "the facilitation of learning in others." He becomes an educational engineer, a contingency manager, with the responsibility of serving the great majority, rather than the small minority, of young men and women who come to him for schooling in the area of his competence. The teacher of tomorrow will not, I think, continue to be satisfied with a 10% efficiency (at best) which makes him an object of contempt by some, commiseration by others, indifference by many, and love by a few.

> No longer will he need to hold his position by the exercise of functions that neither transmit culture, dignify his status, nor encourage respect for learning in others. No longer will he need to live like Ichabod Crane, in a world that increasingly begrudges him room and lodging for a doubtful service to its young. A new kind of teacher is in the making. To the old kind, I, for one, will be glad to say, "Good-bye!" (88-89)

The "superteacher" of the xMOOC, the creator of structures from afar and for the needs of the successful and the rich, can never be the kind of teacher that Keller envisions. That requires constant attention to the individual learner. And it necessitates an unwillingness to accept, unlike the MOOC, a 10% efficiency as sufficient.

Colonialism and its post- and neo-colonial descendants, as Dick implies and Hechter and Rodney argue, is never about the colonies, but about the metropole and its fantasies (though these have changed since the colonial era). I learned this in Peace Corps in Togo, working among the ruins of earlier development projects. Peace Corps was wonderful for me... but was it much good for the Togolese? Similarly, Skinner's "operant chamber" was never about training rats. It was designed to assist in the teaching of students, to help them understand a learning process ("shaping" or operant conditioning) so they could apply what they learned elsewhere. By the same token, the xMOOC is not designed for students but for the people operating it. It is a system for making money and reputations. True, there are some colonized people who actually have benefitted from colonization. Some of the white rats used in experimental psychology classes have had better lives than they otherwise might have. And a certain percentage of students will be autodidactic enough to make excellent use of the xMOOCs. But these, in all three cases, are small minorities of the whole.

What about the rest?

Some people brush the concern aside, including Nathan Harden, a young Yale graduate and spokesperson for the sorts of attitudes Dick lampoons. He writes that

> students themselves are in for a golden age, characterized by near-universal access to the highest quality teaching and scholarship at a minimal cost. The changes ahead will ultimately bring about the most beneficial, most efficient and most equitable access to education that the world has ever

seen. There is much to be gained.... If a faster, cheaper way
of sharing information emerges, history shows us that it will
quickly supplant what came before. People will not continue
to pay tens of thousands of dollars for what technology allows
them to get for free.

Shades of *The Grasshopper Lies Heavy*! Access to what the rich of
the metropole already have... except for the real motivational guidance and individual interaction that makes education possible. Thus,
making this golden age an ersatz, though apparently identical, version
of what the rich already have.

In a 2007 article in response to what was initially envisioned for
OLPC, Binyavanga Wainaina wrote that

> I am sure the One Laptop per Child initiative will bring glory
> to its architects. The IMF will smile. Mr Negroponte will win
> a prize or two or ten. There will be key successes in Rwanda;
> in a village in Cambodia; in a small, groundbreaking initiative
> in Palestine, where Israeli children and Palestinian children
> will come together to play minesweeper. There will be many
> laptops in small, perfect, NGO-funded schools for AIDS or-
> phans in Nairobi, and many earnest expatriates working in
> Sudan will swear by them.
>
> And there will be many laptops in the homes of homeschool-
> ing, goattending parents in North Dakota who wear hemp
> (another wonderproduct for the developing world). They will
> fall in love with the idea of this frugal, noble laptop, available
> for a mere $100. Me, I would love to buy one. I would carry it
> with me on trips to remote Kenyan places, where I seek to find
> myself and live a simpler, earthier life, for two weeks a year.

The OLPC laptop is great for the rich playing poor. When you
already have the best, you can slum a bit, secure. OLPC has fizzled,
for the most part, but the rich never learn—or, at least, never change.
Wainaina could just as easily have been talking about the MOOC, the
technological marvel succeeding the laptop as savior of the downtrod-
den, really proving to be little more than another temporary toy for the
secure well-to-do and a chimera for everyone else.

In his devastating critique of colonialism, *Prospero & Caliban: the Psychology of Colonization*, written during the colonial period, Octave Mannoni points out:

> It is of course somewhat arbitrary to compare educational with colonial problems: the colonial peoples are fully adult, and those who think of them as overgrown children may be accused of harboring paternalist motives or at any rate an unconscious paternalist attitude.... We have long been in the habit of speaking of the colonial peoples as being under our guardianship, and the present troubles are largely due to their struggles for emancipation.... To imagine that it is possible to take direct steps to combat the paternalist behaviour of colonial Europeans while the situation persists is to adopt a purely moralistic attitude, refusing to admit the facts and indulging in futile idealism. (166)

Just so, the fact remains that the power in education rests with today's equivalents of the colonial Europeans, the people with access to money from power bases within entrenched educational institutions. Just as any effective solution to colonialism that does not devolve into post- and neo-colonial situations that are tantamount to the same thing (the irony of Caliban's "Has a new master. Get a new man") requires that action originate on the ground, even at the village level, real education reform needs to start with the student. Certainly, that is true in higher education, where paternalistic and colonialistic attitudes are no longer needed, the students, like colonized people everywhere, being quite as capable (believe it or not) as their colonizers and teachers.

Writing in an essay made famous by "underground" reproduction in the 1960s (I once mimeographed copies myself), Jerry Farber argues, making an implicit connection between colonialism and education through equating students and Jim-Crow-days African-Americans, that:

> Students, like black people, have immense unused power. They could, theoretically, insist on participating in their own education. They could make academic freedom bilateral. They could teach their teachers to thrive on love and admiration, rather than fear and respect, and to lay down their weapons. Students could discover community. And they could learn to

dance by dancing on the IBM cards. They could make coloring books out of the catalogs and they could put the grading system in a museum. They could raze one set of walls and let life come blowing into the classroom. They could raze another set of walls and let education flow out and flood the streets. They could turn the classroom into where it's at — a "field of action" as Peter Marin describes it. And believe it or not, they could study eagerly and learn prodigiously for the best of all possible reasons — their own reasons.

They haven't done that, though, as the very development of the MOOC shows. Defeating oppression is nigh on impossible, for colonialism builds defeatism into the colonized people—and so it takes generations for success to come even in those few cases with positive outcomes.

We see the continuing results of colonialism all over the world, unceasing poverty for vast majorities and a constant stream of wealth away from formerly colonized lands, but few of us pay attention. We also ignore the fate of the rats once the semester is over (many ending up food for snakes). I think I knew, similarly, when I was a kid playing with teaching machines and programmed-instruction material, that these weren't things meant for me, that I was subject, too—as I later discovered through things like the Farber essay when I was in high school. I suspect most who participate in xMOOCs slowly begin to understand the same thing, which is why the completion rate remains low.

The xMOOC, imagined and created far from the learner, cares as little about the student as the metropole does about the colony—or the professor about the rat. If it is to contribute effectively to learning, it is really going to have to evolve toward the student (and toward student control of the learning) and away from its creators and the hegemonic structures of almost all of contemporary education. Rather than simply creating another tool for dominating educational structures, MOOCs of all types could then become simply one more tool available to students in diverse learning environments such as that Keller proposed for his PSI. After all, the students are the ones all of these should be for.

WORKS CITED

Buffett, Peter, "The Charitable Industrial-Complex," *The New York Times*, July 27, 2013, A19, http://www.nytimes.com/2013/07/27/opinion/the-charitable-industrial-complex.html?partner=rssny-t&emc=rss.

Dick, Philip K., *The Man in the High Castle* (New York: Berkeley, 1974). Print.

Farber, Jerry, "The Student As Nigger," http://ry4an.org/readings/short/student/.

Harden, Nathan, "The End of the University as We Know It," *The American Interest*, January/February, 2013: http://www.the-american-interest.com/article.cfm?piece=1352.

Hechter, Michael. *Internal Colonialism: The Celtic Fringe in British National Development, 1536-1966*. Berkeley: University of California Press, 1975. Print.

Keller, Fred, "Good-Bye, Teacher," *Journal of Applied Behavior Analysis*, 1968: 1. Print.

Mannoni, Octave. *Prospero and Caliban: The Psychology of Colonization*. Ann Arbor: University of Michigan Press, 1990. Print.

Rodney, Walter, A.M Babu, and Vincent Harding. *How Europe Underdeveloped Africa*. Washington, D.C: Howard University Press, 1981. Print.

Skinner, B. F. The technology of teaching (New York: Appleton-Century-Crofts, 1968). Print. Wainaina, Binjyavanga, "Glory," *Bidoun*, No. 10, Spring 2007: http://www.bidoun.org/magazine/10-technology/glory-by-binyavanga-wainaina/.

MOOCversations: Commonplaces as Argument

Jeff Rice

For a concept approximately one year old in its current incarnation, there has been no shortage of conversation regarding MOOCs.* A simple Google News search produces over 2,000 hits of recent on-line discussion among outlets varying from *The Huffington Post* to college newspapers. Among education outlets of news, almost daily *The Chronicle of Higher Education* or InsideHigherEd.com publish an op-ed or news coverage of a MOOC related event. In *The New York Times*, Thomas Friedman waxes poetic about MOOCs, and in *The New Republic*, Andrew Delbanco offers a critique of MOOCs via the tongue in cheek title "The MOOCs of Hazard." On my own campus, the dean of the college of Arts & Sciences returns from a trip to Austin, Texas where he serves on one of the University of Texas' advisory boards. The topic of his last visit was MOOCs, and he expresses discomfort over the enthusiasm he encountered among Texas administrators. That discomfort might resemble University of California Irvine Professor David Theo Goldberg's concern that MOOCs are a distraction and possible fly by night idea. Or the University of Texas' enthusiasm might reflect Martin Weller's belief that MOOCs can complement current teaching without harming education. MOOCs, in short, quickly have become a conversation piece. The conversation, however, typically plays out as a binary opposition: One is either for them or against them in the majority of conversations we experience.

In the circulated conversations about MOOCs, we hear the claims that MOOCs will destroy face to face interaction, will liberate education from the university's hegemony, will never be profitable, will be profitable, will change the nature of education forever, or will stumble and fail. For some time now, I've been tracing these conversations by bookmarking them into my Diigo account, an online shared book-marking service: https://www.diigo.com/user/drfabulous/MOOCs . As I save each MOOC discussion I come across, I notice few writers discussing their experiences participating in a MOOC or sharing a critique or interest that goes beyond these circulated tropes I've brief-ly identified. Among the exceptions, A. J. Jacobs writes humorously about his experience taking MOOC courses, concluding "an online college will never crack *Playboy's* venerable annual list of top party schools." And Larry Gordon documents his experience in a Public Health MOOC by noting "this style of online education should be the occasional snack, not the entire meal."

Other than these moments, shared positions on MOOCs are large-ly exaggerated. They build off a base of common, cultural knowledge long associated with new media innovations so that the response is cliché: X will save us or X will destroy us. In that sense, these po-sitions are commonplaces circulated as knowledge. A commonplace represents a familiar knowledge; that is, as a topos (a place of mean-ing), it works from accepted thinking (not new ideas). I've come to think of these bookmarked sites I save and read as the conversation on MOOCs *we all know to date*. In other words, the conversation is epi-deictic. Epideictic rhetoric is the appeal to what one already believes; it is not an effort to persuade in order to change belief. Thus, these pro and con commonplace positions speak to ideas we *already* likely have or that we are familiar with. When an article about MOOCs surfaces online, we know what to expect from the author (hyperbolic embrace-ment or hyperbolic critique).

A brief survey of the conversation's patterns might help. One re-peated claim circulated in the MOOC conversation is that online learning—particularly on the massive scale MOOCs offer—destroys face to face interaction. Writing for *Inside Higher Ed,* for example, University Council-AFT president Bob Samuels offers this common-place response:

I worry that students are losing the ability to make eye contact and read body language, and that they are not being prepared to be effective citizens, workers, and family members.

Edutopia's Mark Levinson produces a similar lament, arguing that the "student-teacher bond is more challenging to develop and sustain through online learning" because "unfortunately, for many learners, MOOCs lack the possibility of mentorship and close guidance that comes through the building of a meaningful relationship between student and teacher." Andrew Delbanco concludes his diatribe against MOOCs with an anecdote from a student whom he has had a "profound effect" upon. Delbanco notes:

> No matter how anxious today's students may be about gaining this or that competence in a ferociously competitive world, many still crave the enlargement of heart as well as mind that is the gift of true education. It's hard for me to believe that this kind of experience can happen without face-to-face teaching and the physical presence of other students.

And describing his experience in Duke University's first year writing MOOC, John Warner comments on his instructor by noting, "she and I don't have a relationship, and when it comes to learning, relationships matter." The list of face to face interaction critiques goes on.

If there is a current MOOC conversation, then, it's hardly a conversation. What we hear is repetition. The discussion regarding MOOCs, as the face to face examples show, tends to repeat itself. But the teaching occurring in some MOOCs—and at the least, in the few MOOC courses I've enrolled in—doesn't reflect these repetitions; these courses don't repeat these critiques. They merely repeat already existing practices. That is, whatever it is a MOOC is *supposed* to do (good or bad), it appears to be merely doing the familiar teaching associated with face to face learning. Face to face courses engage with the lecture format; many MOOC courses do as well. Face to face courses might offer short writing assignments or tests as assessment; MOOC courses do as well. Face to face courses can be terribly boring; MOOC courses can be as well. If, for whatever reason, a student's heart is enlarged (as Delbanco claims) by being in a room with a professor (and I doubt that has ever happened in any course I've taught—unless the student had a heart problem), it will likely occur in an online course as well. What we talk about when we talk about MOOCs is not really a conversation, but an appeal to the known. To get at why the known might terrify or excite, we should, at least, participate in some of the MOOC courses currently offered. That is what I did.

BEING IN THE CONVERSATION

I cannot claim that my MOOC experience is "massive." I have enrolled in only four MOOC courses to date: Listening to World Music, E-Learning and Digital Cultures, and Duke University and Ohio State University's first year composition course. All four courses were offered through Coursera. Alongside the face to face critiques repeated in MOOC discussion, much has been made about the circulated (and repetitive) claim of a 10% completion rate so far witnessed in Coursera offerings, a statistic published by *The New York Times* (Lewin). Columbia University's Engineering College also cites the 10% number (Dyer). In *The Boston Globe*, Northeastern University's president Joseph Aoun puts MOOCs' completion rate at between 5% and 10%. *Forbes'* David Skorton and Glenn Altschuler note that Stanford's first MOOC course on artificial intelligence had only a 13% completion rate. St. Leo's president Arthur F. Kirk, Jr. puts the Stanford completion rate at 10% . *The Chronicle of Higher Education's* survey of MOOC courses and instructors identified a 7.5% completion rate and a "median number of passing students" at 2,600 ("The Professors Who Make the MOOCs"). *The Chronicle* also quotes Coursera's founders as not being concerned with the low completion rates.

> But most students who register for a MOOC have no intention of completing the course, said the company's co-founders, Daphne Koller and Andrew Ng. "Their intent is to explore, find out something about the content, and move on to something else," said Ms. Koller. ("Coursera Takes a Nuanced View")

As a member of the estimated 90% (those who do not complete all of the criteria for course completion), I, too, have enrolled in these courses largely out of curiosity, but also because I have found the circulated conversations—including completion rate issues—regarding MOOCs as unhelpful as face to face debates. I want to understand MOOCs outside of the repeated critiques or praises I tend to bookmark as the MOOC conversation. Another such critique is completion rates. To do that I can offer a small amount of critical thinking. These claims that a 10% completion rate of 20,000 students in a course is unacceptable make little sense when we consider the following:

1. Students are not paying for these courses nor enrolling for credit (low stakes produce low results).
2. Students, like me, may be enrolling for reasons beyond education (i.e., we never intended to complete the course).
3. 10% of 20,000 is 2,000 (which also mirrors the published median number). If such a MOOC course was for paid college credit, the course would still be larger than any face to face lecture course offered in a given university, and at a $300 per credit hour price (a fairly average state university tuition rate), it would generate $1.8 million. That is considerably more money than the average lecture course provides.

That I completed a MOOC course or did not complete the course matters little at this point in the conversation; completion rate is a conversation I am aware of but not in need to critique or extend beyond this simple breakdown. If anything, conversations regarding retention speak more to the commonplace (what we normally discuss as university administrators, of which I am one) and not to the MOOC itself (where participants act as a different kind of student). What I have learned—so far—from this minimal involvement in these MOOC offerings is that the hyperbolic conversations surrounding MOOCs do not resemble what I have experienced. Participants—whether they complete the course or not - do not seem upset at the message forums and limited Google Hangout interaction (used in one course). Nor do they seem upset with the content delivery (video lecture or posted lecture). Nor do they reject the assignments (very short writings of 200 to 600 words or the semester long creation of a visual artifact). The courses tend to end with enthusiasm (at least what is posted on the forums). I, on the other hand, found all of what I experienced problematic. But I wasn't the real audience for the course. Tenured professors enrolled merely out of curiosity are not the long term audience for a given MOOC course, and that is why I am among the 90% who did not complete the four courses. I am not in the course to complete it. This observation does not excuse what I think is bad pedagogical practice, but it also is a part of a larger network of meaning that the conversation must acknowledge.

MOOC Writing

As example of my experience, I offer my most recent attendance in Duke University's composition course, English Composition 1: Achieving Expertise. In the short narrative I tell about this experience, I have no intent to critique the course's professor Denise Comer, who is also Director of Duke's First Year Writing program. In fact, my very short narrative—while likely critical in tone—is meant to be reflective and to exemplify what I might call the "briefly ethnographic." That is, I do not offer a complete ethnography of English Composition 1, but instead a brief circulation of moments, observations, and discussion. By offering only brevity, I want to contribute to the conversations I have outlined here so far and bookmarked in my Diigo folder. Only, I don't want to repeat those conversation as is; instead I want to briefly enter into a limited ethnography so that it, too, joins the conversation and hopefully, in some small way, may impact that conversation as being outside of the repetitions I encounter.

I have taught composition at least once a year since becoming a professor—with the exception of the three years I was the Writing Across the Curriculum Director at the University of Missouri. Twice, as well, I have served as the Director of Composition (at the University of Detroit Mercy and at the University of Missouri). Along with this expertise, I have also published extensively on composition. I joined the Duke course, then, not as a student but as a supposed expert interested in writing instruction's move to a massive online space (Georgia Institute of Technology and Ohio State are two other universities sponsoring first year writing MOOCs). As a supposed expert, I joined the course not to learn how to write. I am looking to extend the conversation, rather than repeat it. I'm joining as a colleague, not as a student.

When I joined English Composition 1, the course was already long in progress, so I had the advantage to move along the three weeks at random, watching videos out of order, and observing the Google Hangout workshops—held as limited peer review sessions and, on another occasion, as a discussion with an author whose work the students had read. The syllabus promised to teach writing as theme—in this case, expertise—an idea I can trace, at the least, to William Coles' *The Plural I*, whose canonical amateur assignment has been influential in writing pedagogy over the last 30 years. Thematic focus is familiar to me as well since I have taught composition courses as thematic (writing about place, about influence, about a local farmer's market, etc.). The four course projects felt like a typical pacing of students through work that builds off of previous assignments. In this way, the course is part of the larger conversation one might identify as first year writing instruction.

When I viewed the Google Hangout for a peer review workshop on the first assignment—a 300 word essay on "I am a Writer"—two things struck me:

1. These are not the students I would see in a composition course I teach. I.e., they were mostly:
    a. Adult, international students looking to improve their English writing.
    b. Composition teachers (who, like me, are curious).
2. Participation in peer review was awkward and cautious. Responses were short. There was silence between responses. As one student said after giving feedback, "Was that ok giving feedback because I've never done it before."

While the first point offers insight into who, besides a fellow composition instructor, is the intended MOOC audience for this course, the second point is a familiar one. Even in face to face instruction, peer review is often awkward, met with caution (students are afraid to offer feedback, are not sure how to do it, and offer brief responses), and short.

The course's second project "Analyzing an Image," too, is familiar; it resembles the visual writing assignment in the textbook *Seeing and Writing*, which I isolated as problematic in my book *Digital Detroit: Rhetoric and Space in the Age of the Network*. In that *Seeing and Writing* assignment, students were asked to examine Joel Sternfeld's photograph "Warren Avenue at 23rd Street" and "notice" what was in the image. In my discussion, I noted the limitations inherent in mere noticing, as opposed to more explorative examinations of a space's meaning (i.e., what noticing cannot account for). In English Composition 1, students are asked to identify an image representative of their area of expertise and write about it. "What does expertise look like," Comer asks in a video introduction to the assignment. "How do we define it? Who gets to define it?" In another video lecture, Comer reminds students, "the more you look, the more you notice." To notice, the assignment directs students to ask themselves while analyzing the image:

- What does the image depict?
- What objects to you see in the image?
- What people do you see in the image?

In the forums, students posted images and followed these guidelines. What we find, then, in the forums is a collection of *noticing*. In *Digital Detroit*, my response to noticing was that such writing questions offer, instead of guidelines or prompts, limitations regarding the network of activities that affect an encounter with an image and that might generate a heuristic. Noticing fails to capture much beyond the immediate and familiar response (i.e., noticing denies the network of interactions surrounding the image or what it represents). Reading through English Composition 1's assignment, therefore, causes me no more discomfort than *Seeing and Writing's* prompt did; that is, they both trouble me, but only in ways that many pedagogical practices trouble me. My troubling is familiar.

This point is exemplified in a specific moment during the Week 4 Reading Visual Images video lecture, Comer asks students to spend two minutes looking at the image of Cory Doctorow writing at his desk (Doctorow's image is shown in the video). In the forums, students offer responses regarding the image, but how would students know to contextualize Doctorow as an editor and founder of the website Boing Boing (whose tagline once was "a weblog of cultural curiosities"), as a sci-fi writer, as a proponent of open source, etc. When only looking at the unfamiliar picture of a man behind a desk, how could they "notice" what is not in the image? And by not "noticing" what is not in the image, how is the response more than a commonplace; that is, the familiar and known way to frame a man sitting at a desk, in front of a wall of books ("he looks busy," "he must be smart," "he must read a lot")? Thus, when Comer traces out for the students what she's noticed, she also cannot connect the odds and ends and clutter in Doctorow's office with Boing Boing's cluttering of odd links. Nor can she connect Doctorow's collection of electronics with his sci-fi or open source interests. Nor can she connect the ways the books on his shelves inform his concept of "whuffie" (online sharing ethos from his sci-fi novel *Down and Out in the Magic Kingdom*). Knowing this network of background, profession, other publications, and ideology, for me, would allow for the conceptual connections I'd ask students to compose. Such connections move beyond mere noticing so that the image (or idea) is put into the larger conversation circulating, so that the patterns that generate any given moment are identified and tapped into, and so that the familiar is not the fall back gesture. That conversation, then, acts as the moment of invention (the ah-ha moment when one sees the contributing idea) so that a writer may move beyond the familiar.

Comer is clear that she does not want students to know such background, but I would. The point is slightly ironic. In Week's 5's video lecture Effective Claims, Comer introduces the 5cs of Effective Claims. Among the five items a writer supposedly needs to do to be effective, one is connecting. As Comer instructs, "connected means. . . is it connected to the work of others." Unfortunately, Doctorow—the writer expert—is left unconnected so that students may notice. And that point does not make Comer's pedagogy wrong nor the MOOC lecture wrong. The point merely illustrates this pedagogy's familiarity to other textbook generated pedagogies. I know I have seen this kind of disconnect previously. I know I have critiqued this disconnect previously. The situation is very commonplace. What we are talking about, then, is not always a degree of correctness (as much of the conversation regarding MOOCs shows), but a conversation that should be about pedagogical sameness.

What We Talk About When We Talk About the Same Things

Thus, there is a conversation occurring about MOOCs. That conversation, however, is not new, not innovative, and not something we have not already encountered. As much of my bookmarking indicates, and as this briefly ethnographic description demonstrates, the conversation is repetitive. If I identify something among the MOOC conversations I bookmark or engage with, I find what I already know. As known positions, alarm and enthusiasm are interesting emotional responses; they depend a great deal on the repetition of previous positions, commonplace situations in which to anchor our reactions. That dependence might suggest that alarm and enthusiasm should always be with us—in the face to face course, the lecture course, the poorly attended course, or the daily activities of a given university campus. As a former writing program administrator, I have seen little previous alarm or even outright enthusiasm regarding these familiar practices on the campuses I worked. If we now are alarmed or enthusiastic because of

MOOCs, maybe we should always have been alarmed or enthusiastic since the discussions and pedagogies we encounter are largely familiar. And yet, we are not. Only now do we feel these emotions regarding the familiar. Only now do we feel as such because *of the large numbers of students involved.*

The known does not vanish once I engage—at some level—with a MOOC course. I find a pedagogy that is familiar to me, and I find a pedagogy I have critiqued previously. If there is anything unsettling for me to date regarding MOOCs it is how I have yet to find the discussion or experience that demonstrates "disruption" (as another conversation regarding MOOCs promises). Maybe I want disruption. Maybe I want innovative pedagogies that utilize the massive online space to do something far more interesting than "noticing" what is in an image. Maybe I want a disruption that goes beyond the message board or peer response genres we encounter in a typical Humanities based MOOC (such as Coursera or other commercially-oriented MOOCs). Maybe I want a disruption beyond the familiar, whether how we evaluate this pedagogy or the pedagogy of peer review sessions occurring in a Google Hangout. Maybe I want a user-oriented disruption. In his most recent book, *Spreadable Media*, Henry Jenkins attempts to rethink the notion of user-centered content so that we consider content users participate in creating and sharing. "In this emerging model," Jenkins writes, "audiences play an active role in 'spreading' content rather than serving as passive carriers of viral media: their choices, investments, agendas, and actions determine what get valued" (21). I want, to some extent, a spreadable MOOC. Of course, I've always wanted a spreadable pedagogy whose content and sharing is determined by students. My desire, too, is familiar.

That spreadable MOOC might, at the very least, work with patterns. Patterns disrupt when they make visible the invisible. In the case of my brief narrative and overview, the patterns I identify among critics and supporters make visible the familiar practices, conversations, and emotions attributed to a supposedly novel approach to online education, but that remain invisible to the emphasis placed on the critique or support. What might have appeared as critique, for instance, the patterns disrupt as commonplace. I am not a passive carrier of such a pattern; I spread it across this short essay to extend the conversation, to disrupt the commonplace if only for a moment, if only to draw attention to how familiarity exists even in supposedly, novel

moments. Cathy Davidson writes that "MOOCs right now have captured attention as a 'disruptor' of higher education because, in form,
they are the least disruptive use of new technology in learning." What
rhetorics or approaches might disrupt? Let's start with patterns. Identifying patterns might assist partly in this disruption, but composing with patterns, as I have even done here when I briefly traced the
conversation and pedagogical experience, might as well tap into the
disruptive nature of media formations that disrupt or interfere with familiar methods of expression and learning. A MOOC—or a Humanities MOOC—that asks students to compose or that itself composes
across patterns might, indeed, be disruptive. I won't predict what that
disruption will achieve since I can't; it hasn't occurred, and we don't
yet know what it will be. The familiar, on the other hand, does little
outside of repeat what we know.

And as I write that final point, I find myself joining a new MOOC:
The Ohio State Rhetorical Composing course at Coursera. I join again
as colleague, not student. I join in search of new or familiar patterns.
I join hoping I can find a moment of disruption, any disruption, any
break with these MOOCversations we continue to have.

Works Cited

Aoun, Joseph. "A Shakeup of Higher Education." *The Boston Globe.*
17 Nov 2012. http://www.bostonglobe.com/opinion/2012/11/17/
shakeup-higher-education/Wi5FQz2JYstDnYDlUaUfdI/story.
html

Davidson, Cathy. "What I Hope to Learn by Teaching a MOOC on
'History and Future of Higher Ed'." HASTAC. 20 April 2013.
http://hastac.org/blogs/cathy-davidson/2013/04/20/what-i-hope-
learn-teaching-mooc-history-and-future-higher-ed

Delbanco, Andrew. "The MOOCs of Hazard." *The New Republic.* 8
April, 2013 (30-33).

Dyer, Nicole. "Making Sense of MOOCs: Columbia Engineering
Jumps into the Market of Massive Online Courses." *Columbia Engineering Magazine.* Spring 2013. http://engineering.columbia.edu/
making-sense-moocs

Gordon, Larry. "Hitting the MOOCs Instead of the Books." *The
Los Angeles Times.* 19 April 2013. http://www.latimes.com/news/
columnone/la-me-online-class-20130419-dto,0,6145509.htmlstory

Jacobs, A.J. "Two Cheers for Web U!" *The New York Times*. 20 April, 2013. http://www.nytimes.com/2013/04/21/opinion/sunday/grading-the-mooc-university.html?smid=pl-share&_r=1&

Jenkins, Henry, Sam Ford, and Joshua Green. *Spreadable Media: Creating Value and Meaning in a Networked Culture*. New York, NY: New York University Press, 2013.

Kirk, Arthur F., Jr. "MOOCs: Game Changer or 'Tech Ed Du Jour'?" *Huffington Post*. 10 April 2013. http://www.huffingtonpost.com/dr-arthur-f-kirk-jr/moocs-game-changer-or-tec_b_3053322.html

Kolowich, Steve. "Coursera Takes a Nuanced View." *The Chronicle of Higher Education*. 8 April 2013.

____. "The Professors Who Make the MOOCs." *The Chronicle of HigherEducation*. 18 March 2013. https://chronicle.com/article/The-Professors-Behind-the-MOOC/137905/#id=overview

Levinson, Mark. "Where MOOCs Miss the Mark: The Student Teacher Relationship." *Edutopia*. 8 Feb 2013. http://www.edutopia.org/blog/where-MOOCs-miss-the-mark-matt-levinson

Lewin, Tamar. "Students Rush to Web Classes, but Profits Might be Much Later." *The New York Times*. 13 Jan 2013. http://www.nytimes.com/2013/01/07/education/massive-open-online-courses-prove-popular-if-not-lucrative-yet.html?_r=0

Samuels, Bob. "Being Present." *Inside Higher Ed*. 24 Jan 2013.http://www.insidehighered.com/views/2013/01/24/essay-flaws-distance-education

Skorton, David and Glenn Altschuler. "MOOCs: A College Education Online?" *Forbes*. 28 Jan 2013. http://www.forbes.com/sites/collegeprose/2013/01/28/moocs-a-college-education-online/

Theo Goldberg, David. "MOOCmania." *DML Central*. 21 Jan 2013. http://dmlcentral.net/blog/david-theo-goldberg/moocmania

Warner, John. "I'm Failing My MOOC." *Inside Higher Ed*. 22 April 2013. http://www.insidehighered.com/blogs/just-visiting/im-failing-my-mooc

Weller, Martin. "MOOCs are Your Friends" *The Ed Techie*. 23 Jan 2013. http://nogoodreason.typepad.co.uk/no_good_reason/2013/01/moocs-are-your-friends.html

MOOC Feedback: Pleasing All the People?

Jeremy Knox, Jen Ross, Christine Sinclair,
Hamish Macleod, and Siân Bayne

While much has already been written about the first wave of MOOCs—their high-profile launch and lauded open enrolment—what is becoming increasingly apparent is that MOOCs are finishing.* The initial surge of courses is coming to an end: final assessments have been completed, feedback surveys distributed, and reams of data are available for analysis and interpretation. As the second and third instances of these courses become available, questions of feedback, development and enhancement will increasingly emerge in MOOC dialogue. However, although perhaps a routine process for courses with small cohorts, these are troubling questions where the MOOC is concerned. Fundamental to effective feedback and improvement systems is knowing who your course is for. Armed with such approximations, what your course is for, and how you might best go about teaching it seem to follow. The sheer number of participants in the MOOC makes such customary procedures rather more challenging.

An established course has processes of recruitment: filtering, selecting and scrutinizing, procedures which, through their search for suitability, attempt to ensure that the final cohort are "the right sort of people," participants who have appropriate background skills to engage effectively, and will make a success of the opportunity. However, the MOOC is an open door where enrolment is concerned, and while this can be seen in a positive light (Carey), it does present challenges. The *who* of a MOOC is, at present only a matter of speculation, and as the first wave of "window shoppers" satisfy their curiosity, tomorrow's enrollees are still unknown. The University of Edinburgh's 2013 report (MOOCs@Edinburgh Group) offers some early insights into MOOC learners, derived from entry and exit surveys created for their first wave of six courses. Nevertheless, the sheer scale of enrolment, we suggest, makes the identification of *what* the course is for, and indeed *how* one might teach it, decidedly more difficult. Thus the *who*, that is the scale and spread of participants, remains despite the attempts at broadcast and automation, the underlying, most extraordinary, and truly disconcerting aspect of this new brand of educational activity.

It is just such dilemmas that we, the teachers of "E-learning and Digital Cultures" face as the deluge of our first MOOC begins to settle, and planning for the second session begins. "EDCMOOC," as it became known, was one of six initial offerings from the University of Edinburgh in partnership with Coursera, and was designed by a team of teachers and researchers already working within the field of digital education, though on a decidedly smaller scale. Fundamental to this work with and around the MSc in Digital Education (MSc in Digital Education) has been the idea that contact drives good online learning, an approach that has culminated in the "Manifesto for Teaching Online" (Ross et al.). Concerted interaction, connection and exchange with our students gives us a fairly accurate idea of *who* our students are, how they have fared, and what to fine tune in the program—a constant and vital process.

If we were to situate the EDCMOOC amongst other Coursera and edX offerings, it might be categorized as requiring more in the way of self-directed study than the average MOOC. The content of EDCMOOC was not a series of pre-recorded video lectures, but a collection of public domain videos and readings, which participants were expected to navigate and digest, and to which they were invited to respond in the Coursera discussion forum or a personal blog. While we presented participants with introductory and summative text and questions on course pages and around the resources, the intention was to be less specific about guiding student activities. Our teaching presence was embodied in the curation of and narratives around resources, and exacted through participation in the forums and comments on our own and participant blogs. While we adopted this approach with

the intention of challenging the idea that pre-recorded videos constitute unproblematic teaching presence online, we were also aware that
it would be an experience that some would find challenging to engage
with. One significant consequence of MOOC-hyperbole has been the
increased mainstream interest in "online learning" in general, such
that well-trodden and much-critiqued debates have resurfaced with
vengeance, most notably the "de-humanizing" of the digital and the
supposed authenticity of the video.

The EDCMOOC formally came to a close on March 3, 2013,
although the resources are still available to those who enrolled. The
Twitter stream (#edcmooc) remains a valuable "go-to" place for interesting news on the MOOC phenomenon. Our post-course evaluation survey indicated that a large majority (82.8%) of respondents
who actively participated in the EDCMOOC found their overall experience to be good, very good, or excellent (see fig 1). Feedback comments were, unsurprisingly, massively diverse, ranging from praise for
innovation and creativity, to criticism for unorthodox course design.
Our initial analysis of participant feedback is available on the EDC
MOOC blog (Ross).

Figure 1. EDCMOOC post-course evaluation survey question: "rate your
overall experience with EDCMOOC."

Given our 'insider' population (60% of survey respondents indicated that they were employed in education), some very astute opinions

surfaced, particularly in the forums and blogs during the course. If we were to categorize this feedback broadly, two approximate categories would emerge: those who would want more direction from and visibility of tutors, and those who enjoyed the flexibility of activities and interaction, and a distributed and amorphous course space. As our preparations for the second instance of the EDCMOOC reveal (Sinclair), we are making some changes to the course design. These include strategies for "managing the massiveness" and video introductions to each week. However, making these decisions about which responses, comments, and criticisms to incorporate into the next session has been challenging.

The variety of feedback, and the irreducible diversity of opinion that the EDCMOOC seemed to provoke—although in some ways reassuring, life-affirming and, quite frankly, delightful to us—creates a problem for routines of feedback and development. Where opinions are so different, as with the question of structure and teacher presence, to satisfy one desire would appear to stifle the other. Stipulate the weekly activities, administer the groups, and delineate the modes of participation, and risk alienating a significant proportion of your curious enrollees. Equally so, guidelines and activities perceived as nebulous, and faith in an emergent community, will frustrate others. So, whose voices should prevail?

We'd like to make a case for *listening* to participant feedback—as much of it as possible, as often as possible—while retaining a skeptical and reflective stance towards it.

Despite the often criticized emphasis on the video lecture format, Coursera, edX and Udacity all play the "student-centered learning" card, describing it as essential for learners' flexibility and empowerment. While the broad shift from "education" to "learning" (Biesta 37) is too vast a topic for this chapter, it may be problematic to place total faith in participant views at the heart of MOOC development. Such faith assumes firstly that "learners" are a distinct group of people with universal qualities (which we have already indicated is problematic in a MOOC context), and secondly that these learners are in the best position to judge the value of the educational activity they have just engaged in.

The quandaries of MOOC feedback and development bring these issues into sharp focus. How can flexibility and personalization, buzzwords of learner-centrism, come to the rescue of MOOC improvement? To address the division of opinion described earlier, the answer would have to be to create a single course that allowed for both (and in reality all) methods of participation. While this may be an interesting, if not exhausting, way to develop the MOOC, the second assumption begins to loom large. What is the justification for assigning responsibility to learners to decide how courses should play out, perhaps in minute detail and without much, if any, space and time to gain perspective on the experience?

Where this particular take on "learner-centeredness" is privileged, not only are learners assumed to be able to guide themselves through the learning activity, but they are also imagined to be able to step out of themselves, to that objective "view from nowhere" (Haraway 1988), and perceive precisely what it is they have or have not learned. It is the assumed ease with which this takes place that seems problematic, rather than its possibility.

More humility, recommended for teachers and learners alike, might allow us to move beyond what seems to be a current obsession with "satisfaction" surveys. Enjoyment is an anticipated outcome of the educational experience, not a measure of it, and neither should "dissatisfaction" indicate a failure of course design—discomfort and disequilibrium can be vital to learning (Macleod and Ross). Satisfaction, to be clear, was not the intended outcome of the EDCMOOC, and we suggest the futility of engaging exclusively with such feedback; a process which can only result in pleasing some and exasperating others. Indeed, we might even venture to say that we are comfortable with the love/hate relationship that appears to have developed (see Parr) so long as, even if participants claim to have found the experience insufferable, they learned something. However, the open design of MOOCs does mean that participants can easily unenroll if they find the experience unpleasant, therefore losing the potential benefit of dissatisfaction. Of course, that should also include the caution that if you enjoyed the EDCMOOC, that does not guarantee that you had a worthwhile learning experience. We might even go as far as suggesting that expressions of disappointment are indicative of profound learning opportunities. Disagreement suggests entrenched positions, and in contrast, places where your thought is not willing to go. Affirmation seems rather dull in comparison. This doesn't mean that we shirk the responsibility of responding to negative (or positive) feedback, but we are interested in contextualizing feedback to understand how it also might relate to learning experiences in indirect ways.

Student feedback matters a great deal. However, the scale of the MOOC presents an opportunity to think through this vital component of course development. The division between students who prefer independent learning and those that crave direction is a red herring. What massive participation highlights is that there is no consensus of opinion on how learning experiences should unfold, no collective body of "learners," and no impressive feats of mastery through which participants can impartially judge their experience. People are different, from others and from themselves. This is, we suggest, what the "massive" tells us, and what we might consider to be the real value of the MOOC to education. Unfortunately for the advocates of singular strategies and blanket blueprints, there are no solutions to making the MOOC a universal and absolute form of education. This is not to be fatalist: we urge MOOC teachers to continue to engage with feedback, to experiment, to comment and to seek to explore this new educational arrangement. However, we also urge them to be humble and acknowledge that there is no "one way." Innovations which sit at the boundaries of established practice, such as the MOOC, provide fertile occasions to *do* education differently; in ways individuals feel passionate about and committed to. Attempting to please all the people all the time, at MOOC scale, risks diluting the convictions that bring educators into new territory in the first place. Education is not a popularity contest. Let us not be swayed by ostentatious enrolment numbers, but rather by the opportunity to develop educational experiences that click for some people, and challenge or perhaps sometimes frustrate and disappoint others. This mix of the advocates and the skeptics is what makes education interesting. The conversations that emerge from this mix are what propel us forward.

WORKS CITED

Biesta, Gert. "Giving Teaching Back to Education: Responding to the Disappearance of the Teacher." *Phenomenology and Practice,* 6(2), 2012. pp.35-49.

Carey, Kevin. "The MOOC-Led Meritocracy." *The Chronicle of Higher Education,* 29 August 2012 <http://chronicle.com/blogs/conversation/2012/08/23/the-mooc-led-meritocracy/>

Haraway, Donna. "Situated Knowledges: The Science Question in Feminism and the Privilege of Partical Perspective." *Feminist Studies,* 14(3), 1988. pp.575–599.

Macleod, Hamish, and Jen Ross. "Structure, Authority and Other Noncepts: Teaching in Fool-ish Spaces." In R. Land & S. Bayne (Eds.), *Digital Difference: Perspectives on Online Learning.* Rotterdam: Sense. 2011. pp. 15-28.

MOOCs@Edinburgh Group. MOOCs @ Edinburgh - Report #1, 10 May 2013 <https://www.era.lib.ed.ac.uk/bitstream/1842/6683/1/Edinburgh%20MOOCs%20Report%202013%20%231.pdf >

MSc in Digital Education. *The University of Edinburgh.* 2013. Web. 29 October 2013 <http://online.education.ed.ac.uk>.

Parr, Chris. "How was it? The UK's first Coursera Moocs Assessed." *Times Higher Education,* 18 April 2013 < http://www.timeshighereducation.co.uk/news/how-was-it-the-uks-first-coursera-moocs-assessed/2003218.article>

Ross, Jen. Digesting "EDCMOOC Feedback." *Teaching E-learning and Digital Cultures: Thoughts and Reflections on Teaching on the EDCMOOC.* 02 April 2013 http://edcmoocteam.wordpress.com/2013/04/02/digesting-edcmooc-feedback/

Ross, Jen, et al. *Manifesto for Teaching Online. Part of the MSc in Digital Education at the University of Edinburgh.* 2013. Web. 29 October 2013 <http://onlineteachingmanifesto.wordpress.com/the-text/>

Sinclair, Christine. "#EDCMOOC: Shifting and Reshaping." *Teaching E-learning and Digital Cultures: Thoughts and Reflections on Teaching on the EDCMOOC.* 06 September 2013 < http://edcmoocteam.wordpress.com/2013/09/06/edcmooc-shifting-and-reshaping/>.

More Questions than Answers: Scratching at the Surface of MOOCs in Higher Education

Jacqueline Kauza

Rewind time a year, and I already had a few questions about MOOCs—
though admittedly most of those questions could be summarized as a
quizzical "What on earth *are* they?" and then easily answered by a suc-
cinct and fact-laden paragraph.* Since then, I have moved a bit beyond
that. I've read some about the subject, written a little, and discussed
quite a bit. I've done some snooping, prodding, and poking. I even
tried my hand at taking a MOOC, enrolling in Coursera's "E-learning
and Digital Cultures," a five-week course taught by five faculty members from the University of Edinburgh, that scratched at the surface of
what it meant to learn online, an intriguingly self-reflective topic for a
Massive Open Online Course.

Firmly back in the present day now, having both researched
MOOCs and experienced one first-hand, I am nevertheless left with
a strange sensation of knowing more but perhaps understanding less
than when I began. My comparatively simple question of a year ago
has been replaced with much thornier prospects: who are MOOCs for,
what are MOOCs actually trying to accomplish, and what stands to
be gained or lost in the MOOCs' meteoric rise into the spotlight of
pedagogical discourse and policy. The uses of MOOCs as a form of
digital learning, and their place in online education, have been sub-

---

jects of sometimes heated debate—and after engaging with MOOCs as a scholar and a student, I agree that their usefulness is very much debatable. The E-Learning MOOC (EDCMOOC) in which I participated handled some pedagogical elements well, but left me decidedly unsatisfied with others. Though some of the issues I encountered may be resolved when and if this fledgling form of education develops further, others seem almost inherent to the format. And after my initial foray into this biome of the massive open online world, the question most on my mind is what place the MOOC could occupy in the world of higher education.

To give credit where credit is due, EDCMOOC did offer a refreshing variety of course content, taking advantage of the opportunities afforded by its online format rather than limiting itself to traditional, print-based, words-in-a-row readings. By including these diverse materials, the instructors modeled a stance advocated for by digital literacy expert Cynthia Selfe of Ohio State University: that communicators, especially those acting in digital environments, should "acknowledge, value, and draw on a range of... modalities" (642). The assortment of genres—from print to video, from audio to visual, from popular culture film clips to perspectives-on-education pieces—spoke to the value the instructors placed on multiple forms of literacy and the need to provide students with an occasion to develop "a respect for and understanding of the various roles each modality can play in human expression" (Selfe 626). Students were encouraged to sample and engage with the clips and readings that seemed most interesting to them: some might gravitate more toward video, others toward more traditional academic writing, and still others toward the education-focused articles. In providing such a diverse array of content, the MOOC creators may have been looking to engage many different factions of the titular "massive" audience of the Massive Open Online Course, by including resources that would appeal to a broader cross-section of students.

Presenting this variety of course content also served to model some of the different kinds of composing that can take place in digital environments, which helped to set the stage for the MOOC's final assignment. To complete the course, all participants needed to create a "digital artifact" that demonstrated an understanding of the material covered in the class. Described by the instructors as something "designed to be experienced digitally, on the web," this artifact could take nearly any form, provided it was stable enough to be accessed online for several weeks and included some combination of two or more of the following: text, image, sound, video, or links (Knox et al, "E-Learning"). Aside from these instructions and a few examples of possible digital artifacts, students received very little guidance regarding the MOOC's one and only required project. However, despite the slight vagueness of the assignment parameters, I liked the idea of creating a digital artifact, and I thought it appropriate for both the subject and format of the class. Such a final assignment provided students with an avenue for experimenting with some of the genres and modalities they had been listening to, reading, and watching over the past five weeks. It encouraged students to "communicate in ways that are 'born digital'," to explore the possibilities for meaning-making and communication afforded by different digital genres (Knox et al., "E-Learning"). Yet while I personally enjoyed the creative freedom of this project, I can also see how its lack of specificity might have been overwhelming, especially when the MOOC provided little opportunity for a confused student to contact an instructor for individual advice.

In regard to the instructors, I am of two minds concerning their presence or role in the MOOC classroom. I think of Todd Gilman— an online instructor and the author of the article "Combating Myths About Distance Education" for *The Chronicle of Higher Education*— and his assertion that instructors in an online setting must endeavor to seem engaged and approachable, even more so than in a face-to-face classroom, in order to connect meaningfully with students they may never physically meet. The EDCMOOC instructors did write with a friendly, enthusiastic voice in their weekly notifications and summaries, giving me as a student the impression that they were indeed a likable group. I also appreciated the fact that the instructors added some initial posts to the forums that were meant to serve as the anchoring point for class discussion; doing so gave them some presence (however minor) as conversational participants.

However, I cannot say I felt any real connection to the instructors—a significant strike against this MOOC for me, as I value the student/instructor relationship in any classroom. This course lacked what Douglas Hersh might call "the human touch." There was little opportunity for the discussion and conversation one might have with an instructor in a smaller class. Yet, it also felt far removed from a large lecture experience, for even in a large lecture hall, a student can see and hear the professor, the person, discussing the material, despite op-

portunities for one-on-one conversation being more limited. There are
ways to create meaningful connections between students and instructors online, of course, and Hersh, the dean of educational programs
and technology at Santa Barbara City College, expounds upon several
of them; for instance, he encourages online instructors to incorporate
video and audio clips of themselves to personalize the otherwise face-
less text (Kolowich). While I have not always been the biggest fan of
"talking head" videos, they might have proved beneficial to students
had the instructors of the MOOC chosen to utilize them. Being able
to see a face or hear a voice might help a student feel more connected
to the instructor, even if that student never communicated with the
instructor directly—as such one-on-one conversation would prove difficult if not impossible in a MOOC class of thousands.

That class of thousands, that ability to reach so many students,
seems a major selling point of the MOOC. Yet I feel that it is also
one of its pedagogical weak points. Hersh suggests that part of what
contributes to students' successful engagement in an online class is
a feeling of connection not only with their instructor, but with their
classmates (Kolowich). However, the only MOOC classmates that I
truly felt a connection with were a few fellow graduate students from
my university, who were also enrolled in the EDCMOOC course. It
did not seem to be for lack of trying on the part of the MOOC instructors. They emphasized discussion as one of their "primary pedagogical activities" and attempted to enact it through the forums on
the Coursera site (Knox et al.) Yet with the sheer number of posts, I
found it difficult to sustain any discussion with another individual,
or even with a group of the same people, on a day-to-day or week-to-
week basis. I got very little out of posting to the forum and eventually stopped, simply giving it a cursory skim-through each week. The
forum discussions seemed far removed from the real give-and-take of
genuine conversation; it was more like casting words and ideas into a
void. The MOOC did offer other opportunities for web-based connection—Twitter, blogs, etc. But with thousands of people potentially
using edcmooc hashtags or blog post tags, these strategies did very little to foster in me any feeling of true connection or community with
my fellow students. In my experience, one of the main advantages of
classroom (whether brick-and-mortar or smaller online) learning over,
say, teaching oneself from a book is sharing in the learning with others, both instructors and fellow classmates. It is a chance to not only

learn the material, but also to make connections with others through that learning. So this leaves me with another thorny question: is it worth having several thousand students in this digital classroom if those students lose out on one of the elements that I have found makes classes most worthwhile?

In addition to finding few opportunities to meaningfully connect with my teachers and fellow students, I encountered several other troubling issues while participating in this MOOC. These would not necessarily cripple the MOOC as it is now—a free resource for students interested in learning more about a certain topic. They could, however, cause significant problems if a MOOC were to be instated as a credit-bearing course. The EDCMOOC seemed to hold students accountable for very little and offered few structured opportunities to practice learned skills. The only required assignment, in fact, was the final project, the digital artifact. While I engaged with many of the course resources, I feel that it would have been very possible to skim just one or two articles, then spend only an hour or so in Prezi or Wordle or Animoto to handily pass the course. While I know methods of assessment vary from MOOC to MOOC, my own experience raised worrisome questions about what skills MOOCs are really trying to teach and how knowledge is really being measured. Again, with MOOCs as free learning-for-learning's-sake options, this matters less. But should reading two or three articles and making a Wordle be worth college credit?

And if success in online learning can be attributed "not to technology but to time," with online students spending more time on a task than those in face-to-face classrooms and consequently learning material better, how can that be reconciled with the low-stakes assignments and assessments of this MOOC (Jaschik)? MOOCs seem tolerant, almost encouraging, of students picking and choosing which readings to do, as well as when to do them and when to skip them altogether—again, perfectly acceptable when one is learning strictly for one's own edification. But in a credit-bearing course, at what point does not doing the readings become non-participation? When does it become unacceptable?

The question of whether completing only one project should warrant credit notwithstanding, the methods of assessing the digital artifact raised some concerns. The instructors did not participate in the grading of these artifacts; instead, each artifact was assessed and assigned one of three grades (0, 1, or 2) by three fellow MOOC students. While peer review can certainly provide a student with useful input that can then be used to revise his or her work, peer *grading* presents an assortment of problems for students in any classroom, digital or otherwise. Yet, the sheer number of students in a MOOC leads to few other viable options for grading and assessment. While the instructors suggested that peer review of the final digital artifact would create dialogue about e-learning, I saw little possibility for this in practice (Knox et al, "E-Learning"). There were no structured opportunities for students to revise their artifacts after receiving peer feedback, and there was no ready avenue for continuing conversation with my peer graders or with the students whose artifacts I assessed. Peer feedback was a one-shot deal, a one-time, one-sided "conversation." Additionally, the fact that all students are not assessed by the same person, or even the same core group of cooperating people, leads to questions of fairness. Having each student assessed by three peers counterbalances this somewhat, but in the back of my mind, niggling questions persist. Would students rate one another more highly, more charitably, than the work deserved? Would they do so out of perceived solidarity, unwillingness to criticize, or simple unfamiliarity with grading and assessment criteria? On the other hand, if a MOOC stood as a credit-bearing course, would a student receiving a low grade from peers then appeal to an instructor? Could an instructor not then receive several hundred or even several thousand appeals? Who, in a credit-bearing MOOC, would be the final authority on issues that students themselves cannot rectify?

The present-yet-absent instructor(s) of MOOCs are particularly problematic for me. As a student, I have always found relationships with my instructors to be very valuable, and in this, I am not alone. Reggie Smith of the United States Distance Learning Association notes that "the learner-instructor interaction is the most critical one to the success of the learning experience" (Kolowich). While student-centered classrooms have their proponents, I believe there is a difference between student-centered and student-only classrooms, and MOOCs run the risk of being the latter. Without some form of leadership, I feel that a class, especially in low-stakes, low-consequence social environments like those afforded by the Internet, could unravel very quickly into tangents at best and bitterness, sniping, and mud-slinging at worst. Gilman does note that an instructor in an online course should strive to be less a "sage on the stage" and more a "guide on the side," but the keyword here is *guide* (Gilman). Instructors should still participate in and help to steer conversation and critical engagement with course resources; however, the number of students participating in a MOOC makes it impossible for instructors to interact, let alone take part in meaningful conversations, with even a small percentage of their students. While this lack of instructor guidance may not adversely impact some students, it would likely put others at risk. According to Rosanna Tamburri, author of the article "All about MOOCs" for the Canadian website University Affairs, MOOCs might "work well for the 10 percent of highly motivated, independent learners who are likely to succeed regardless of circumstance," but might not be as helpful to the 90 percent of other students who require more guidance, assistance, and support (Tamburri). And so I balance another question precariously atop my ever-growing stack: are MOOCs, as a form of education that reaches thousands of people, worth pursuing if the students they are most likely to benefit are generally the students who would have succeeded in education regardless of its format?

And so I am at that point of knowing without fully understanding, surrounded by several teetering towers of questions, both about MOOCs in their present form and about how MOOCs would need to evolve if they were to be integrated as credit-bearing higher education courses. When, I ask myself, are MOOCs as I observed them truly useful, or when could they be truly useful? Yes, I personally got something out my participation in a MOOC—but it certainly was not anything like what I would get out of a smaller class (whether online or face-to-face), or even what I would get out of a large lecture with accompanying smaller discussion sections. While the MOOC proved an interesting experience, the knowledge I gained is, I feel, more analogous to the knowledge I might gain from reading an anthology of texts relating to a particular topic rather than from taking a class on the same topic. Someone with expertise in a subject compiled these readings or resources; someone felt that considering them together might have educational benefit. However, that person never then actively led others to see those same benefits, nor readily facilitated the close conversation and collaboration between learners that might in turn lead to critical analysis and discovery. Despite the thousands of people participating in the EDCMOOC, it failed to create true collaborative learning and human connection for me. For students like me, for whom sharing learning experiences with others is a significant facet of education, I am not sure where MOOCs would fit in, aside from as compilations of readings that might be slotted, almost like a textbook, into a smaller-sized class.

Yet, there may be an opening MOOCs could fill. As they are, MOOCs present a worthwhile option for genuinely curious learners, those who are interested in a topic for learning's sake or for their own edification. Like Tamburri, I can also see MOOCs being useful for continuing education; my mother, who was a teacher, and my friend, who is a nurse, are always on the lookout for classes or lectures that they could attend to keep their certifications valid. MOOCs also have the potential to be valuable to "new groups of learners" or those for some reason "ill-served or... shut out of the current system" of education (Knox et al. "MOOC Pedagogy", Shirky). Despite her reservations about the numbers of students who might truly benefit from MOOCs, even Tamburri acknowledges that the low cost and easy, flexible accessibility of these courses might well-serve non-traditional students in a variety of circumstances, like the Afghan soldier or the single mother, motivated individuals who, because of time, distance, or commitment, are unable to partake in more traditional education. However, even in these instances, I have a hard time conceptualizing a completely MOOC-based education. These measures still seem stopgap and temporary, filling the education void until one has the time and flexibility to pursue face-to-face or smaller online options that allow for greater connection to and engagement with both instructors and other classmates.

At this juncture, the questions I have are still too thorny for me to envision MOOCs in their current form replacing college classes or even being credit-bearing in the way of many decidedly less massive online courses. I've seen some good aspects in them, yes, but not enough to quash some lingering skepticism. I'm still not sure who MOOCs are really for; I'm still not sure who they are really benefiting. From my own experiences, I'm still leery about the casual way in which my work in the EDCMOOC was assessed, and I'm still hesitant to consider giving institutional recognition for something that, in the end, required very little engagement or effort. I'm still not sure if MOOCs are providing wider, more equal access to quality education, or if they are peddling a watered-down product disguised in a well-wrapped package. But I find that, to me, what most cripples MOOCs is the lack of true connection that comes from trying to both address and be accessible to thousands of people at once. In trying to be so "massive," to reach so many people simultaneously, the MOOC sacrifices many of the benefits of smaller courses—human interaction, individualized instructor attention, ongoing peer collaboration, and even a simple sense of camaraderie. And so, despite having many yet unanswered questions, I think that, for myself, I can answer a few. Do MOOCs present interesting material? Yes. Can people learn something from them? Definitely. Are they, as Berkeley doctoral student Aaron Bady says, "better than nothing," education-wise? In some instances, probably. But being better than nothing is not, I feel, high enough praise to warrant a place for MOOCs in their current form as free-standing, credit-bearing classes. So while MOOCs as they stand now might have *a* place in higher education, I cannot see them filling *the* place of higher education.

Works Cited

Bady, Aaron. "Questioning Clay Shirky." *Insidehighered.com*. n.p., 6 Dec. 2012. Web. 5 Mar. 2013.

Gilman, Todd. "Combating Myths About Distance Education." *The Chronicle of Higher Education*. The Chronicle of Higher Education, 22 Feb. 2010. Web. 5 Mar. 2013.

Jaschik, Scott. "The Evidence on Online Education." *Insidehighered. com*. n.p., 29 June 2009. Web. 5 Mar. 2013.

Knox, Jeremy, Siân Bayne, Hamish MacLeod, Jen Ross, and Christine Sinclair. "MOOC Pedagogy: The Challenges of Developing for Coursera." *Online Newsletter*. Association for Learning Technology, 8 Aug. 2012. Web. 5 Mar. 2013.

Knox, Jeremy, Sian Bayne, Hamish MacLeod, Jen Ross, and Christine Sinclair. *E-Learning and Digital Cultures*. Coursera, 24 July 2012. Web. 5 Mar. 2013.

Kolowich, Steve. "The Human Element." *Insiderhighered.com*. n.p., 29 Mar. 2010. Web. 5 Mar. 2013.

Selfe, Cynthia. "The Movement of Air, the Breath of Meaning: Aurality and Multimodal Composing." *CCC* 60.4 (2009): 616-663. *EReserves*. Web. 5 Mar. 2013.

Shirky, Clay. "Napster, Udacity, and the Academy." *Shirky.com*. WordPress, 12 Nov. 2012. Web. 5 Mar. 2013.

Tamburri, Rosanna. "All about MOOCs." *University Affairs*. AUCC, 7 Nov. 2012. Web. 5 Mar. 2013.

Those Moot MOOCs: My MOOC Experience

Melissa Syapin

As a student that has followed the "standard" learning path of graduating from high school, attending a 4-year institution, and then moving on to a Master's, I am no stranger to the traditional college experience.* I am currently enrolled at Eastern Michigan University, working on my Master's in Written Communication. Before taking English 516: Computers and Writing, Theory, and Practice in the winter of 2012, I had not heard of the emerging phenomenon called MOOCs. After my initial exposure to them, however, I feel like I am surrounded. They are certainly taking the world by storm, and I can see why. For some, MOOCs are heralded as the free, open-access way to get higher education to those that were previously denied it (Koller; Shirky). They are supposed to be the world's cheap resource for education, or at least help in the battle against the cost of higher education (Shirky). I think there is a grain of truth to this sentiment, though I am not convinced MOOCs will solve the problems of affordability or access to higher education among the poor and uneducated. If one is dedicated enough and wants an education enough to accomplish it outside traditional means, however, MOOCs are a fantastic first option. But it is only those that really want the education who are going to get the most out of MOOCs.

My experience with MOOCs is based off my class readings on the subject and the MOOC, "E-Learning and Digital Cultures," (EDC)

---

* This work is licensed under the Creative Commons Attribution-Noncommercial-ShareAlike 3.0 United States License. To view a copy of this license, visit http://creativecommons.org/licenses/by-nc-sa/3.0/us/ or send a letter to Creative Commons, 171 Second Street, Suite 300, San Francisco, California, 94105, USA. For any other use permissions, contact the original author.

taught through Coursera that we were required to take as part of my class. As a student in a Master's degree program with a traditional background, I felt I was in a different category from the targeted audience. MOOCs are in the introductory or undergraduate phase of their evolution. It is hard to imagine getting any degree from a MOOC-only education, though this appears to be an issue companies like Udacity and Coursera will eventually tackle (Wildavsky; Tamburri), finding ways to (attempt to) overcome accreditation issues without sacrificing their popularity or enormous class size. Early in its evolution, MOOCs still have to figure out the best online platform for teaching. There is a lot of discussion about e-learning—how best to do it, what techniques or tricks to use, how to structure the class, how to get educators on board—and where MOOCs fall within this broader discussion. I think many of these bigger teaching issues will need to be fully thought-out before popular platforms like Coursera and Udacity will fully take off.

My impression of MOOCs, based on tidbits from class readings and blogs, was that the majority of MOOCs follow an online lecture format, followed by some quiz or assessment to see if you've learned the material. I do not feel comfortable saying the EDC MOOC I participated in is indicative of most MOOCs, if they tend to follow this format. I do, however, think it is indicative of the humanities MOOCs out there, which tend to fall under the "connectivist MOOC" category, or MOOCs that promote self-assessment and open curricula (Knox et al.). If a student were trying to gain an education equivalent to a degree via MOOCs, I feel it would only be possible among certain subjects—humanities definitely being out. The humanities rely too much on discussion and subjectivity to thrive in a large-scale, online classroom. Much research into the online realm of assessment and distance or online learning (Vojak et al. 101; Cope et al. 81; Jones 214) has been done showing that online learning can and does happen. It is not the online classroom setting (the OOC) that made my experience less than satisfying, but the Massive part, which was not helped by the tool used to present the class.

In my experience, the discussions were too vast to be of any real use. Not only was it hard to find a thread you had posted on, but it was too much to follow. The sheer quantity of posts made for a very discouraging and tedious experience. To its credit, however, the EDC MOOC did provide for more interactivity such as Google Hangouts and suggested ways to deal with the massive number of students, such as joining a study group.

The biggest problem with the classroom setup, however, was there weren't enough chances to feel heard. For me, part of learning has always been the chance to have an active role in the learning process from which I come out feeling accomplished and like part of the 'in crowd' that shares a certain knowledge. But when you don't feel you have a voice, or a chance to participate actively in the learning happening around you, you lose some of your motivation to be a part of the class and lose out on the learning opportunities within the class. Furthermore, the classroom provided many resources and suggestions for how to go about finding meaning or insight, but they did not go beyond suggestions. The resources and connections were laid bare for all to see, but it was up to the student (and the student alone) to make sense of them. This might seem like a strange statement given that MOOCs offer thousands of students the ability to make sense of these resources with their classmates, but I found myself feeling like it was just me in the class. I would seek out comments or discussions on the videos or readings I chose to read in order to find connections, but I rarely felt I was connected to another student. The closest I got was the peer review of our projects at the end of the class, most likely because it was a small, one-on-one interaction between me and my assigned peer reviewers. Otherwise, I felt as if everyone was individually learning the content as opposed to a classroom learning the content together. So if you are a person that is used to independent study and prefers that format, then this is your kind of class. But if students with less traditional education backgrounds are the main target audience for MOOCs, is this independent study style the best for them? Or do they perhaps need more help learning the content?

If you are a student that prefers to discuss things with others to help find your way, then perhaps this isn't the best model. I fall under the "discussion" type of students, often gaining my best insights from a class through discussion. While the EDC MOOC offered more discussions than I could follow, none of it felt like a true discussion. This is not just a fault of MOOCs, but one of all online education platforms that I have participated in. Discussion online is not equal to discussion in person. I have found with all online experiences that to participate in a discussion is more or less like a writing assignment. Try as I might, it is hard to write a response on a discussion board like I would say the response in person. It's as if the discussion forums are too formal by their mere format. A discussion session that involved a live chat, however, would be more similar to a person-to-person discussion and would, hopefully, satisfy my need to discuss more.

Some of the problems I encountered in the EDC MOOC could be fixed in future versions. For instance, creating smaller chat rooms or having a live chat session for those that are online would help to solve the problem of sheer size. This did happen outside the classroom among some students, but it was not necessarily a part of the class. Students wishing to do this would have had to find the group on their own (which might or might not be an easy thing to do) and would have had to put in the extra effort in order to make the size of the class work for them. More Google Hangouts might also engage the students more with the teachers, so students feel they are learning from someone instead of sifting through a database of resources. As I said earlier, I do also think these are problems that have to do with the subject matter, as the humanities tend to cover more fluid concepts that can have different interpretations based on who is teaching them. Research on MOOCs leads me to believe that more quantitative and definitive subject matters, such as math and the sciences, could do well in this sort of online environment where the platform is more geared toward videos and assessments. These subjects lend themselves to concrete ways to test knowledge because there are objective and absolute answers (i.e., there is often a right and a wrong answer that is not seen as much in the humanities)—at least at the introductory levels that most MOOCs are covering.

I believe that the EDC MOOC was following the connectivist format, deliberately trying to steer away from a more traditional style of teaching (lecture) and embrace the cybersphere. But, a middle ground is needed. The lack of structure to the class was a hindrance to the learning process because it was too open, with too many options to choose from. I would have preferred less options and more emphasis on readings that the teachers, in their expertise, saw as more substantial or helpful to learning the concept. On the other hand, however, online classes should not replicate bricks-and-mortar classrooms and I was glad to see an online class attempting to ground itself in the pedagogy of cyberspace.

The teaching pedagogy I experienced, however, didn't make the most positive impression on me. I found myself wondering what the teachers actually did in, and for, the class. It seemed as though the instructors gathered the material and setup the class, but then most of their work was done. Yes, they took part in discussions and had their two Google Hangouts, but I didn't get a sense that I was being "taught" anything by them or really that I even had teachers. This is most likely due to my background rooted in traditional education and students without this background most likely did not feel this way. Coming from a traditional background, I suppose you could say I am used to teachers that have opinions. I would have liked to see the instructors of the EDC MOOC insert themselves more into the classroom, something I think could have been accomplished with a more structured format. As it stands, I felt as if I stumbled across a site of resources and activities because the only sense of my instructors I received was an overview of each topic and the occasional response in the discussion boards. I am used to much more intrusive, hands-on instructors and it was hard to wrap my head around a class where the instructors took a backseat to my learning (on my own).

I believe this aspect is very important to consider in the ongoing debate about MOOCs. Yes, it is great to get access to education for the public, but is this really an "education?" My experience seemed more like spending time in a warehouse of knowledge rather than being part of an educational setting. I've always thought of education as an activity that requires engagement, both on the side of the student and the educator. I found myself bowing out of the engagement in my role as student because I did not feel heard in the class and knew that I would not be missed among the thousands of other voices. I never made a connection with the instructors of the MOOC and, therefore, never felt engaged with them. As mentioned above, this is something that I think might have been resolved with a different classroom format for the EDC MOOC.

Though I know the educators worked much harder on the course than it appeared from my end, the lack of engagement I felt seems to be of importance to the discussion of e-learning, including MOOCs, and how to do it. The online setting is such a far cry from the traditional classroom setting that I can see the resistance on the part of educators. Something in the middle is necessary, however, to reach students with all types of educational preferences and backgrounds. As students become more acquainted with technology, they will expect not only that their teachers will know how to use that technology, but also that they will learn how to apply it as well. This means that teachers will need to be technology-savvy in order to relate to their students—they cannot teach something if they are unfamiliar with its practical uses outside the classroom. It also means that teachers will need to apply the latest technological advances, or at least find ways to incorporate them in some small way, in their classroom. This is a reality I do not think can be denied or overlooked—and MOOCs realize this. They seem to understand what underlies the social media phenomenon and are attempting to incorporate it into higher ed.

In today's online landscape, society seems to have undergone a shift in its thinking about knowledge. Knowledge has not been an "it" to capture for a long time; it has become something that is seen as constantly surrounding us and consistently at our fingertips. In fact, it's to the point that most people carry "knowledge" with them everywhere they go and are anxious if they forget it. In one sense, this seems like a good thing for education because it appears to demonstrate an eagerness to learn and a desire to satiate curiosity. On the other hand, this constant link to "knowledge" gives people the sense that they do not need a teacher—the Internet becomes their teacher. Constant Googling or YouTube tutorials satiate curiosity, but they also deny creativity and true learning that comes with trial and error as you problem-solve your way through a new experience alongside the guidance and assurance from your teacher that it is possible.

It occurs to me that MOOCs are trying to bridge this gap between having knowledge at your fingertips and actually learning from that knowledge. The platform is online and some classes, such as the EDC MOOC I took, are trying to tap into the nature of the Internet that people have become so accustomed to. The EDC MOOC was built in an almost "browse-mode" structure where students could browse until they found something they liked, as if they were on Google. The Internet has let people tap into their interests, and effectively let them ignore the things they don't think they are interested in. This is another problem with an online class "structured" like the EDC MOOC: in an attempt to open the class up to as many interests/possibilities as possible, you risk students potentially pigeon-holing their time in the course on select interests.

Higher education is about broadening horizons by introducing students to subjects they never thought they'd learn (or requiring them to learn things they have no interest in to make them more well-rounded, if only for an exam). MOOCs do not fulfill this part of higher education. And I'm not sure this is a problem that can be overcome in the future. The learning we do online is thought about differently from the learning we do in a classroom. This isn't a bad thing. Online learning has become something that is associated with flexibility. In the case of MOOCs, it is not only associated with flexibility but with possibility—they offer such a variety of courses from all subjects that students could easily go through their "education" without taking a class they didn't want to. Or students can drop out if the class doesn't suit them, as is often the case. This is fine on a class by class basis, but if we look at the big picture, at the type of education one can receive via MOOCs, it becomes a problem. Without the structure that a degree program provides, students miss out on a big chunk of the higher ed experience.

So while my MOOC experience was not a good one because it didn't really ring true to what I consider an educational experience, I see the benefits of taking them for a certain demographic of students. I can also see MOOCs evolving into a sort of giant, online college or repository of online classes that could take the place of community colleges or handle some transfer credits before moving on to a different college. This would still help the cost of education, one of the tenets of MOOCs. I cannot, however, get on board with MOOCs being the new higher ed. And I don't think most students serious about an education will either.

WORKS CITED

Cope, Bill, Mary Kalantzis, Sarah McCarthey, Colleen Vojak, and Sonia Kline. "Technology-Mediated Writing Assessments: Principles and Processes." *Computers and Composition* 28 (2011): 79-96. Print.

Jones, Donald. "Thinking Critically about Digital Literacy: A Learning Sequence on Pens, Pages, and Pixels." *Pedagogy: Critical Approaches to Teaching Literature, Language, Composition, and Culture* 7.2 (2007): 207-21. Print.

Knox, Jeremy, Siân Bayne, Hamish MacLeod, Jen Ross, and Christine Sinclair. "MOOC pedagogy: the challenges of developing for Coursera." *ALT Online Newsletter.* Association for Learning Technology, August 8, 2012. Web. June 10, 2013.

Koller, Daphne. "What We're Learning from Online Education." TEDGlobal 2012. Edinburgh International Conference Center, Edinburgh, Scotland. June 26, 2012. Presenter.

Shirky, Clay. "Napster, Udacity, and the Academy." *Clay Shirky.* n.p. Blog. May 25, 2013.

Tamburri, Rosanna. "All about MOOCs." *University Affairs.* Association of Universities and Colleges of Canada, November 7, 2012. Web. June 5, 2013.

Vojak, Colleen, Sonia Kline, Bill Cope, Sarah McCarthey, and Mary Kalantzis. 2011. "New Spaces and Old Places: An Analysis of Writing Assessment Software." *Computers and Composition* 28 (2011): 97-111. Print.

Wildavsky, Ben. "Making MOOCs Mainstream: Will Accreditation be Next?" *The Quick and the Ed.* Education Sector at American Institutes for Research, November 14, 2012. Web. June 3, 2013.

MOOC Assigned

Steven D. Krause

One of the often-noted problems of MOOCs is they tend to confuse the delivery of content with teaching and education. In that sense, MOOCs are more often like a textbook than like a course.* After all, textbooks are mass produced collections of content created and assembled by experts (and often notable scholars) of the field with particular pedagogical strategies and courses in mind, which are then used by other instructors who usually do not have the level of expertise as the textbook authors. The "freshman comp" textbook is a classic example: written by experts and experienced teachers and scholars in composition and rhetoric, they are consulted/taught/assigned at many different kinds of community colleges, colleges, and universities for the universally offered—but certainly not standardized—introductory writing course, a course made up of smaller sections taught (often under the indirect supervision of a faculty "Writing Program Administrator") by inexperienced graduate assistants and adjunct instructors.

With this textbook analogy in mind, I decided to assign a MOOC. Specifically, I assigned the Coursera MOOC "E-Learning and Digital Cultures" (EDC MOOC) as a part of the course "Computers and Writing, Theory and Practice" I taught in the winter 2013 term. EDC MOOC was taught/organized by faculty at The University of Edinburgh's Digital Education program, which I learned about via their provocative "Manifesto for Teaching Online" (Ross, Bayne, and Mc-Leod). Among the many phrases and philosophies that intrigued me were:

- Distance is a positive principle, not a deficit. Online can be the privileged mode
- Text is being toppled as the only mode that matters in academic writing
- New forms of writing make assessors work harder: they remind us that assessment is an act of interpretation
- Online teaching should not be downgraded into 'facilitation'."

My course was a graduate-level offering in our MA program in Written Communication required for students in the teaching of writing emphasis and an elective for those in the professional writing emphasis. The title, "Computers and Writing, Theory and Practice," is a bit dated and misleading in that the course concerns topics about technology that are much broader than what we think of now as "computers," and it is also a course with a specific pedagogical emphasis. For example, even before I decided that my students and I would take EDC MOOC, I knew that we would be reading about and discussing online pedagogy and the rapid emergence of MOOCs.[1]

Another important aspect (twist?) to this experience was my course was online, which meant for this portion of the semester, we were simultaneously experiencing, studying, and discussing MOOC pedagogy while we were ourselves within a MOOC—we were the rats in the maze and simultaneously we were the scientists watching how that rat negotiated the turns. Further, we were also studying MOOC pedagogy while being within a MOOC that itself was described on the introductory page as a course that would "explore how digital cultures and learning cultures connect, and what this means for the ways in which we conduct education online" (Bayne et al.). In other words, the content of the MOOC we were studying also promised to be relevant to the purpose and curriculum of the course I was teaching. And finally, I assigned EDC MOOC blindly in anticipation (hope?) about what it was to be about since there was no way for me to review the course content before it began. This is a point I will return to again in a moment, but in very real ways, my students and I were both approaching EDC MOOC with the same lack of knowledge as to what would take place.

Jeremy Knox and his University of Edinburgh colleagues who facilitated EDC MOOC have essays in this collection called "MOOC Feedback: Pleasing All the People?" and two of my graduate students who also took part in this MOOC, Melissa Syapin and Jacqueline

Kauza, have written from their perspectives on the MOOC experience. So with that in mind, I want to focus here on my experience as the professor who assigned this MOOC to his students in the first place and the effectiveness of EDC MOOC as a "textbook" of sorts. What happened with this experiment of the "MOOC Assigned," and what did I (and of course my students and the folks at Edinburgh) learn about the potential of a MOOC as a textbook?

Getting Started

My graduate students and I jumped into the MOOC experience by both enrolling in EDC MOOC and discussing several introductory readings from sources about MOOCs generally and EDC MOOC in particular. All of my students were new to MOOCs and several of them were also new to online courses of any kind, and the initial conversation was a mix of excitement and apprehension. While students generally seemed willing to give it a try, there was also a lot of concern about the logistics about being a part of a "class" that had tens of thousands of other students.

But as the professor, I had two concerns about EDC MOOC, problems that were never really resolved. First, while the description of the course strongly implied an emphasis on pedagogy, the real emphasis was on digital *cultures,* with the major units focusing on utopias and dystopias and humanism (along with post-humanism and anti-humanism). The readings and discussions on pedagogy were few and far between. The EDC MOOC was not a complete mismatch for the course I was teaching, but it was tangential in relation to the main topic of "Computers and Writing," which is on *teaching* writing with technology. I blame myself for this mismatch; after all, I had assigned EDC MOOC based only on the description available before it began, and while I have done similar things in the past with assigned readings and it has generally worked out, it certainly would have been preferable in this instance to have known more about the cultural focus of EDC MOOC before I assigned it to my students.[2]

Second, there were many ways in which the EDC MOOC organizers were consciously working against the organizational structure of previous MOOCs I had read about, visited, or experienced as a student. For example, Knox and his colleagues worked hard at decentering the class by dispensing with the usual "talking head" style of video lecturing that is usually the focus of instruction in MOOCs. In fact, the EDC MOOC instructors were barely visible at all outside of the Google Hangout Chats filmed live and made available to students on the site. I'll come back to this issue later in my essay, but my point in bringing it up now is that their lack of video lectures was certainly atypical of most MOOCs I had seen previously, which again made EDC MOOC a less than an ideal example of what MOOCs are "like" to share with my students.

EDC MOOC HIGHS AND LOWS

EDC MOOC moved quickly—it was only a five week course—and as it moved along, my students and I did our best to hang on to it and the more traditional online course I was teaching, a course that was separate but that overlapped the MOOC. I think the experience was successful in that it immediately conveyed to my students what a MOOC was (none of them had heard of MOOCs prior to EDC MOOC) while immersing them in the experience. We weren't just reading about MOOCs abstractly; we were experiencing one directly. While the EDC MOOC focus on digital culture wasn't an ideal fit, my students and I did have engaged discussions about the material that we were ultimately able to connect back to the other readings I had assigned.

But there were challenges, and as I reflect back now on the on-line discussion within our course about EDC MOOC, I think there were two basic problems with my plan of using the MOOC as text-book-like space. First, there was a recurring challenge of diversity in terms of student expectations and abilities in relation to the readings and discussions for the MOOC. We regularly segregate students into particular groups in education based on age, grade level, prerequisites, majors, and so forth, with the goal to have students within a partic-ular group at the same level of ability and experience. But like most other MOOCs, EDC MOOC took the opposite approach, welcoming one and all regardless of experiences, expectations, abilities, language abilities, etc. While that openness might be a value worth embrac-ing with MOOCs (especially MOOCs focused explicitly on build-ing learning communities rather than granting transferrable credit), it made my assigning sections of EDC MOOC to my students difficult and participating in the discussions on the MOOC intolerable. Many of the videos and readings the EDC MOOC organizers selected would be perfectly appropriate for a section of first year writing and were simplistic for graduate students. Other readings selected by the EDC MOOC organizers were too difficult or too far afield to be of much use in my class. Of course every textbook includes readings and activities teachers skip, but the percentage of those skipped and off-target readings in EDC MOOC was a little too high for my purposes.

Second, the lack of regular presence of the EDC MOOC leaders and the general "de-centeredness" of the pedagogical approach made for an experience more like a loose collection of happenings that might (or might not) be shared through the Coursera site rather than something like a class or a textbook driven by a authorial and curricular goal. I realize that the EDC MOOC organizers were trying to problematize the assumptions of online pedagogy and actualize the proclamations of their manifesto. But the problem for my students and me was the pendulum seems to have swung so far toward upsetting the paradigm that it was difficult to get a hold of EDC MOOC as a complete experience. Student-centered courses still require a *teacher* to be a facilitator, a guide, a mediator, and that is even more the case in an online class. In normal "face-to-face" class experiences, a successful teacher facilitates conversation by moderating student comments and mostly staying quiet. In an online class, if the teacher doesn't say anything, students think that the teacher is either absent or doesn't care.

And there's also the inescapable problem of scale: with tens of thousands of students, Coursera's MOOCs are obviously more similar to lecture hall courses than they are to small group discussion courses. The student-centered/de-centered pedagogy of EDC MOOC works with a small group of students in face to face or in online environments, but with tens of thousands of participants and nearly absent teachers, the student-centered/de-centered online course becomes less an experience of student empowerment and more one of chaos.

MOOC TEXTBOOKS: HOW THEY MIGHT WORK

I want to close by returning to the basic premise I began with, the value of MOOCs assigned in connection with a more traditional course. While I've already described some of the challenges I faced as a teacher trying to make EDC MOOC work as material for my class, it seems to me that MOOCs generally have some potential as textbooks (or courseware-like resources), with some modifications to the general format.

First, let's make that C stand for "content." MOOCs need to give up on the idea of being "courses" offered during a particular "semester" or similar period of time; rather, MOOCs should focus on providing quality and interactive content, and they need to organize themselves less around an academic calendar and more around topics of content that users can select as modules. Actually, this is already happening to some extent with Udacity MOOCs, which rely less on the synchronous experience of Coursera MOOCs, and sites like Khan Academy, which dispense entirely with the "course" approach and focus specifically on providing content in short segments to be used by curious learners or teachers to supplement lessons.

This is how conventional textbooks work, but there are tremendous advantages to presenting this content electronically, advantages that frankly have not been actualized in MOOCs to date. Rather than relying on amateurish productions of lecturing professors speaking to a webcam (or, in the case of EDC MOOC, choppy rebroadcasts of Google Hangouts of the facilitators speaking with each other) or embedded YouTube content, MOOCs could be presenting higher quality and interactive lectures, learning games, exams, and so forth, and they could be providing exclusive and constantly updated content. Depending on the course and its "production values," I think a MOOC that had the design and delivery sensibility of sites like Facebook and Netflix would have a tremendous advantage over traditional print (expensive, single-media, quickly out of date, heavy) textbooks.

Second, MOOCs as textbooks could facilitate community building, both within an institution and beyond. One of the reasons many first year writing programs have program-wide textbook adoptions is to connect dozens of different sections of the same course. A MOOC as content would do the same thing, and it would have the added advantage of being an interactive space where students could connect with others outside of their specific group of 20 or so students, other students at the same institution, or, depending on how these discussion forums were managed, students at other institutions. As a common and centralized space, a MOOC could essentially serve as a broadcast site to a large group of different sections in the same course. Let me focus for a moment on first year composition and rhetoric, a course that is almost universally required in American universities, taught in small sections (25 or fewer students and often by non-tenure track instructors and graduate assistants) which usually have similar readings, assignments, and outcomes across these many different sections. Imagine a scenario where the Writing Program Administrator, the faculty member usually charged to guide and supervise the instructors of these dozens of different section sections of the course, could post a message accessible to all of the students and instructors in the program calling out particular examples of excellence from specific students, updates on institutional issues, connections to current events, and so on. Peer review of particular assignments could be facilitated across "sections," something logistically challenging in conventional writing courses, or even across institutions. In other words, in the case of first year writing, MOOCs could facilitate community among students and instructors in a program at different scales: within a particular section, within a program, and more broadly and beyond the institution and the "freshman comp" community across the country, a group of students that is several million strong across the U.S.

Finally, MOOCs as interactive textbooks could provide a space for common experience across many sections like lecture presentations and discussions. I'm not suggesting that *all* lecture would be a good idea obviously, and that is especially true in the kind of courses we currently teach in small group discussion formats. But at least some lecturing and leadership by the MOOC professors can lend structure, authority, and capture attention. As I pointed out in the beginning of this essay, textbooks are useful—especially for instructors relatively inexperienced with teaching generally or the subject matter specifically—because they lend structure, curriculum, and expertise. It seems to me that one way to emphasize these textbook elements is through at least some lecturing—again, not merely a "talking head" professor speaking extemporaneously into her laptop's camera one day, but polished and produced talks. I'm imagining something more akin with a "TED Talk," because even though there are problems and simplifications in most of those presentations as well, they are clearly engaging and even "entertaining." So I am suggesting here not that MOOCs as textbooks should rely solely on lectures as a means of delivery of content; rather, I am suggesting that MOOCs should include expert lectures as a way of *framing* content, activities, and discussion.

NOTES

1. See http://engl516.stevendkrause.com.
2. The merits of this practice of assigning previously unread texts is something I've debated with my colleagues for some time now, and I am always intrigued by the responses. I have been doing this to some degree every since I began as a graduate assistant in 1988, particularly for courses I haven't taught before, and I have many colleagues who do the same thing. But I also have colleagues who find the whole idea of "blindly" assigning any text like this at best horrifying and nerve-wracking and, at worse, unprofessional. While I still believe that assigning a mostly unfamiliar text or project can be effective, I will admit that this experience is a cautionary tale I will remember the next time I take another similar leap.

WORKS CITED

Bayne, Siân, et al. "About the Course." *E-Learning and Digital Cultures Course Site.* Coursera. Coursera. Web. 12 May 2013.

Ross, Jen, Siân Bayne, and Hamish Macleod. *Manifesto for Teaching Online.* Jen Ross, Siân Bayne, and Hamish Macleod. 2011. Web. 12 November 2013.

Learning How to Teach . . . Differently: Extracts from a MOOC Instructor's Journal

Denise K. Comer

The following is based on a teaching journal I kept during the design and development of the first-year writing MOOC I taught: English Composition I: Achieving Expertise.* The course ran for 12 weeks (March 18, 2013-June 10, 2013) with an enrollment of 82,820. It was offered through Duke University in partnership with Coursera, and was funded primarily with a grant from the Bill & Melinda Gates Foundation. Some journal entries have been slightly revised, abridged and/or updated where necessary for publication.

MONDAY, 1/28/2013: KEEP A JOURNAL

"Keep a journal," Cindy Selfe suggests during a Google Hangout chat with fellow Gates grantees who are, like me, designing several of the first-ever batch of writing MOOCs. I've kept journals twice in my adult life, both connected to learning how to teach writing: during my first semester as a Ph.D. student when I began teaching composition and a few years later during a semester when my class served as an on-going exhibit for other new graduate-student teachers. So I suppose a return to journaling at this juncture makes sense, when the experience

---

designing a MOOC is new, exhilarating, frustrating, and complicated in so many expected and unexpected ways … even though I'm not sure where I can find the time.

Foremost on my mind right now is trying to gain consonance between my interests in designing a MOOC and the MOOC itself. My priorities for teaching a MOOC are twofold: (1) to cultivate global conversations about writing so more people around the world can grow as writers and learn about writing from each other; and (2) to conduct research on how the MOOC impacts the teaching and learning of writing.

These priorities, though, are proving difficult to focus on because I'm busy wrestling with some seemingly unresolvable paradoxes: The MOOC is not credit bearing, yet I'm told it should resemble as much as possible a residential first-year writing course. The ideal MOOC length seems to be six or seven weeks, but the writing courses I teach are normally sixteen weeks. The MOOC should not be watered down, yet it must accommodate the reality that some learners will be doing coursework while washing dishes, or at 1:00 a.m. after a long day of work. The MOOC should teach first-year writing, yet learners may have Ph.D.s, or no high-school diploma, and will likely range in age from pre-teen through retired. One marker of a MOOC's notoriety is massive enrollment, yet retention is something I shouldn't worry about (apparently half of the enrolled students might not even click into the class on the first day).

Thursday, 1/31/2012: "I want to improve my writing so I can …"

On the landing page for our MOOC, which offers potential enrollees a video and a written course description through the Coursera site, we[1] created a survey asking people to indicate why they want to improve their writing. We made the running survey results public as part of our larger effort to cultivate a sense of camaraderie over writing. Thousands of people are posting about why writing matters to them. I love reading through the many responses:[2]

"be more confident when expressing my ideas"
"be heard"
"help my grandchildren with their homework in English"
"teach my high school students how to write better"

"improve my critical thinking"
"not fail again in writing exam"
"change the world"

Although conversations in national media seem to be pitting MOOCs against what are now termed "residential" college courses (aka face-to-face courses), most of the responses I have encountered through this query seem to suggest that potential enrollees are adult learners hoping to grow as writers in order to be more successful in their career, educational, or personal aspirations. These learners, it seems, want the structure, space, and time to work on their writing. I have not seen any of the respondents indicate that they are interested in *replacing* what would otherwise be a first-year writing course by using the MOOC, for example, to earn course credit for first-year writing or fulfill a college curriculum pre-requisite.

Mostly I am just moved to see how powerful writing can be, how much it can accomplish, and how many different people see the value of writing and want to work on their writing.

Tuesday, 2/5/2012: The Tail Wags the Dog

I find myself stymied in course design by limitations of the MOOC Coursera platform. In the fall I had been led to believe through conversations with MOOC developers at my institution and Coursera representatives that no writing assignment could be more than 500 words long, and that writing assignments could only be pasted in as text to a submission box rather than formatted as a pdf and uploaded. As a writer, I am well aware that form can often determine parameters, but the rigidity of the possibilities for writing assignments due to platform limitations is increasingly frustrating for me in designing the course. Of equal concern is that pdfs are vital if we want learners to attend to matters of document design and adhere to rules of citation.

At last, after my repeated assertions in these conversations about how and why longer project possibilities and pdfs are central to the work of the course, I finally got the go-ahead for freedom of constraints with page lengths and the capability of uploading documents.

Now, though, having just resolved these matters, I am facing another, even less flexible platform hurdle: pacing. Astonishingly, it seems that the first project will require about five or six weeks of the course calendar. Normally, I would devote around three weeks to a first writing project. But the MOOC requires a full week for each stage of the process because the course is organized by week instead of by class period. I need to accommodate learners who choose to log on right when a new week becomes available (i.e., Monday morning) as well as those learners who will not be visiting the course website until the following Sunday evening. Thus, in order to do a full cycle (reading and discussing material, pre-writing, drafting, peer review, revising, and editing) students need the following: at least one week to read, discuss, think, and pre-write, one week to draft, one week for peer review, one week for revising and editing, and one more week for peer grading. This drawn-out pacing limits drastically how many projects I can assign in the course. It also makes smaller, sequenced writing assignments difficult because I cannot guarantee feedback for sequenced writing.

The platform presents other challenges regarding class design as well. One of these involves peer feedback. Since it is randomized by the computer, I am unable to have the same peers give feedback on drafts and final versions of projects. I am also unable to invite the students within Coursera's platform to create a portfolio of their writing. If I want a portfolio, I must go outside of the platform to find a portfolio tool. Perhaps most jarring in terms of platform constrictions involves the timing of the videos and material development. The development team asks that we film all the videos first, then upload course content. Editing the videos takes a very long time (my online course associate, Kendra Atkin, does all the editing). So her editing timeline is driving the production schedule. Since everything is traveling at warp speed, this means that I find myself preparing and filming videos before I have fully designed the course projects. In some videos I'm even coached to remain deliberately general in order to accommodate the possibility (likelihood) that I will shift the course content.

Monday, 2/11/13: On Hairstyles and PowerPoint

Today was another marathon recording session. I spend three or four hour chunks recording videos for the class. My first such session was on January 18, 2013. It was terrible. I was awkward and uncertain of what to say. Each time I record, I find myself overly concerned with what I am wearing and with how my hair looks. Another instructor I know recorded all of his videos on one day, but brought 15 or so different ties so he would look different in each video. While I should have been spending time doing something more intellectual, I've instead been rummaging through my wardrobe for different outfits, doing research on best color patterns for the camera. I haven't been this concerned with my appearance as a teacher since the first weeks I stepped in front of a classroom.

My discomfort puts me in the mind of several points Michael Wesch makes in "An Anthropological Introduction to YouTube." Wesch suggests that webcams create "hyper self-awareness" and make the speaker feel "as if everybody is watching where nobody is." Exactly my problem. My colleague said that several people in our CIT department were considering posting photographs of students on the wall above where the camera was so faculty recording videos could pretend they were speaking to students.

I suppose as a response to my incredible awkwardness in front of the camera, Kendra, my online course associate, suggested we record the videos in a more relaxed setting, such as in my office, where I could be sitting down and surrounded by a warmer background than the clinical environment of the state-of-the-art CIT recording lab. Yes, that should work better.

But, perhaps the worst part is that I have to create PowerPoints to accompany the videos. For the first such video, I had to create a PowerPoint about the writing process, when normally I would spend time with students encouraging them to have a conversation about their writing processes. While my faculty colleagues in Chemistry or Biology are flipping their classrooms by recording lectures and facilitating student discussion during class, I'm busy learning how to unflip, creating PowerPoints and lectures out of content that would generally be class discussion. I don't know how to lecture about writing. I certainly don't know how to turn dialogic conversation into PowerPoints.

It feels so awkward to speak to the camera. I hope I get more accustomed to this.

I hate PowerPoint.

And we lost several videos. That's seven hours of lost time. Plus my hair looked really good that day.

WEDNESDAY, 2/13/13: HOW ACCESSIBLE IS THE INSTRUCTOR?

Normally, I value instructor accessibility outside of class as a feature of effective teaching. The MOOC, however, operates on a different paradigm. I'm receiving Facebook and Linked In requests, phone calls and emails from people enrolled in the course or considering enrolling. People involved with MOOCs at my institution are suggesting I not respond. They say that answering students will become too time consuming, and that if students know I will respond, it will become a deluge. In truth, I don't mind responding to emails (within reason), but I don't feel comfortable opening my FB page to potentially thousands of people. But even as I decide this, I wonder if I should be using social media more effectively to complement my teaching persona? I'm flummoxed by the competing aims of presenting myself as accessible through videos, presentations, and forum participation, but inaccessible for direct access outside of class.

THURSDAY, 2/28/13: ALIGNMENT

I thought that throughout my career as a teacher I was fairly deliberate in creating course materials for students. I spend a lot of time thinking carefully about my assignments, and working with other faculty as they design theirs. However, crafting course materials for thousands of people has really heightened my awareness of learning objectives. It has made me make a much more concerted effort to align objectives and criteria within assignments and across the course. As part of the grant, I needed to create an alignment framework where I listed my learning outcomes and indicated how I would teach toward these outcomes through the assignments, technology, peer interaction, and assessments. Making visible for thousands of learners the purpose of assignments, and the sequencing of assignments has encouraged me to be more deliberate in naming learning outcomes for each project and making certain that they are directly connected to the larger learning outcomes for the course. This renewed and strengthened attention to alignment is something that will benefit all my teaching, MOOC-based or otherwise.

MONDAY, 3/18/13: DAY 1

I am so nervous. I feel so exposed.

I actually stayed home all day so I wouldn't be seen. The thought of more than 70,000 people starting this course feels like such a large responsibility.

Learners are pinning their locations on a Google map, greeting each other on the forums. People are joining the course from all over the world. I've seen postings from learners in Brazil, Japan, South Korea, Spain, the United States. The Google map image really emphasizes for me how global this MOOC is.

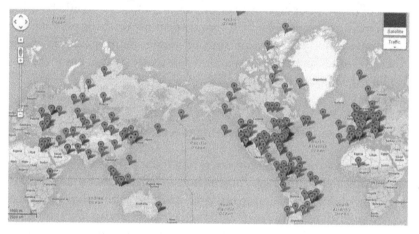

Figure 1: Course participants enrolled from all around the world, making this a highly global and cross-cultural experience. Map Data: Google, INEGI, SK planet, Zenrin.

Participants seem so excited about writing and about the course. In their exchanges with one another they are sharing their hesitations and insecurities as writers, and others are responding with support and encouragement.

But *I* remain so, so, so nervous! I can't even write any more right now...

SUNDAY, 3/24/13: WISHING I KNEW MORE...

The other day I was desperately rifling through my office bookshelves looking for the only textbook I own on technical writing, a text I used for the one technical writing course I taught back in 1997 or 1998. I couldn't find it. I need a technical writer and an information management specialist. I did not anticipate how much confusion there would be or how crucial and difficult information flow would be to this endeavor. As confused as I was about MOOCs and about the peer feedback mechanism in particular, one would think I would have intuited the degree to which the 70,000+ learners in the course would need untold levels of clarifying information across areas of the course site. Of course I have tried all along to provide clear materials and instructions, as did our entire team of course developers. And, having taught across many institutional contexts for 18 years now, I also have considerable experience designing teaching materials that are, hopefully, clear and helpful. But at this scale, and with this range of online mechanisms (many of which are new to both learners and developers), there seem to be an endless amount of ways in which we are unprepared to anticipate the many possible sources of confusion. I can now understand why politicians and business leaders resort so often to adages—they deliberately decide to pare ideas down to the least complicated denominator in order to reach the largest number of people possible.

But I think this issue of information flow has more to it. If you aggregate anxieties about writing, with anxieties about technology and school, you get the perfect trifecta for some highly anxious —and vocal —learners. Students call out to me with angry headings on the discussion boards: "Staff! I need an answer." Or "PROFESSOR COMER PROVIDE AN ANSWER." Feedback, forums, time zones, deadlines, late work, word count ... there is no end to the amount of information needing to be clarified, re-clarified, and managed. Our team from the Center for Instructional Technology, Elise Mueller (CIT Project Manager) and Kendra Atkin (CIT Online Course Associate) are doing their best to answer questions and manage information, but it is proving to be an impossible task. Even in a 12-person class it's likely that at least one student might have difficulty understanding an assignment or process, despite the most careful written and verbal information. If we multiply that by the tens of thousands enrolled in the course, it's of course understandable that there will be a large cohort of people who are confused at any given time.

I think I will strive for more consistency in communications, and use more elements of document design—bolded sections, color coding. People will route themselves to many different places and will learn in different ways so we can post the same information in a variety of different formats in a variety of different places.

I need to order a new technical writing textbook. I need a degree in technical writing.

TUESDAY, 3/26/13: ON SHYNESS

Every time I venture onto the discussion forums I feel so shy. In my face-to-face classes, I sometimes feel shy the first day, but generally get over that feeling within a few minutes as I begin interacting with students. On these forums, though, I'm continually —perpetually — not sure what to say. My routine seems to be to go on the forums, look around, think about things to say, reject my ideas, then leave and return a few hours later. I feel like anything I say will need to be enormous, profound, and True. This is the same reason I do not post to Facebook. Nothing I can think of to say seems worthwhile enough to be posted to the world.

The other difficulty is that in the forums when I participate, it's not so much a conversation as me swooping in to say something and then leaving. I cannot engage in sustained conversations with the students. It's not that they need me; they do fine on their own. The forum conversations are lively, engaged with course material, self-driven and autonomous. It's just that I want students to know that I'm interested in them, and the course, and in what they have to say. I am uncomfortable giving off the impression that I'm just an occasional drop-in supervisor. Maybe the role and position of the instructor matter less in some disciplines' MOOCs (though I doubt it), but in a writing course I am accustomed to thinking that cultivating shared learning and building relationships between teacher and students is particularly crucial. The MOOC asks me to reconsider the relationship I have with students and a course by both elevating and de-authorizing my role as instructor and facilitator.

We had a conversation among the MOOC team about what the purposes might be for our forum contributions: clarifying confusion, answering questions, maintaining a visible presence, and drawing attention to compelling exchanges. We decided to create tags so that learners could search for instructional team posts through a tag with our name and be able to track our contributions. I think what will work best for me is to use my posts to highlight what a student has said. If someone makes an astute comment, or raises a compelling question, then I will draw attention to what they said. This, I hope, will take the pressure off of me to be saying something of value.

MONDAY, 4/1/13: HANGING OUT

I facilitated our first Google Hangout on Thursday, March 28, 2013. We invited members of the class to volunteer to participate in a virtual writing workshop with me, and we chose five people. We all discussed one student's draft of the Unit 1 paper. I loved the experience. It was such a pleasure to meet and talk with people from all over the world about writing. The workshop participants gave strong feedback about L's draft; they offered suggestions for how he might improve it, and they shared what aspects they found worked really well. We focused our conversation around the ideas in the text, and I really felt like we were accomplishing something as writers. The Hangout offers me a chance to have a visual, real-time connection with members of the class.

More importantly, for others in the course who watch the Hangout, it offers another way for students to move forward on their revision processes, and it offers a model for how students can provide feedback to one another on their drafts. Although participating in the actual hangout enables those few individuals to have an engaging experience and make gains as writers, my hope is that the hangouts have measured traction for all the learners in the course. This mirrors my goal for writing workshops in my residential seminars, where even an hour-long workshop on one writer's draft functions primarily as a way for all writers in the class to think about themselves as writers and about their own writing projects. After the hangout was recorded, we posted it as a video for the course, and invited people to watch the hangout and then share their reflections on a designated forum about what they learned from watching the hangout. The postings in that forum suggested that learners appreciated having the chance to see a draft in progress, and they came away with ideas for how they could revise their own first drafts, such as other aspects of the text that they might address and strategies for citation. Some people posting in this forum wrote out specific revision plans for their own drafts. Within this forum we also created a space for learners to network and arrange times to hold their own Google Hangout writing workshops. So far I can see that several groups of learners are trying to coordinate.

Beyond my own experience getting to connect with writers from around the world through a Google Hangout, I am so thrilled to see people watching other writers at work, learning more about the process of feedback and revision, and then thinking about their own writing. That some of these learners are actually going to take this experience and replicate and build on it by creating their own Google Hangouts makes this even more rewarding. These kinds of writerly conversations across the world are exactly the kind of thing I had in mind when I decided to create a writing-based MOOC.

FRIDAY, 4/5/13: NEGATIVE, NEGATIVE, NEGATIVE, NEGATIVE, NEGATIVE, NEGATIVE

Negative. I feel overwhelmed with negative feedback. I've certainly received lots of positive feedback, from people in the course, colleagues, and friends, but my natural inclination in life is to focus more on what's not going well than what is going well. It's an unfortunate disposition made more unfortunate with a MOOC since everything is scaled on massive levels.

Negative feedback is coming from many directions: some learners in the course who post complaints on forums; writing program administrators around the country posting to the Writing Program Administrators Listserv (WPA-L); commentators and pundits posting online and in publications. Some of the negative feedback from students involves confusion with the course site or critiques about course design. This is easier to deal with than the negative feedback on a professional level. Professional negativity appears from many domains: Some is based on well-reasoned concerns about the impact and place of MOOCs in higher education. Some, though, is from people unfamiliar with what MOOCs are, and who are therefore operating under misguided assumptions, such as that MOOCs cannot have communities of learners or that students writing in MOOCs will not get responses. Some of the heat is from people who are so vehemently hostile to MOOCs that their comments border on rage.

I'm getting exhausted by the energy it takes to process this negative feedback: MOOCs are elitist; MOOCs are colonial in nature; MOOCs will render writing teachers jobless; MOOCs will destroy higher education as we know it; the writing assignments are too long; the writing assignments are not long enough; the videos are too dull; the videos are too distracting; the content is too conventional; … What do I respond to? How do I respond? Which misconceptions do I clarify? Which ideas will help me as I develop the course? Which ones can help me as a teacher in the longer term? Which comments are useful for me as a researcher studying the impact of the MOOC on the teaching and learning of writing?

I anticipated that there would be professional debates over MOOCs, particularly as they are at this stage new and gaining considerable traction. And I am a proponent of vigorous conversations and disagreement, especially about MOOCs since they stand to have some measure of impact for many stakeholders. However, I did not anticipate that these debates would often conflate *me* as a person with *MOOCs* as an initiative. I also didn't anticipate that by teaching a MOOC so many people would assume I am therefore an unalloyed proponent or staunch defender of MOOCs. I am teaching a MOOC because I was intrigued by the prospect of facilitating a cross-cultural exchange for writers around the world; I was extremely attracted to the idea of creating a space where so many different thousands of people could improve as writers; and, as a scholar-teacher, I was excited about the range of possible research opportunities with writing pedagogy in this new context. Just because I am teaching a MOOC, though, does not mean that I am not also very concerned about the impact MOOCs may have higher education and, more specifically, on the landscape of residential first-year writing courses. Teaching a MOOC does not mean that I devalue residential first-year writing seminars or believe that MOOCs should replace these courses.

Similarly, I anticipated that there would be some negativity in my course's discussion forums among learners, but I did not fully appreciate how much that would expand given the size of the class. And I didn't anticipate how to address the spread of effect when the negative voices are as loud or louder than those who are engaging more positively with the course.

I've decided to change my WPA-L setting to digest and take a break from the discussion forums in the course. I'm doing exactly what I would advise new teachers against: instead of focusing on the positive and remaining engaged, I'm disengaging. Maybe next week I will find a way to regain my enthusiasm.

Negative.

Monday, 4/15/13: Who is the Teacher in this Course?

Although I created the first draft of course content and assembled
our team, the product is most certainly the result of many different
contributors. Although all teaching is collaborative, the MOOC is so
much more collaborative than any endeavor I have taken on. And yet
this collaboration is also so much less visible. The MOOC emerges
through such a complex network of contributions, and yet it seems on
the surface that I, as instructor, am in a position of much more prima-
cy than I actually feel. True, I am in the lead, but I am unaccustomed
as a teacher to needing so much active assistance during a semester.
Perhaps teachers of large lecture sections are more familiar with this
model.

Our team of online course associates and managers really is running this course. They drive the production, the timeline, they write
drafts of the weekly updates. They create the working schedule; they
answer questions on the forums. They shape and re-shape course
content, materials, and ideas to make them more MOOC-ish. Elise
Mueller, Shawn Miller, and Kendra Atkin, from Duke's Center for
Instructional Technology, are really central to the endeavor.

The disciplinary consultants, Maral Erol, David Font-Navarrete,
and Rebecca Vidra, are contributing in many of the same ways that
I am: Google Hangouts, forum posts, sample commentaries. Our assessment consultant, Edward White, has worked with me on designing
the assessment and feedback aspects of the course. Our ESL consultant, Paul Kei Matsuda, has shaped our approach to English Language
Learners. We have a librarian, Greta Boers, a guest expert on Op-Eds,
David Jarmul, and a guest visit by one of the authors whose text we
read, Daniel Coyle, and an undergraduate peer writing tutor, Thomas
Kavanaugh. Joe Moxley and his team with *Writing Commons* created
links to relevant textbook content that can supplement the course material.

Students are teaching each other too. Some learners in the course
are actually teachers, but others are not, and even so teach one another. In my residential courses I encourage peer-to-peer learning, but in
the MOOC it happens in so much more profound ways. The MOOC
is disrupting conventional binaries of teacher and student. It's not so
much that my expertise or authority is missing, but it's radically decen-
tered. Students give feedback and grade one another; when they have
questions about course material or strategies for assignments, they help

one another. Many of the "students" in the class are also (quite literally) teachers —teachers of writing or other disciplines, from K-12 to postsecondary, in the U.S. and around the world. Although all of these enrollees are technically "students" in the MOOC, I think the term, "student" carries with it certain assumptions, albeit problematic assumptions, about one's level of power or expertise in a given context. These assumptions do not hold true in this context. It also suggests a counterpart entity known as "teacher" and I certainly do not feel like the same kind of teacher in this course as in other courses. My role is more of facilitator in this MOOC.

I think I will refer to those enrolled in the course as "learners" instead of "students," since this seems a more apt term that is inclusive of everyone in the course.

MONDAY, 4/16/13: FIRST WRITING PROJECT.

The first project was a success (mostly)! I asked learners to write a critical review of a text by Daniel Coyle on expertise (an excerpt from his book *The Talent Code*). Although the remainder of the course will invite learners to tailor their writing projects along an area of expertise of particular interest to them, I wanted the first project to offer a common starting point that we could all use to build from. Learners were to write and submit a draft, then the platform would randomly distribute that draft to three peer responders (only those who also posted a draft were allowed to respond to peers). Each of the three responders would have one week to provide formative feedback according to a specific rubric that Ed White and I developed. Then, the original writers would receive back the three sets of peer feedback, and would have one week to revise and then submit the final version

Going into the first project, I was very worried about the logistics: Would the directions be clear enough for people to figure out where on the platform to submit their projects? Could the platform sustain the number of submissions? Would it appropriately turn around the submissions and push them out to three peer responders, who would then respond? I was also curious about the writing itself: Would people follow the assignment prompt? What would be the range of responses? Would responders follow the peer feedback rubric?

The logistics, for the most part, worked out well. Some users had difficulty identifying the right buttons to click, but we offered clarifications and are now planning to create screen capture videos to demonstrate the upload process. Some users did not receive a full set of three peer responses (presumably because these peers did not complete the work for that week). However, for the most part—and I've come to decide as a MOOC instructor that my goal is "most" or "many" rather than "all"—the system worked and those who submitted drafts got feedback.

Of course, peer feedback in the MOOC context is bound to be uneven given the number of learners and their ranges of experiences and expertise with academic writing. From the forums, I am sensing that although it was not a productive experience for all who submitted drafts, the feedback process worked very well for many people. One learner posted the following on a forum where some other learners were discussing the results of their peer feedback: "I've submitted 3 peer-feedbacks too, and also received 2 responses to my review. I understand the disappointment that some of you feel when having 3 proper feedbacks can mean so much to an aspiring writer. I would like to encourage my fellow classmates to continue to do the good effort that you've made to give proper feedback to the reviews you've received. I, for one have been blessed by the 2 who chose to put in their effort to properly critique my writing, enabling me to learn and improve from my mistakes." I'm especially gratified to see from the following post that one of my main points is getting through to learners: "Professor Comer is right when she said reading and grading your peers paper will help you in your own writing. I already write a lot better. I spend five hours a day Mon-Fri on my work."[3]

I wanted to see what the experience was like in my course, so I have adopted a pseudonym and am writing the assignments along with students so I can better understand what the course feels like (and also so I can improve as a writer). I submitted my first writing project draft and three members of the class read it and gave comments according to the peer-response rubric. The feedback I received from peers indicated that they understood the points I was trying to make and that I used enough evidence. Here is an excerpt from the peer feedback I received (the second peer quoted my draft):

> *Where does the author go beyond summary of the text to pose a question about Coyle's text, raise a limitation about Coyle's argument, or make some other point about Coyle's article?*

peer 1: The author shows many great examples of his/her own considerations about what Coyle was about. The main point was about making failures and lack of time for deep practice. The Talent Code is indeed something that makes deeply thinking about human possibilities. Apparently, the author was also deeply engaged by thinking about people and their ability to become more successful and the role of mistakes in it. The author stressed out that having time for 'deep practice' is an affordance that not all people are able to have.

peer 2: Here, the author shows a very good understanding of Coyle's chapter. Coyle also seems to be suggesting that mistakes are ok, but the end result is success. In the end, the people who can be great (because of circumstances) have a better chance of actually becoming great. And those who have less potential to be great will still have not as much a chance of really doing enough deep practice to be great.

Seeing firsthand this kind of engagement with peer response makes me so hopeful —not necessarily that everyone enrolled in the MOOC will have a valuable experience (I cannot control that) —but that some people can really grow as writers in this MOOC.

TUESDAY, 5/21/13: LEARNING WHEN AND HOW TO LISTEN

I was recently in a meeting with a colleague, an excellent teacher who teaches a face-to-face first-year writing seminar. She had written in her teaching portfolio that, over the past year, she had spent time "learning how to listen" more closely to her students.

Halfway through the MOOC as we spoke, I was struck by a distinct difference in experience from hers. In fact, I had probably spent the past eight months as I designed and delivered the course learning *not* to listen. I had to learn not to listen to some of my knowledge of best practices in writing instruction when the platform limited what I could do and when I could do it. I had to learn not to listen to colleagues when I experienced intense professional backlash. I had to learn not to listen to unproductive MOOC discussion forum complaints. Perhaps most strangely, I had to learn not to listen to student confusion. Well, perhaps that's too extreme. In some cases, with hostile individuals, I needed to not listen at all. In other cases, I had to listen without any expectation of responding. In my seated classes, I have 12 students and I am accountable to every one of them. If one or two do not understand an assignment, it is my responsibility to try to help. In the MOOC, by contrast, I needed to rely on others to answer questions, or students to find their own way through the fog. And, for the most part, this worked fine.

So it's not that I am trying not to listen at all, but rather that I am learning to listen differently. I need to try to hear what I need to and filter out what I do not need. I need to maintain silence. I need to listen to myself and privilege my own intuition. So this has been an experience of learning how to listen differently, deciphering more clearly what is or isn't valuable, what does or doesn't need response, what does or doesn't enhance my vision and goals.

Wednesday, 6/5/13: Again?

They've asked me if I am interested in running the course again. Contrary to what some who are not involved with MOOCs may think, the course cannot run again on its own. My involvement through Hangouts, forum participation, in-time modifications and adjustments ... all of this is crucial to the running of the MOOC. It cannot be simply put on re-run status, played and re-played for eternity. Plus, as with any class I have taught, it's only after teaching it that I realize how I want to revise and improve it.

If I do it again, I would change the format for the low-stakes introductory assignment at the beginning of the course. I would try to facilitate more structured feedback on forum contributions. I might tweak the readings. I would probably modify the assignments, reducing the length of the course and the number of projects. I would work harder at contributing on the forums in a sustained and less shy way (my brilliant idea about participating on the forums only by highlighting what students had to say still didn't make it any easier for me). I would continue to think about the cross-cultural components of the course and about the significance of having so many English Second Language learners in the course. And I would make the idea of portfolios more explicit and visible throughout the entire course.

Still, I'm not sure I am ready to process the negativity, which will surely resurface to some degree from enrollees and members of the larger professional community again.

Reading the forums this final week, however, suggests to me that perhaps those who are discontented have the loudest voices and thereby make a disproportionate impact. The forums this week are replete with not only positive feedback and expressions of appreciation, but posts that suggest an ongoing interest in developing as writers: "Improving as a writer, needs time and the right attitude, so I'm very enthusiastic because I consider that to participate in this course has just been the first step. I want to keep on writing, reading and learning thanks a lot to the Duke University staff, to the Coursera staff and all students and people who have made this course a reality."

Comments like this make me feel, despite the platform adaptations, the negative feedback, and the exhausting workload, somewhat positively about the experience: Thousands of people talked about writing with each other who otherwise might not have. Some people made lasting relationships with one another, and may remain in ongoing writing groups. One student, in a Google Hangout, referred to several peers as her "MFFs (MOOC Friends Forever)." Here's another post from this week's final discussion forum:

> I just got my peer reviews for my op-ed project and my reviewer said "Your opinion is clear and your arguments, well defined and also interesting". Now compare this to "You don't explicate your argument very much" and "there were only a few sentences where the writer expresses his/her opinion" which I got for my first project. I have been able to deliver a much more polished final version after every peer review of my drafts. For my op-ed, I got valuable suggestions from the discussion forum. Peer reviews consistently strengthened my writing. I can see so much value in these peer reviews. I was thinking if we could form an online community, maybe a Google group, where we could continue submitting our future writing projects for peer review. My thanks to all my peers who reviewed my work over the last twelve weeks, and for all the reviews on the discussion forums, from which I learnt so much.

Comments like these make me appreciate the possibilities of the MOOC experience. As the course draws to a close, we have over 80,000 people enrolled. That's 80,000 people who thought about writing, or watched a video on writing, or contributed to the forum, or drafted a writing project, or gave feedback to another writer. Some (granted, not very many) even did all the work of the course. It looks like only around 1300 people may be earning a Statement of Accomplishment. But my intention was never to have high retention or rates of completion. My intention was to create a learning experience for writers centered on academic writing. Forum posts suggest that even if someone participated in one segment of the course, they had the opportunity to think about themselves as writers: "I have always had the fear of rejection whenever I write a paper, may it be academic or literary. Because of this I have been timid to share my works with others. Through this course, I was able to slowly overcome that fear. To know that people around the world are actually reading my work is still something new to me. And I am very thankful for all the comments that I received."

One of my other main intentions was to conduct research on the impact of the MOOC platform on the teaching and learning of writing. Ed White will soon be running a holistic scoring session of learner's portfolios, and I am eager to learn more about students writing as measured against the learning outcomes.

Mostly I just keep thinking about what a truly incredible opportunity it is to be able to teach a writing course to learners from over 187 countries around the world. This is remarkable, and exciting. Yes ... I am interested in doing this again. Yes...

Acknowledgments

Thank you to the other contributors of this collection who made comments on earlier drafts of this article: Jacqueline Kauza, Steve Krause, Alan Levine, Charlie Lowe, Robert Samuels, and Ed White. My appreciation also goes to those involved centrally with the design and development of the English Composition I MOOC: Kendra Atkin, Yvonne Belanger, Greta Boers, Maral Erol, David Font-Navarette, David Jarmul, Paul Kei Matsuda, Shawn Miller, Elise Mueller, Lynne O'Brien, Marcia Rego, Rebecca Vidra, and Ed White. I am grateful for the grant from the Bill & Melinda Gates Foundation for the development and assessment of the course. And, much in this article bears the imprint of my ongoing Google Hangouts with the other writing-based MOOC Gates grantees: Rebecca Burnett, Kaitlin Clinnin, Susan Delagrange, Scott DeWitt, Andy Frazee, Kay Halasek, Karen

Head, Pat James, Ben McCorkle, Jen Michaels, Cynthia Selfe, and Louis Ulman.

NOTES

1. I use the plural pronoun here because, although I was the primary instructor, a team of over 20 people contributed to the design and development of the course. My project manager at Duke University's Center for Instructional Technology (CIT), Elise Mueller, and CIT Director Shawn Miller were especially central to creating the landing page materials.

2. Excerpts selected from https://duke.qualtrics.com/WRReport/?RPID=RP2_9tVOvczFExmWknP&P=CP

3. Student comments drawn from the discussion forums and peer review are included anonymously and in accordance with Coursera privacy and permission policies. Where necessary, we have made some minor corrections for grammatical correctness but without changing meaning. See: https://www.coursera.org/about/terms (look for the User Material Submission section). Here's a relevant piece:

With respect to User Content you submit or otherwise make available in connection with your use of the Site, and subject to the Privacy Policy, *you grant Coursera and the Participating Institutions a fully transferable, worldwide, perpetual, royalty-free and non-exclusive license to use, distribute, sublicense, reproduce, modify, adapt, publicly perform and publicly display such User Content.*

--- also ---

We may also use or publish posts submitted on the forums without using Personally Identification Information.

WORKS CITED

"English Composition I Map." Map Data: Google, INEGI, SK planet, Zenrin. maps.google.com. Web. 3 Sept. 2013.

Comer, Denise. "English Composition I: Achieving Expertise." *Coursera*. Web. 3 Sept. 2013

Wesch, Michael. "An anthropological introduction to YouTube." *YouTube*. Web. 23 Aug. 2013.

MOOC as Threat and Promise

Edward M. White

I was surprised and pleased when Denise Comer, teacher of record for the Duke MOOC Composition 1, asked me early in 2013 to join her team.* Would I, she asked, develop a feedback and assessment design for what turned out to be a truly massive enrollment of students from around the world? I knew next to nothing about MOOCs but the challenge of integrating modern concepts of assessment on such a scale got my blood racing and my retired energies revivified. Knowing, as I did after more than fifty years teaching and writing about writing, writing research, and management of writing programs, that college writing instruction requires personal communication, expert responding, and careful attention to reading, how, I asked, could I accomplish such a task with integrity? There was no way writing teachers could respond personally to over 64,000 students (the initial enrollment). And personal faculty attention could hardly be attempted, outside of images on the screen.

At the same time, many of my colleagues—and they are nicely represented in this book—saw all MOOCs as an unmitigated evil, about to swallow serious college education for lunch and many of their jobs for dessert. Most seriously, I wondered, would there be pressure to award college credit for student work never actually evaluated by a faculty member? (There was and is, but more on this later.) One condition I did stipulate: we could help students prepare materials to be submitted to a college or university for evaluation for credit, but the institution would have to make the credit decision. Our job would be

---

* This work is licensed under the Creative Commons Attribution-Noncommercial-ShareAlike 3.0 United States License. To view a copy of this license, visit http://creativecommons.org/licenses/by-nc-sa/3.0/us/ or send a letter to Creative Commons, 171 Second Street, Suite 300, San Francisco, California, 94105, USA. For any other use permissions, contact the original author.

to provide a free, or virtually free, educational experience for those seeking it, to give a taste of college-level reading and writing to anyone with a computer and access to the web. Shades of John Dewey and Paulo Freire stood at my back as I agreed to develop the design.

But before I go into the assessment design, I want to address the concerns about MOOCs, some of them justified but most not. I can speak with authority only about the one MOOC I have helped develop, but I think it is probably pretty typical. The initial enrollment of more than 64,000 defined itself ranging from age 11 (5 were under 13) to 143 over the age of 65, with 77% of them speaking English as a second language. It dropped rapidly to 3,311 completing a draft of the first assignment and only 375 of them signing on for the signature track ($39), which provides secure materials for an authentic E-Portfolio suitable for presentation to a university for evaluation for credit. In addition, 1,289 received a "statement of accomplishment" from Duke Professor Comer. In short, it is likely to have much less effect on enrollments in first-year college required composition courses than the College Board College-Level Examination Program (CLEP) or Advanced Placement Programs (AP). These programs make claims for college course equivalency, based on evaluations of college-level performance through tests and the AP Language and Composition test alone enrolled this year almost 480,000 students. Two other AP tests enrolled even more. We should also note that CLEP and AP scores depend wholly on tests which ask for timed impromptu writing on set topics, as opposed to more valid writing portfolios.

Duke's Composition 1 MOOC makes no such claims, since our peer-evaluation system provides much feedback, but no faculty evaluation. Since American colleges and universities have learned to live at peace with AP and CLEP, they should be able to cope with a handful of applicants asking to have their E-portfolios evaluated for credit without much of a problem—as long as the campuses are prepared for such evaluations by their faculty.

However, MOOCs are a potential threat to higher education. It is already clear from actions taken in legislative committees in California and Florida that MOOCs offer ways to further lessen state support for education and to debase college education through even more budget cuts than they have already made. These efforts are based on a vision of MOOCs as offering college credit on the cheap, without paying for faculty, buildings, or research. Most of those offering MOOCs in writing at present have a different vision, based on models of education rather than off-shore business production, but it is possible that the other model might prevail. It is up to everyone involved with education to protect the enlarged view of education that is embodied by faculty-student interaction and faculty research from such an impoverishment of the concept of a university and of a university degree.

But if we see the MOOCs, not as a replacement for college, but as an expansion of what used to be known as community education or adult education—learning for its own sake—then the promise of the MOOC becomes clear. The immense numbers of people of all ages and from many countries who sign up for these courses are clear evidence of a wide-spread, international hunger for learning. The entrepreneurs who began edX and Coursera recognized the threat and promise of this hunger by insisting that only what they called high prestige universities offer MOOCs and requiring systematic and careful evaluations of the quality of the courses; since Comp 1 was funded in part by the Gates Foundation, it also required even more detailed evaluation through its Quality Matters program. I suppose that this was Coursera's way of protecting the quality of the courses, though many of us will question the relation of research universities to the best college teaching, particularly for a much wider population than they are accustomed to. At the same time, the business people supporting MOOCs are not likely to be above looking for a return on their investments. And the only currency we have to offer in business terms is college credit toward graduation. I foresee some conflict between those of us trying to defend that currency against debasement, as we offer college-level work without college credit.

Which brings us back to assessment. It is more in the European tradition than the American one to value performance assessment above seat time, but we do remain committed to asking more of students than spending time and fulfillment of requirements, whatever the attention to the material, however low the quality of the work. In campus courses, we do trust (more or less) the professor to monitor the quality of student performance, since we expect that professor to know the students and to uphold the standards of his or her field. But with thousands, nay tens or hundreds of thousands of students in one course, such monitoring is impossible. With the aid of clever software, we can monitor whether students have submitted the required work, even check against plagiarism and impersonation, but we cannot certify that the quality of the student performance is at the college level, no matter how advanced the course material or how outstanding the qualifications of the teacher of record. For this basic reason, MOOCs cannot and should not certify college credit.

What then is the role of assessment under these conditions? It turns out, it seems to me, that MOOC assessment is liberated to function at its best, to be an incentive to improve, to be most useful for learning. Assessment has two functions, often not entirely compatible: certification and feedback. Thus the teacher puts a grade on a paper but also writes some useful comments to help the student do better on the next paper or, if possible, a revision of the original. For many students, the grade is not only a judgment of quality but the only feedback that counts, and they ignore the comments. But the best students have always valued the written or oral feedback more than the grade, for that is what stimulates learning most effectively. MOOC assessment, liberated from grading and certification, can concentrate on feedback, lots of feedback, and hence be a powerful learning tool.

So that is how we set up the assessment design for Composition 1, which consists of four separate but linked units, each with reading and writing assignments. The field of rhetoric and composition has developed consistent learning theory about how to help students improve as writers. That begins with well-constructed reading and writing assignments, continues with structured peer-group responses to early drafts, leading to revisions and constructive evaluations of later drafts. Thus, for our MOOC, on the first due date for unit 1, the student submits the required essay to a specific web site; the computer picks at random three other students to be the first peer responders and sends that essay out to them. Their responses, following a set of directions keyed to the assignment, are returned by computer, stored and sent to the original writer, who later posts a revision, along with a separate note on how the peer responses helped (or not) to improve the writing. The computer then sends the revision to four new students to rate on a highly structured 6-point scale. Their consensus rating becomes the rating for unit 1. Every student writer thus is responding to and evaluating other students' work, even as he or she is receiving feedback from eight other students about his or her own writing. At every stage, students are required to write short think-pieces about how responding to the writing of other students also affects their own progress. This assessment process reverses the usual class assessment, putting the emphasis strongly on feedback, with the numerical rating, of dubious authority, coming at the end. Finally, in order to complete the class, the student must compose a reflective letter, demonstrating understanding of the course goals, ability to create an argument, and effective use of sources. The software gives each student an opportunity to put all the writing of the course, the drafts and revisions, the responses to the writing of others, the reflective notes on the writing process, and, oh yes, the ratings awarded by fellow students, in a single document, an E-portfolio to be saved and treasured, even perhaps to be presented to a faculty committee on some campus which may, perhaps, award college credit.

Since feedback is more important to most writers than assessment, why, you may ask, do we call for the last group of student respondents to place a rating on the papers they are asked to read? While we felt it important to emphasize feedback and de-emphaize grades, we also felt it important to maintain a felt sense of quality, distinguishing a college course from, say, library writing groups. Thus an essay that responds fully to the assignment is, for college writing, a better paper than one that does not; an essay that uses sources well is better than one that does not; an organized essay is better than one that is incoherent and ineffectively argued. We asked those putting a numerical rating on other students' work to follow a specific scoring guide that referred specifically to the goals for the course. The rating assignment was another way of emphasizing that the course did have specific goals for writing and asking for particular rather than generalized feedback.

After the course was over, at the end of June 2013, I read through about fifty of the completed portfolios, with particular attention to the reflective letters, to see what a random sample of the most committed students, those who stuck with the class to the very end, had to say about the assessment design. To my surprise, not one of the fifty had anything to say about college credit and only two complained about the quality of the peer responses. (One included an illiterate and irrelevant sample.) All the rest found much to praise about the feedback they received, though numbers of them disliked giving and receiving ratings.

I suspect that few MOOCs, at this very early stage in their development, have such an elaborate assessment design, but a writing course without student-faculty personal communication requires no less. Thus, the promise of the MOOC is to widen educational access, introduce college-level reading and writing to those seeking it, and provide a community of readers and writers for those eager to learn. The threat of the MOOC is to debase the quality of a university education by awarding credits and degrees without faculty evaluation, student-faculty interaction, or the experience of an academic environment. It is up to all of us to preserve the promise and defeat the threat.

A MOOC With a View: How MOOCs Encourage Us to Reexamine Pedagogical Doxa

Kay Halasek, Ben McCorkle, Cynthia L. Selfe,
Scott Lloyd DeWitt, Susan Delagrange,
Jennifer Michaels, and Kaitlin Clinnin

Through the spring and early summer of 2013, a team of five faculty and two graduate students at Ohio State University designed and taught a ten-week Massively Open Online Course.* Originally envisioned as a second-level college writing course, the MOOC, "Rhetorical Composing," taught us all a great deal about the ways we understood—and sometimes failed to understand—our roles as teachers of composition and our students' roles as writers and learners. In short, the MOOC learning environment resisted the professional narratives we collectively brought to the class and prompted us to seek and then embrace new discourses and narratives of teaching.

Even as professional educators, we often carry with us unexamined notions about what constitutes effective teaching. As the philosopher and social critic Michel Foucault reminds us, we are always caught up in regimes of truth, constrained by the very discourses and mentalities that give shape to our professional identities because to unravel those gossamer-like strands might undo our otherwise stable subject positions. Similarly, as the postmodern theorist Jean-François Lyotard

---

reminds us, grand narratives are powerful forms of doxa, deeply embedded ideologies that constantly and quietly inform our conscious thoughts and actions. They sustain commonsense ways of thinking and understanding our reality. Such narratives or discourses generally function with conservative force, given that they are aligned with and supported by existing cultural formations. In the context of postmodernity, with its rapidly shifting cultural, educational, economic, and philosophical landscapes, the breaks in such narratives often become apparent, and the value of reformulating our understandings can emerge. The MOOC became for us one such force, a disruptive presence that encouraged us to interrogate pedagogical habits of mind that we had long assumed and left unquestioned.

Grand Pedagogical Narratives

Of the many narratives that shape our professional work as compositionists, one has assumed a central doxological status. The plot of this narrative is relatively simple, even if the implications are complex and far reaching: Composition faculty are experts best positioned to teach writing; we accomplish this activity in small, carefully-designed classes where we shape instructional spaces for students, who ideally function in the role of attentive learners. As a shorthand description, we refer to this plotline as the "Teacher Knows Best" narrative. Composition teachers, this narrative suggests, provide instruction and insightful feedback on students' work with the goal of encouraging students to become critically aware of and reflective about their writing.

A second narrative correlated closely with the first can be termed the "Attentive Student" narrative. According to this narrative, responsible students listen closely to instructional content created and delivered by teachers—primarily in the form of lectures and readings—and follow the instructors' directions for completing each successive task through the duration of the course, regardless of their individual interests or motivations. Taken together, both of these entrenched narratives rigidly define the respective roles of teacher and student alike, making it difficult to imagine alternative learning dynamics in most educational contexts.

In April of 2013, when our Rhetorical Composing MOOC went live, no narratives were more firmly ingrained in our consciousness than these linked professional understandings, these doxological

touchstones: The knowledgeable teacher, the careful classroom manager, the adult who leads attentive students along a carefully crafted
intellectual path. Set firmly in this disciplinary context, we began designing our Rhetorical Composing MOOC along relatively familiar
lines. As faculty, we began by taking responsibility for the curriculum,
designing a carefully sequenced set of assignments and tasks that started with "Getting to Know You," a literacy narrative. Subsequent assignments (titled "Getting to Know One Another," "Making a Visual
Argument," "Composing a Researched Argument") built on one another, focused on different rhetorical contexts, and were informed by
different learning outcomes. We created a walk-through video lecture
for each major assignment and assembled a set of core and enrichment
materials to support each instructional unit, replicating to some extent
what we might do in a conventional classroom.

If our curricular design for the Rhetorical Composing MOOC was
relatively conventional at the outset, the realities of the course and its
participants quickly challenged our assumptions. The initial demographic survey, for instance, indicated that the majority of participants
already held college or professional degrees (72%) and were *not* traditional second-year writing students but instead identified themselves
as teachers, scientists, database administrators, heads of research or-
ganizations, veterinarians, engineers, waitresses, artists, travel writers,
and receptionists. Only 15% of participants were college-aged. [1]

Confronted with these data, we began revising our sedimented professional narratives about teaching and learning for the new MOOC
environment. By the time the class opened, for instance, we found ourselves increasingly reluctant to refer to the individuals enrolled in the
class as "students" and had started referring to them as "writers." And
when our conception of this audience changed, our narrative about
ourselves as teachers also began changing. When we reviewed our
introductory video about the Rhetorical Composing class on Coursera, for example, we were struck by our own unexamined bias toward
conventional collegiate teaching contexts: We referenced "students,"
"classrooms," "undergraduates," and "the second-level college writing
course." In this early video, we had assumed a student body that mim-
icked our traditional student populations at OSU. We had not anticipated the people who enrolled in the Rhetorical Composing MOOC.
Only a few weeks later, we re-recorded and re-edited the video to re-

flect our new thinking and approaches—our new understanding of our "audience" for the course.[2]

These changes led to others. We recognized early in the course, for instance, that the numbers of individuals enrolled in the class—27,000 by the opening day and over 32,000 by the end—would require us to rethink our responsibilities as expert evaluators and graders. Facing this reality and with some forethought, time, and a skilled programmer (Corey Staten) on staff, we designed WExMOOC, a software engine and peer review platform (WEx: The Writers Exchange) to which authors submitted essays for anonymous review and rating by four readers, each of whom was given careful instruction about responding productively to authors and each of whom used a common rubric to structure their ratings. In turn, the author of each essay employed WExMOOC to rate the readers' feedback according to its degree of "helpfulness" to them. Additionally, we designed an Analytics Engine for the course that allowed individual students to compare their own performance with aggregated data across a number of different features (average ratings, reading ease, overall length, and so on). Within this context, the writers themselves assumed full responsibility for rating other writers' essays, responding to others writers' feedback, thinking about their own performance in the class, identifying some of the characteristics—both productive and unproductive—of their own written work.

Still another characteristic of the Rhetorical Composing course that resisted the professional narratives we collectively brought to the class were the Discussion Forums. We were all familiar with how discussions often proceeded in classrooms—carefully controlled exchanges, shaped and guided by teachers and constrained by the cultural politeness requirements of face-to-face discourse in university settings and oriented toward assignment expectations. The Discussion Forums in the Rhetorical Composing class, however, bore little resemblance to these orderly exchanges. From the beginning these arenas were actively occupied by class participants, who—as adults and professionals and learners—engaged and even tested the faculty team by making their needs explicit and articulating the problems the instructional context posed. By the third week of class, for instance, participants and teachers had visited the Discussion Forums 116,845 times and created 2,679 threads; 2,322 different participants had posted 11,222 messages; 1,035 participants had commented on posts 4,815 times; and 1,369

individuals had voted posts up or down 10,448 times. The Discussion
Forums were not the only means employed by participants enrolled in
the class. Students created additional learning spaces, exchanging information within the Google + community and on Facebook.

Initially, used to the model of guiding discussion in a face-to-face
class, we tried to both monitor and shape discussions, but they rapidly
expanded beyond our ability to do so. We tried to answer questions,
help frustrated writers who had lost their way in the complexity of
the course, and give advice on draft ideas for the first assignment.
But the ideas multiplied far too quickly. We couldn't keep up with
the suggestions of how to improve the course, the questions students
had about assignments, the pleas for people to read drafts. This was a
phenomenon we came very quickly to accept—in part because (as we
soon learned) the "wisdom of the crowd" took over. The participants
solved one another's problems and answered one another's questions
with an alacrity and care at which we marveled. The crowd began to
manage many of these tasks for us. Participants, for instance, took on
the task of introducing themselves to each other and identifying who
they were, what they did for a living, and where they were located geo-
graphically. One participant created a Google map for individuals who
wanted to place a pin on their home country. Participants were also
incredibly kind, helping each other and answering questions of writers
who seemed lost. They seemed genuinely happy to review each other's
writing and embraced the possibilities that activity offered for improving their understanding of writing, as Mama D wrote:

> I am a happy reviewer! It is not so bad! I have done six now
> and will try to add some more. I am finding that it helps me
> to see my own writing better. I will now have to force myself
> to do the necessary editing of my own work!

What became evident, in sum, during the first weeks of Rhetorical
Composing was that the intertwined professional narratives to which
we subscribed—the Teacher Knows Best narrative and the Attentive
Student narrative—were being revised around us, regardless of our
plans. In this environment, we were still teachers and retained the responsibility for designing the course, but we were no longer solely (or
even largely) responsible for the *shape* of the course, the direction it
took, or how the participants engaged the material. They were determining which course content they needed and assuming much of

the responsibility for responding to questions and even complaints. In the context of a course that did not offer formal university credit or a conventional grade and was not held in a setting where teachers monitored the actions of students, knowledgeable participants felt perfectly free to explore what the course offered, bound only by the designers' expectations. Many of these participants resisted working systematically or steadily through course content in the order we had planned it—a point they made quite clear to us in the Discussion Forums. As busy professionals and as voluntary writers, they focused on meeting their own goals, allowing their interests to determine how they engaged the course. The reasons behind this "sampling" varied quite dramatically. We know, for example, that although 17,982 participants were active in the course in some way (i.e., accessing instructional materials on the Coursera course website), many others were observing the course as educators interested in MOOCs but did not assume the role of student; other participants were clearly reading or watching the course materials but not posting their written essays for review; others completed the writing assignments and selected individualized sets of enrichment materials provided by Bedford-St. Martins and Joe Moxley's open-source textbook *Writing Commons*. Still other participants avoided the enrichment materials and turned the discussion forums or the Google + community into their own reviewing community.[3] By the third week of class, the instructional videos associated with the course were watched 91,880 times and downloaded 33,266 times by 9,296 participants. During that same period, only 1,657 participants completed Assignment #1 ("Getting to Know You," a literacy autobiography) and 1,182 participants completed Assignment #2 ("Getting to Know Each Other," a reflective synthesis essay about the literacy narratives) and 944 participants peer-reviewed Assignment #2.

Although these figures are large in comparison to the numbers of students we reach in face-to-face classrooms, the statistics reveal that the vast majority of the participants enrolled in the course did *not* watch the instructional materials, turn in an assignment, or review a paper. To be frank, these statistics don't alarm us. Students aren't officially enrolled. Attendance isn't taken. We weren't giving grades for class participation. The course is voluntary, and we recognize that the MOOC platform as an innovative and controversial learning technology invites many "drop-ins" who are simply interested in seeing what the MOOC and our course were all about. In short, the notion of "dropping out" simply does not apply in the Rhetorical Composing MOOC as it functioned in the Spring of 2013. Participants' interests and personal motivation determined whether and how they engaged with course materials—and exactly what they took from the class instruction and interaction. And honestly, we learned to embrace this phenomenon, as well. Rather than secretly express frustration that participants didn't all complete a given activity, we came to recognize that the activity we designed may not have been suited to the interests and motivations of these individuals, and we moved on.

The one-size-fits-all model of teacher-based instructional design, we discovered, was a cultural and economic artifact of bricks-and-mortar universities, the assumptions we make about the students who attend those institutions, and the ways in which such environments (and the cultural formations associated with such environments) have informed, and been informed by our collective professional thinking: historically, economically, culturally, and ideologically. In part, for instance, this model (and the expectations that inform it) has been shaped by a consumerist culture and a relatively stable population of fee-paying students expected to come face-to-face with instructors twice or three times a week for a semester. The efforts of such students are shaped and regulated by a complex and interlocking economy of letter grades, tuition payments, graduation timelines, behavioral expectations, and major requirements. In the absence of these regulating forces, we learned, it was quite possible for self-motivated students to take responsibility for their own learning, provide their own motivation, set their own timelines, select their own learning opportunities, and determine their own level of involvement—according to their individual needs, which they knew so much better than did we. And although we cannot attribute writers' investment and involvement in this course to any single structural feature or set of forces, we can suggest complex linkages that need to be explored further—between the diminution of our own control as teachers and the increase in writers' responsibilities and intellectual investments in the course, the lack of a lockstep curriculum meant for all students and the freedom to choose content and activities, and the absence of conventional grades. We don't claim that these linkages function in the same way in all contexts or that they were the only forces that shaped the course, but for us and for OSU's Rhetorical Composing MOOC, they seemed to be keys to understanding the complex dynamics of the course as it unfolded in the time and space of that first online offering in 2013.

Concluding Thoughts

> *At a time when amazing new forms of connectivity are made possible by new digital technologies and when much of the best recent work in the humanities has made us more aware of the social and collective nature of intellectual work, we still think of teaching in ways that are narrowly private and individualistic, as something we do in isolated classrooms with little or no knowledge of what our colleagues are doing in the next classroom or the next building and little chance for each other's courses to become reference points in our own.*
>
> —Gerald Graff

In 2009, Gerald Graff encouraged teachers to connect—to reach out to our colleagues and infuse our teaching with a sense of collaboration, to move away from "hermetically sealed classrooms" that incline us toward a "Courseocentrism," "a kind of tunnel vision in which our little part of the world becomes the whole." We can state definitively that our experiences collaboratively conceiving, creating, and delivering a MOOC to nearly 33,000 participants have made tunnel vision impossible.

In commentary on various listservs and discussion boards in the months preceding the launch of Rhetorical Composing, colleagues from across the country declared that teaching writing could not "scale." Certainly it seems counterintuitive to the grand narrative we interrogate here—as well as our current practices and years of advocacy for small class sizes (arguing, as we have, that a teacher cannot effectively teach writing in a theoretically-informed and pedagogically sound manner if teaching more than 20-25 students in a college writing course). As we embarked on Rhetorical Composing, however, we felt obliged to question these kinds of assumptions—not because we felt they were incorrect, but because we recognized that through informed investigation and research developed from that investigation we might be able to better address challenges to our practices. In other words, we sought to learn from our MOOC experience lessons that might come to bear on our understanding of writing instruction in a range of educational contexts.

We don't yet have answers to the question, "Does the teaching of writing scale?" because the MOOC has motivated us to reframe the question. We're no longer asking whether the teaching of writing scales but are, instead, asking such questions as "In what instances, for which learners, or for which kinds of instructional or institutional purposes might the teaching of writing scale?" We haven't fallen victim to an infinite regress of self-questioning—but we have begun to acknowledge (as we do here) that many of our assumptions about our roles as teachers and the roles we assume students will take on stem from the narratives we have inherited about teaching and learning in face-to-face classrooms. And these narratives are complicated in a MOOC in ways we find compelling and challenging—both personally and professionally. For example, with the "Teacher Knows Best" narrative firmly in mind, we have often attempted to empower students our classrooms—encouraging them through student-centered activities such as peer grading as means of enacting the critical pedagogies to which we subscribe. In this context, in our classrooms, peer review is always already situated in terms of *teacher* feedback. (And even if we were to employ methods that validate peer feedback—such as responding only after peer review has been completed and situating our responses in terms of the reviews composed by peers, feedback from the teacher remains privileged.) What would happen, we asked, if we instruct students in creating effective peer review but don't enter the process ourselves? In a MOOC with 6000 or more active writers, we can *see* what happens: Teaching and learning happen. New narratives about teaching learning created.

We have, however, come to a clearer understanding of a question posed by Jim Porter in response to this essay, "Does the Rhetorical Composing MOOC serve the purpose of, accomplish the goals of, and substitute for a second-level writing course at a traditional brick-and-mortar institution such as Ohio State University?" To this question, we would say, "No, nor should it." The Rhetorical Composing MOOC was so very different in its form, its goals, its participants, its structure, the cultural formations that shaped its operations, the things it accomplished that it is impossible to make such a claim (e.g., an online writing MOOC substitutes for a face-to-face writing course) with any degree of certainty. This caution, however, does not diminish the fact that that designing and working with the Rhetorical Composing MOOC taught us a great deal about teaching and learning, perhaps more than any of us expected or hoped.

Certainly, the process of designing and teaching a writing MOOC is neither seamless nor without difficulty and controversy—but it is (our early observations tell us) meaningful, and the MOOC gives us the opportunity to investigate further the possibilities for peer review in an online course environment. We've also learned that it's important to loosen the reins, to let go. It's been challenging and humbling—but we've come to recognize the rewards and outcomes of waiting and listening, of letting the wisdom of the crowd to rule. This isn't an easy or comfortable proposition for us *or* the participants in the MOOC because the MOOC challenges participants' doxa as well. For example, many of the participants ascribe to the "Teacher Knows Best" and "Attentive Student" narratives and the related assumption that the instructor serves as the locus of assessment and evaluation, a kind of "black box" of grading. When they discover, as we did, that the fabric of this narrative has been rewoven, that the lines between teacher and student have been blurred—they too have to create new narratives about how teaching and learning take place. The teacher as expert/student as apprentice model doesn't apply in the same way or to the same scale. And, we've begun to ask ourselves what it means to assume that only an authorized expert can give advice about good writing or that a teacher's advice is more valuable than students'. And, as we increase transparency for students, ("allowing" them to see a series of their own discourse analytics and scores relative to the whole), they're making their learning and opinions more transparent to us.

Because our first experience curating the Rhetorical Composing MOOC is, as of this writing, still unfolding, we are still gathering data—qualitative, quantitative, and anecdotal—that are helping us make sense of this new pedagogical format. Thus, it's still premature to make definitive claims about how (or how effectively) MOOCs will transform the teaching of writing. We can, however, take advantage of the opportunity afforded by the MOOC platform to take a sober look at what we've been doing in our classrooms, about the inherited narratives and assumptions that have shapes our approaches, and ask sometimes uncomfortable questions about our motives and motivations.

The aforementioned points only begin to scratch the surface of the productive disruptions of which MOOCs are capable, especially the ways they compel us to re-think traditional pedagogical practice. There are, of course, many other examples we could point out: the idea that a quality educational experience is necessarily tied to a financial cost, or the correlation between class size and pedagogical effectiveness. In some of these cases, we might actually end up galvanizing our previously held views, while in others we might radically up-end them, but the point is that the relationship between MOOCs and traditional classrooms doesn't necessarily have to be adversarial or agonistic, as much of the current discourse on the topic suggests.

Notes

1. We define as "college-aged" those participants born between 1990-1995, assuming a six-year matriculation. If limited to a four-year span (1992-1995), the figure falls to less than 8%.

2. Both videos are available on YouTube, as is a short "mash-up" created by Kay Halasek that demonstrates our changing understanding of the course and our roles in it. View the original video at https://www.youtube.com/watch?v=2FzDXvGSSLk. The second video may be viewed at https://www.coursera.org/course/writing2. The mash-up video is available at https://www.youtube.com/watch?v=C2bCyo-gOc-E

3. Over 3200 participants "unenrolling" from the course completed an exit survey in which nearly 20% indicated that they were "just dropping in to see what [the couse] was like and am ready to leave."

Works Cited

Gillam, Ken, and Shannon R., Wooden. "Re-Embodying Online Composition: Ecologies Of Writing In Unreal Time And Space." *Computers & Composition* 30.1 (2013): 24-36. Print.
Graff, Gerald. "It's Time to End 'Courseocentrism'." *Inside Higher Education.* 13 January 2009. Web. 10 May 2013. <http://www.inside-highered.com/views/2009/01/13/graff>.

Putting the U in MOOCs: The Importance of Usability in Course Design

Heather Noel Young

Over the past year of declarations for and against massive open online courses (MOOCs), news sites and blogs alike have been compelled to playfully reword the MOOC acronym. Ranging in severity from M is for Monstrous to M is for Meh, the most recent M, Messy, provides an entrance to the larger pedagogical problems underlying MOOCs (Krause, Stommel n. pag.).*

In early February 2013, a MOOC offered by the Georgia Institute of Technology through the Coursera platform closed within the first week of class, leaving a crashed Google server and 40,000 plus students in its wake. The crash of "Fundamentals of Online Education: Planning and Application" (FOE) compelled articles like Scott Jaschik's *Inside Higher Ed* piece to discuss the implicit irony of this "MOOC mess." He offers a student tweet that seems to capture the mood of the event: "'Fundamentals of Online Education' MOOC, broke down in the first week. Cue scathing declarations of symbolism" (Jaschik).

While the demise of this particular MOOC was mostly attributed to technological problems and structuring by the teacher Fatimah Wirth, online instructional designer and FOE student Debbie Morrison cites such pedagogical problems as "lack of instructions for the assignments and the group activity" as a key factor "contributing to this course calamity..." Such pedagogical issues seem secondary to the closing of FOE; however, they are significant to the students, who frequently post on discussion boards about their struggle to find assignment information and other course materials. These problems are not limited to FOE. Other MOOCs, perhaps more quietly, have similar issues relaying course materials and information to students in effective ways.

MOOCs' problems with design and delivery of course materials might bear some resemblance to problems in face to face and traditional online courses. However, as the FOE MOOC has illustrated, problems with technology are closely connected with pedagogy and interface design, which begins to point to the qualities that afford MOOC-specific usability issues.

The closing of FOE does not merely represent a failure of design. Instead, this breakdown has created an opportunity for usability testing in current and future MOOC courses. By questioning, investigating, and ultimately testing the usability of course materials in MOOCs, educators, course designers, and user advocates can make the learning experience more accessible by appropriately addressing the rhetorical situation of this digital medium.

USABILITY: A QUICK DEFINITION

The concept of usability is challenging to define because of its involvement within multiple discourses practical and theoretical, professional and scholarly. I want to focus here on usability that moves beyond mere functionality of technology towards questions concerning the design and arrangement of course materials in MOOCs. That is not to say that the technological functionality of MOOCs is insignificant. Without technology, the delivery of these materials (and many other critical functions that make the MOOC world turn) would be impossible. Because of the vast strata that MOOC instructors must be responsible for (working within the constraints of a MOOC platform, organizing discussion threads, sidebar navigation, any basic HTML formatting of Coursera wiki pages, producing lecture content, incorporating outside content into the course, etc.), I feel that focusing on course materials best allows for workable solutions for instructors. Course materials are under complete control of the instructor. I also feel compelled as both a writing instructor and a technical communicator to scrutinize the usability of materials that I provide students.

The definition of usability adapted from Susan K. Miller-Cochran and Rochelle L. Rodrigo's *Rhetorically Rethinking Usability: Theories, Practices, and Methodologies* is especially useful when discussing the arrangement and design of course materials because it focuses on 1) the text (text here meaning everything from words on a page to software) 2) the audience 3) the space 4) the design and 5) the purpose. Usability is

> concerned with anticipating users' needs and expectations, as well as designing texts, documents, systems, platforms, spaces, software–and many other things–with a purpose in mind that is appropriate to and tailored for that audience of users. (Miller-Cochran, and Rodrigo 1)

While the term user is an apt phrase (students are using course materials, after all), the term student suggests a specific purpose, environment, and sequence of events.

In this essay I will address MOOC usability in two parts. First, I question the usability of organized information and navigation in MOOCs that I have participated in as a student. Second, I will question the usability of assignment "sheets" in MOOC courses. As problems of usability arise in cluttered navigation and text heavy, traditional classroom documents, I will investigate solutions that take into account the possibilities of web-based assignment design.

USABILITY OF COURSE MATERIALS

For this section I will be referencing two MOOCs, Duke University's "English Composition I: Achieving Expertise" and Ohio State University's "Writing II: Rhetorical Composing," both offered through Coursera.

"Start Here?": Information Dumping and Navigation

Both home pages of the Duke's and OSU's MOOCs illustrate one of the many problems in designing and presenting course material through MOOCs. So much information about the course is necessary and required for the student to view. However, they are often compiled in such a way that is overwhelming, confusing, or inaccessible. One of the most important parts of the Coursera MOOC homepage, the navigation sidebar, is just one example of usability problems.

The instructor support literature from Coursera on navigation bars states "Although the navigation bar comes pre-populated with a few links when you first log in to your session site, it is customizable and you can delete/add links as you want, even to external sites." This suggests navigation bars have no requirements, but Coursera liaisons still have the ability to strongly encourage such links as an "About Us" tab. While I do not have the research or instructor experience to comment on the tensions between MOOC platform requirements and encouragements, as well as the effects it has on an instructors' pedagogy, I can see the importance of such information to this study.

Duke's course homepage contains a massive sidebar proceeding down the lefthand side (see Figure 1). Tabs include:

- Home
- Professor Comer's Corner
- Start Here
- Frequently Asked Questions
- Syllabus
- Learning Objectives
- Schedule
- Video Lectures
- Readings & Resources
- Discussion Forums
- Writing Projects & Peer Feedback
- Self-Reflections
- About Us
- Course Wiki
- Join a Meetup

The tabs do not appear to have a specific hierarchical order, other than the implied importance of tabs at the top, which in itself seems confused. For example, "Professor Comer's Corner" is tab two so it must be more important than tab three "Start Here," thus undermining the explicit message of the "Start Here" tab to beginning students. Interestingly, in the "Start Here" tab, Dr. Comer explains that the "Video Lectures," "Readings & Resources," "Discussion Forums," and "Writing Projects & Peer Feedback" tabs are the most important while they are located near the bottom of the navigation sidebar.

Further investigation of the tabs continues to reveal partial, redundant, and misplaced information, which inhibit student navigation through the course. When I examined the content of tabs that seemed to overlap, like "Video Lectures" and "Readings and Resources," which I assumed would be found also under "Schedule," or "Syllabus," things did indeed get messy. "Reading & Resources" provide links to readings organized by project, but do not link to these projects or provide dates for readings. The dates for readings can be found in an easily digestible form under the "Schedule" tab. However the "Schedule" tab mentions the video lectures but does not link to them explicitly, though the schedule does link to the readings, writing assignments, and forums, all of which have their own navigation tabs. Partial information on multiple tabs is not only confusing, but does not provide a logical order for the flow of information across the course.

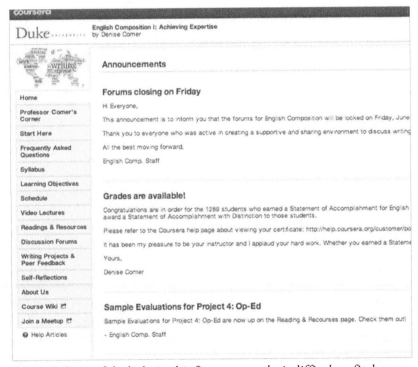

Figure 1. Some of the links in this figure can make it difficult to find course information. For example, where would a student go to find course reading due dates? "Schedule," "Readings and Resources," "Syllabus," or maybe even "Start Here"? From "Announcements;" *English Composition I: Achieving Expertise*; Coursera.

While OSU's homepage was similar with seventeen tabs down the left hand navigation bar, organized in a similar way to Duke's site, there are two additional features. First, the the "Start Here" page offers a legend on the righthand side that provides identifiable icons for certain actions within the course, an eye for "Watch It," a pencil for 'Compose it/Check Your Progress," a person holding an open book for "Read It" (see Figure 2). These icons appear every week of the course, providing simple instructions for students. Instead of traveling to multiple tabs, students can find links to their lectures, readings, and assignments in one location, which seems like one possible solution to overloading students with links. While this legend is not on the homepage, perhaps something similar could be incorporated to visualize information for easier access for students.

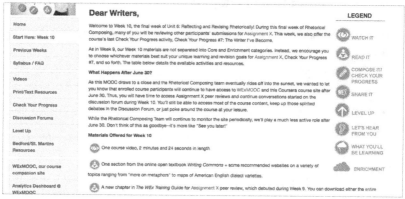

Figure 2. OSU's "Start Here" page incorporates a helpful, visual legend that allows students to quickly locate information visually, instead of reading text heavy pages. From "Start Here: Week 10;" *Writing II: Rhetorical Composing;* Coursera.

In addition to OSU's Coursera homepage, there is a companion website called "WexMOOC." This website offers a sleek, interactive, and simplified version of the Coursera MOOC homepage. Instead of a lefthand navigation bar, there is a slim navigation bar across the top of the page with links to lectures, assignments, analytics, level up challenges, and the forums (see Figure 3). Emphasized in the center of the page are four simple tasks that are hyperlinked, "Watch the lectures," "Do the assignments," "See the data," "Level Up your skills," and "Discuss with others." This companion site not only affords nav-

igation, but it also encourages students to navigate by allowing information to be easily available.

Figure 3. OSU's companion site provides easily navigable links by pairing
down the information to five concrete steps, as well as presenting this information in such a way that takes advantage of the web medium. From
"WExMOOC;" *WExMOOC*; WExMOOC team.

While the companion site is certainly an interesting solution to
the problem of a cluttered platform, perhaps there are other solutions
to affording easier navigation strategies within the MOOC platform.
From the simplistic idea of limiting the number of similarly titled links
on the navigation bar, to the more moderately difficult task of creating
a completely interactive syllabus page which acts as the central hub
of the course, to the even more complex solution of restructuring the
platform to include individual, personalized paths that track the progress and provide links for the student.

The way information is organized and presented to students affects not only the usability of the information, but the usability of the
course itself. If students cannot find assignments or other vital course
materials based on the navigation design, then it becomes a technical
issue equal to not being able to submit an assignment, and thus not
being able to participate in the course.

Assignment Sheets

The assignment sheets and websites of the Duke and OSU courses offer two different snapshots that form a composite view of writing assignment instructions in MOOCs. Duke provides students with a PDF text similar to traditional face-to-face class assignment sheets. OSU gives students a hyperlinked, interactive web page that provides students with direct access to multiple types of information at multiple locations. The usability of a text depends on appropriate considerations of the expected medium as well as expectation of the user. The difference between the PDF and the web page begin to illustrate the importance of crafting course material with the user and medium in mind.

Duke's "Writing Projects & Peer Feedback" tab contains headings for each of the four course projects. Under each heading are the due dates for the required tasks: draft, peer feedback, final, and peer evaluation. The words *draft*, *peer feedback*, and *peer evaluation* hyperlink to PDF instructions. These PDFs look like assignment sheets found in face to face classes (see Figure 4). The "draft one" assignment sheet has an extensive list of bolded headings:

- Project Components and Key Dates
- Purpose
- Learning Objectives
- Assignment
- Grading Criteria
- Readers
- Questions to Help You
- Integrating Evidence and Citing the Evidence
- Drafting and Revising, and Grades
- What file format should I use
- Creating a PDF
- Using the editor box

Some of this information is mentioned elsewhere on the site ("Learning Objectives") or would be better placed elsewhere ("Creating a PDF" and "Using the editor box" do not necessarily need to be on the assignment sheet). Some headings have bulleted points and multiple asterisks to denote very important information. In total, this pdf is almost four solid pages of text, which seems a bit text heavy for an online course.

Denise K. Comer
English Composition I: Achieving Expertise
Critical Review of Daniel Coyle's "The Sweet Spot"
Writing Project 1

Project Components and Key dates
Project 1 will be completed in sequenced stages so you can move through the writing process
and have adequate time to draft and revise by integrating reader feedback.

All times for open and due dates – 9:00 AM EST
- Critical Reading Forum Discussion: (due March 25)
- First draft due, with "note to readers": (opens March 25, due April 1)
- Respond to Peers (formative feedback): (opens April 1, due April 8)
  - Note: You MUST get your comments back to the writers on time so they can
    meet the next deadline!
- Reflect on Responding to Peers
- Revise and Edit
- Final draft due, with reflection: (opens April 8, due April 15)
- Evaluate and respond to Peers (evaluative feedback) (opens April 15, due April 22)

Purpose
Learn how to read critically, integrate evidence, and engage with the work of others. Begin
considering hypotheses about how people become "experts" in their chosen pursuits.

Learning objectives

- summarize, question, analyze, and evaluate written text (read critically);
- engage with the work of others;
- understand the stages of the writing process;
- provide feedback on others' drafts to help them revise and improve;
- incorporate reader feedback;
- revise and improve drafts of your writing;
- integrate quotes/evidence;
- cite the work of others; and
- craft effective titles.

Assignment
For this first writing project, I am asking you to write a 600 - 800 word critical review of Daniel
Coyle's article, "The Sweet Spot." You are likely already somewhat familiar with critical
reviews through movie or book reviews, where a writer summarizes what a movie or book is
about (and offers some details), but also conveys what the uses and limitations are. For this
project, I am asking you to do the following:

Figure 4. While Duke's PDF assignment sheet is a helpful option, utilizing the online medium by incorporating links to helpful information like schedules and readings would make this more usable. From "Project 1 Instructions: Draft;" *English Composition I: Achieving Expertise*; Coursera.

Offering a downloadable version of an assignment sheet is a nice option to have for students who need access to assignments offline, or who value the kinesthetic experience of holding, scribbling, and annotating instructions. However, making a single PDF the sole location of the assignment guidelines becomes problematic for a number of reasons. First, this course is conducted in an online environment, through a digital medium, with the possibility to link to other resources that students could use. Inserting links into a PDF is not a difficult problem to solve; however, it does make a significant difference.

Instead of MOOC course materials being as dynamic as the medium they use, materials are like static, transplanted documents from face-to-face courses. This PDF assignment does not provide an interactive text that links to such requirements as the "note to readers." Students are forced to locate the guidelines for this secondary task (which are not listed textually anywhere, but are embedded within a video). And in place of extemporaneous text on citations and integrating evidence, perhaps an interactive resource or video would have been a more effective way to relay such information. The rhetorical situation of the web needs to be the foundation of course material design instead of repackaging typical face-to-face classroom assignment sheet and expecting them to fit into digital, interactive spaces.

The OSU MOOC offers assignment websites instead of PDF assignment sheets (see Figure 5). For "Assignment 2: Getting to Know One Another," section headings include:

- What Am I Doing?
- What Am I Making?
- What Should I Be Learning?
- Level Up!
- When is this assignment due? When are peer reviews due? When can I expect to get feedback?
- How to Submit Assignment 2 to The Writer's Exchange at WExMOOC
- How to Complete Peer Review in The Writers Exchange at WExMOOC
- How to Access Feedback on Your Assignment 2 Submission

The headings are hyperlinked so that students can skip to parts they are less familiar with. Sections under the headings contain hyperlinks back to forums for reflections, to the companion website, and even to a website that calculates differences between time zones. While this assignment website is still heavily text-based, the function of the digital medium makes this text more interactive and student-centered, thus more usable.

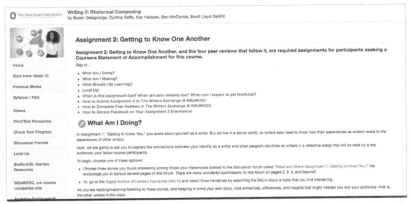

Figure 5. OSU offers an "assignment page" that contains hyperlinked headings so students can skip to sections that are most useful. From

Both Duke and OSU are only the beginnings of Composition's integration into MOOC formats. Just as FOE's usability issues afford a dialogue for usability studies in MOOC classes, Duke and OSU's courses work toward possible solutions for future MOOCs.

CONCLUSIONS AND SOLUTIONS: THINK DESIGN, THINK INTERACTIVE

Unfortunately, simply encouraging usability testing of course materials and course design will not solve usability issues in MOOCs. The relationship around usability and MOOCs is a mostly grey area demanding more research and more attention. For instance, the tension between platform usability and pedagogy is an issue already being briefly discussed. Karen Head's "Lessons Learned From a Freshman-Composition MOOC" from *The Chronicle of Higher Education* addresses the difficulties she faced when trying to modify some of Coursera's typical features to suit her pedagogy. As MOOCs continue to develop the questions remain to what extent should experts in writing pedagogy also be asked to be experts in usability in online courses? And to what extent can instructors work outside of the constraints of MOOC platforms, as well as learning management systems like Blackboard?

Whenever such questions begin to surface, I always look to the students of MOOCs, who arguably know just as much about MOOC instruction as the instructors do. MOOC students are such a diverse wealth of knowledge that most sources seem to ignore or discount. Perhaps MOOC veterans could earn badges by participating in usability testing a week before a course launches. Maybe courses could do a soft release (open the course, unannounced, a few days or weeks early) so that the students who do poke around can test the waters. Until then, instructors must consider the rhetorical situation of the MOOC class they are teaching, construct materials with this foundation in mind instead of transplanting (or remediating) face-to-face materials into the online medium, and critically think about the visual organization of information as a necessary requirement for course planning. Principles like design, interactivity, and multimodality can become concretized components of course planning. Instructors can utilize the ability to connect their work to other, useful materials in such a way that is navigable. They can also present material in formats (other than text) that are appropriate to their courses' purpose, audience, and medium. Maybe then the M in MOOCs will shift from Messy to Manageable.

WORKS CITED

"Announcements." *English Composition I: Achieving Expertise*. Coursera, n.d. Web. 21 Jun. 2013. <https://class.coursera.org/composition-001/class>.

"Assignment 2: Getting to Know One Another". *Writing II: Rhetorical Composing*. Coursera, n.d. Web. 21 Jun. 2013. <https://class.coursera.org/writing2-001/wiki/view?page=assignment2>.

Jaschik, Scott. "MOOC Mess." *Inside Higher Ed*. 4 Feb 2013: n. page. Web. 21 Jun. 2013. <http://www.insidehighered.com/news/2013/02/04/coursera-forced-call-mooc-amid-complaints-about-course>.

Krause, Steve. "E-Learning and Digital Cultures ends with a Meh #edmooc." *stevendkrause.com*. N.p., 6 Mar 2013. <http://stevendkrause.com/2013/03/06/e-learning-and-digital-cultures-ends-with-a-meh-edcmooc/>.

Head, Karen. "Lessons Learned from a Freshman-Composition MOOC." *The Chronicle of Higher Education*. N.p., 6 Sept. 2013. Web. 8 Oct. 2013. <http://chronicle.com/blogs/wiredcampus/lessons-learned-from-a-freshman-composition-mooc/46337>.

Miller-Cochran, Susan K., and Rochelle L. Rodrigo. *Rhetorically Rethinking Usability: Theories, Practices, and Methodologies.* 1st. New York: Hampton Press, 2009. 1. Print.

Morrison, Debbie. "How NOT to Design a MOOC: The Disaster at Coursera and How to Fix It." *Online Learning Insights: A Blog about Open and Online Education.* N.p., 1 Feb 2013. <http://onlinelearninginsights.wordpress.com/2013/02/01/how-not-to-design-a-mooc-the-disaster-at-coursera-and-how-to-fix-it/>.

"Project 1 Instructions: Draft." *English Composition I: Achieving Expertise.* Coursera, n.d. Web. 21 Jun. 2013. <https://spark- public. s3.amazonaws.com/composition/writingprojects/project%201%20 revised.pdf >.

"Start Here: Week 10." *Writing II: Rhetorical Composing.* Coursera, n.d. Web. 21 Jun. 2013. <https://class.coursera.org/writing2-001/ wiki/view?page=week10 >.

Stommel , Jesse. "The March of the MOOCs: Monstrous Open Online Courses." *Hybrid Pedagogy: A Digital Journal of Learning, Teaching, and Technology.* (2012): n. pag.. Web. 21 Jun. 2013. <http://www. hybridpedagogy.com/Journal/files/MOOC_MOOC.html>.

"WExMOOC." *WExMOOC.* WExMOOC team, n.d. Web. 21 Jun. 2013. <https://wexmooc.osu.edu>.

"I open at the close": A Post-MOOC Meta-Happening Reflection and What I'm Going to Do About That

Elizabeth D. Woodworth

"I open at the close." These are the words inscribed on the snitch that Professor Dumbledore leaves to Harry Potter in the last book in that series (the snitch is the golden orb in quidditch that, if caught, often means a team wins). Inside the snitch is the Resurrection Stone, one of the Deathly Hallows—it's the one item that allows Harry to survive the killing curse, Avada Kedavra, cast upon him by Lord Voldemort. Why is this metaphor important to you in this article about a Massive Open Online Course? Because I'm writing about my post-MOOC experience, the end of it all, the close, the thing it was, and then the thing it became—a resurrected thing that continues to have a life. And the Resurrection Stone, as a metaphor, works for me particularly, because my work life often feels like a fatal curse that gets in the way of my life-long learning plans. MOOCs may be the magical "elixir" that allows me to stay alive intellectually when I might otherwise have few options.

I expected to take the E-Learning and Digital Culture Massive Open Online Course (EDC MOOC), offered through Coursera and the University of Edinburgh, to learn a little bit, see what MOOCs might be like, meet a few folks, have some fun—and that would be that. Instead, this MOOC developed into something I did not expect at all. In some way, then, my first MOOC opened me up to the possibilities of MOOCing at the close of the course, and what I thought would be an awful experience—so many students, so much confusion, surely a deathly educational happening—turned into a new kind of online life for me.

I'm writing about all that, but I also want to speculate about why my first MOOC was so MOOC-tastic and how my experience could translate into how others (especially teachers) could approach MOOCs and make them productive aspects of a higher educational environment—personally or professionally, individually or in small groups. My great MOOC time was all about my investment, finding like-minded collaborators, and determining what matters to me as a learner (then as a teacher).[1]

A MOOC Virgin No More

As a writing program administrator, I wanted to try one of these massive courses that so many in and out of my field were talking about (especially on list servs in my community). I dove into the EDC MOOC early on 8 December 2012 even though the course wasn't set to begin until the end of January 2013. I thought spending some time digging around the environment might help me to navigate the course once it started.

What I found immediately was that Facebook and Google+ groups had already been formed and were active. Go figure. Students starting to talk about the course before it began? What? Sort of crazy, but I was there to be part of it; I joined both. I used Facebook more often, and that continued to be the case in this course, but what applies to Facebook applies to Google+ (just not in the same magnitude).

From my Facebook EDC MOOC friends (pop. 4,383 as of 3 June 2013),[2] I learned about dozens of productivity and writing web sites or apps; I took tours of study rooms provided for the course and some provided by the Facebook group members; I had conversations (synchronous and asynchronous) with many about how things worked inside the course, or outside the course, as the case proved to be more massive than promised (there was a LOT going on outside the course); I read and worked on a dozen peer-created and edited pieces housed on our Facebook page: #EDCMOOC; and we shared our blogs, our successes, our failures, our worries, our frustrations—and no matter what, someone answered our questions. Together this small group (relatively small—just over 4,000 compared to the course enrollment which was in the tens of thousands) came together to create dozens of documents that guided, informed, taught, and inspired many of us—through the course and beyond.

As one example, an early administrator of the Facebook group page (administration duties rotated), created a visual graphic of the course as it was evolving so those of us who were visual learners could "see" what we were doing—a sort of web which connected various paths we were taking and tools we were trying to enhance our communication and help us create representations of our thinking (Facebook, Google+, Wix, Diigo, Prezi, Animoto, Popplet, Glogster, Storify, and 48 more tools). Another member created a map where each Facebook group member could pin his/her location—this became our page banner. And yet, another member of the Facebook group started a thread challenging everyone to create a playlist for the MOOC (pulled together in a thread but also in a file on Facebook called "Let the Music Play!"). Many of us created EDC MOOC playlists. We encouraged each other to share our final artifacts for the course on the Facebook group page, too. Many of us posted links to our blogs through Facebook, too, in case our members didn't want to wade through other media to find out what we were writing/thinking/doing. And again, some one in the group gathered links and created a file for all that blog work (and Twitter work, too).[3]

Group members continued to post queries well after the course concluded, share information, and connect with each other. I noticed the group actually gained seven new members in the space of one day in early June (the 3rd through the 5th). I've never participated in any online groups before, so this was baffling to me to see how this group flourished, took a semi-rest, but really kept itself alive as a post-MOOC hub.

As I've been thinking about the afterlife of this MOOC, I've come to some conclusions about why this active post-MOOC life may have happened, why I value it, and why I think it's something writing teachers can and should think about more as teachers of higher education (especially writing).

EARLY ADOPTERS ARE BRAVE

We all know the early adopters—those folks who own the first of any new tech. I'm not one of them. I think they are brave, though, and look forward to their reports, because they get the kinks out so when I get the second generation product, it's cheaper and better.

In the case of this MOOC, though, I totally went the early adopter route. I joined the Facebook group seven weeks before the course started. At that time there were less than 150 members of the group, and in some ways, we got a lot of communication issues handled. We bonded. We taught each other vital things about ourselves and how we worked. I then decided to friend a bunch of my fellow students. I had some down time between semesters, so I could be a brave early adopter and add to my Facebook world. But I must say this: I was scared. I was shy. I was worried about reaching out to others, allowing myself to be seen. I am fairly bold in some circumstances, but I was a bit reluctant to be so in public, in this way, in a way I could not entirely control with gestures or visual cues to further explain my communications. Thinking about the huge numbers in a MOOC was unpleasant for me, but the Facebook group members who had taken other MOOCs earlier in 2012 were terrific mentors—just jumping into it and asking questions: "What are you all doing this for? What do you want out of it? How can we help? Hey, I have a great tool that worked for me to manage the overload." They made it easy to get over myself and put aside my fears in order to find ways to begin engaging.

When early adopters added into our Facebook group, they might receive a half dozen welcome messages and have questions answered right away by their predecessors.[4] (It was much harder to connect later when thousands were adding in weekly at the start of the course.) One of the benefits of my early adoption was that many with educational tech savvy suggested multiple ways of handling the massive part of the course. Working with 50,000+ students was not going to be easy for some of us, or even close to anything we'd done before. I certainly freaked out about the size and expectations of what I might find amongst a group that large and online. I found the suggestions to dial it down, made by veteran MOOCers, very helpful. One suggestion was quad-blogging (see http://quadblogging.net for more info). We didn't do this exactly as described—we would adapt. In essence, four students in our MOOC put their names onto a document in our Facebook page and those four would be a quad blog. Whoever signed up in order got that group of bloggers. Very simple. The four members of the quad blog would link to each other's blogs and decide each week what to focus on and give each other special attention—sometimes following the course exactly, sometimes not. We could expand our connection beyond the blog, of course, and some did—my quad blog did, adding many others to our blog rolls and linking freely within our posts to others in the course who we found intriguing thinkers. I was and still am a member of my original quad blog.

I Am Quad Blog 3

The four members of Quad Blog 3 created our own Facebook page (agreeing that since we were all on Facebook a great deal of our on-line time, we'd just go with it—besides linking our blogs). Through Facebook, the four members of Quad Blog 3 stayed connected regularly in the preceding weeks leading up to the course start—through the course, and also continued to connect to each other through that group after the MOOC ended (we used that space to talk about more than the course, too—discussing trends in higher education, news, courses we are teaching, and sharing some personal information as well).

Other quad blog groups were formed (a total of 16 quad blogging groups from our total Facebook group). These were all randomly put together—whoever signed up did so in the next available slot. Because these 64 students were among the early adopters, I often included them on my own blog roll (and friended them on Facebook, too). I cannot speak to all the quad blogs and their success or whether the relationships have been maintained, but I can say that a collaborative effort was mounted to write an article by several of these early-adopter quad bloggers from several different quads—one author from our quad blog, Emily Purser, was an author of a subsequent article about MOOCs and successful engagement.[5]

Through Facebook and my quad blog, I learned a great deal about the content of the course via a more focused lens but also about how to function in a network beyond my physical reality. As well I sustained my interest in the course by staying connected to the three others who, while being randomly put together, had some important things in common: interest and commitment. What we also found was that we were all invested in higher education—as teachers, as students, as life-

long learners. These are a few things that kept us going in the course
and together:

- Mutual interests (history, writing, English, linguistics, digital
  writing, teaching online and more).
- Similar capabilities (mostly reliable internet, some computer/
  tech savvy, equipment that worked most of the time).
- Willingness to commit to a process of learning (set aside time
  to blog, to write, to think, to share, to post on Facebook to the
  large group site, to our small quad blog site, to interact with
  other quad blogs).
- Time to do the work, think about the work, and share it.
- Admiration and respect (it might not have been necessary, but
  it sure is helpful to sustain the connections before the course
  and during the course and beyond).
- Freedom (we felt like we could talk more personally and with
  less circumspection to each other in our very small group than
  we could in front of 4,000 people, or ten times that number,
  in public).

Such social media connections also made it easy to invest in our
collaborative learning, but investment wasn't just related to our pro-
fessions. I watched with interest as any number of students with vastly
different professional and personal lives from around the world interacted on our Facebook page (and through Google+).[6]

While I was enrolled in the MOOC, I adopted (and adapted) the
concept of quad-blogging to my writing classes, my writing-intensive
literature classes with blog requirements, and have encouraged composition instructors using blogging to consider this small-group interaction as a way to manage what can be an overwhelming online
component of their composition courses—even for a class of twenty.
The close connection between a few students, online, can facilitate remarkable discussions (online) and when used to prompt in-class face-
to-face conversations.

INVESTMENT IS THE THING, BUT IT'S NOT THE ONLY THING

MOOCs can be terrific for a motivated learner, but what might not
work for some students is making a light investment. I can see how
easy it is to lose interest and opt out of the thing completely—success
seems to be mostly about the student staying in touch with others,

sustaining that connection, and keeping up with the work. Lack of any of those may account for the high rates for non-completion I've seen others talking about: anywhere from 90% to 70% non-completion. Whatever. What's significant, though, is the 10-30% who stick it out. If these numbers are even close to accurate and not just chatter on social media I've picked up here and there, then in a class of 50,000, 10% is still 5,000 students hanging in through it all. Impressive. That's 5,000 more students who learned something they might not have been able to learn otherwise. That might be as many students as I could ever come in contact with in 100 semesters of teaching (and I guarantee I will not be teaching for 50 years). And what else might the others have learned by only being involved for a few weeks? Perhaps enough to keep learning on their own or enough to spark an interest to try again (at NO cost other than in time).

I invested, but I did not invest enough. I did not complete my first MOOC. My life and my job pulled me away from my MOOC affair. But I remain kind of sort of in love with the whole concept of MOOCs. As a writing administrator, I love the idea of MOOCs as supplementary instruction, but I wonder if I would accept such a class in lieu of a face-to-face composition course. I'm not sure I would. I might refuse to take MOOC courses for credit in lieu of required writing courses, unless I'm forced to by an overzealous administration or state legislature—but then I'll try my damnedest to construct HOW I'll accept the credit—on my terms. For instance, if a student was clearly invested in learning and could present a portfolio of work, I could be assured was the student's own, I might accept a MOOC comp course in lieu of a composition course on a case-by-case basis. But a wholesale—"we'll take your MOOC in place of our core course"—I doubt that will happen anytime soon at my institution without some kind of substantial persuasion (or coercion). But as a way to extend writing instruction? Oh yes. It's remarkable potential.

And I want MOOCs to keep growing in the field of composition and rhetoric—it's vital to share what is known about writing with more students than the twenty who show up in one bricks and mortar classroom. Why? Because many in the world do not yet know what composition instructors have been doing in US universities for decades. Sharing a composition philosophy with 50,000 students at a time? Yes. That has to be a win, no matter what the completion rate ends up being. Epic. Win.

But. Everything depends on the investment of the student in a particular MOOC (or the investment of the teacher who's using the MOOC to take his/her class beyond the physical classroom—so maybe we need a MOOC to teach composition teachers how to use comp MOOCs to help teach comp classes).

It takes more than a few hours to learn what's available to learn in a MOOC. And those students who completed EDC MOOC did a lot of work and much of it was fine—university-credit quality work, in my informed opinion. I was impressed with the final projects many of my MOOC friends created for this course—really impressed by much of it (some of it was meh—but how is that different than any college course?).

But I was not impressed by me. I didn't finish. I created an artifact that I might share with my Facebook co-MOOCers and on my blog—maybe, some day—but it will be months past the "due" date, or never. I was too busy when the course ended to manage it with my classes and my administrative duties. Yet in some sense, I got enough from the class before it even started to keep me going all year, to continue exploring e-learning and digital community. During the class, I learned to open my eyes to more e-learning tools and the creation of digital communities through a common learning goal, and I used what I needed to enhance the learning environments in my life with my own students, sharing and playing with ideas and digital community.

No Certificate for Me, But I Won Anyhow

As the EDC MOOC course progressed, my spring semester began, which essentially meant that my investment as a student was substantially less than in the weeks before the actual start date. Truly, through the interaction of my fellow MOOCers on Facebook, I felt like we had done a couple of things I'd hope to see happen in the course proper:

1. We formed an e-learning and digital community dedicated to sharing educational technology and personal/professional knowledge about teaching and learning.
2. We investigated various ways to communicate digitally in larger groups, in smaller groups, individually.
3. We also talked about and learned from the course itself.

I even adapted several weeks of curriculum from the course to supplement a unit in my honors freshman comp course on open education, digital learning, and the future of writing and the book (for some of my students, the book is a medium that sometimes feels like an ancient technology). It was a lovely lot of juxtapositions and interactions and interstices in which we talked about the meta-ness of my taking the MOOC and their learning through the curriculum of the course I was participating in, how it was open, how it was online, how it was a connection for them to 50,000 (approx.) other students wanting to learn something/anything, and how such learning could transform their futures. It changed us. They had (of course) not really heard much about MOOCs (they are freshman and were worried about other things). But when we were finished with that unit—they knew exactly what was possible in their learning futures. Three of them signed up for the Duke University Composition 1 MOOC with me that began halfway through our spring term—just because they wanted to see what it was all about.

And that amazing happening in my composition course was something my fellow quad bloggers and I talked about on our Facebook page and in Google Hangout. Each Sunday night for the run of the course, we had a standing appointment to meet and talk synchronously. I made it a couple of times, but always there were two or three of us from our small quad who were on board. One member was able to record the sessions so that those of us with other obligations could catch up the next day—as it should be in a digital world. It was brilliant. We were in the US (California, Alabama, Virginia) and Australia. We had to wrangle a bit with the time zones at first, but we got that handled, and then it was just a thing that we did. If anyone needed to rearrange or cancel, it was not a hassle to accommodate change, but because it was all getting recorded, the pressure was off.

If the MOOC professors decided to Twitter with 1,600 students, that was great, and it was fun to watch that happening, but the members of Quad Blog 3 could have an intimate connection with each other and share reactions and thinking and plans for projects and even continued learning, in a little environment, a manageable space. We often talked about what MOOCs we wanted to take next or even which ones we were signed up for contemporaneously. And what's the most important part of this for me: we talked about what we wanted from the courses we were signed up for or going to sign up for. We wanted what we wanted—not necessarily what was offered. We didn't necessarily all want the whole course, nor did we want to commit to completion, we often just wanted to see if the course might be interesting, and if there was anything within a course that thrilled us, but there was no guilt or worry if we didn't achieve completion. We achieved learning anyway. And there was no outrage if the course was not fantastic. We just let it go if it needed to go.

When I got all I could out of the EDC MOOC, I let it go. I had to. But I also wanted to. I did not earn a certificate of completion. I was okay with it then, and I still am.[7]

No, Elizabeth, No, Don't Go

But here's where it all gets super amazing to me. The EDC MOOC class officially ended after five weeks (from late January through the end of February/early March), but it didn't really end there. I still talk to my quad bloggers. We still Facebook message. We may take other MOOCs together—and we share what we're taking currently or not, or what we're reading. The EDC MOOC Facebook page was still slightly active post-course. On 2 June 2013, for instance, someone posted a query—within minutes six members of the group had responded. New files were continually posted to the page every week by members. Questions are asked—and answered—regularly. Status updates continue to be shared. Seven new members were added from 3 June 2013 through 5 June 2013—in just a matter of a few days—well after the class was closed and well before the next one opened.

Why did this happen? Why this continued interest or investment?

Just like in my assessment of why and how Quad Blog 3 ticked, there seems to be something connecting us (still) in EDC MOOC through our Facebook page that has to do with interest, capability, will, time, admiration. "We are the 4,000." Is it that simple?

But just as fascinating, there is a personal afterlife as well. A few folks that I've friended are active on Facebook, and we've continued to have conversations and follow one another. I have my Quad Blog 3 friends, but also many more folks from around the world who do any number of things for a living—only a few connected to higher education. These are people to whom I would be glad to say: "Hey, I'll be in Sydney next spring, would love to meet you for dinner." Or "I'm headed to Singapore (or China or Bulgaria) next year, would you want to meet for a visit?" Or "Guess who's going to Buenos Aires in a month?"

In few of my professional experiences have I been in touch with so many all over the world. When I dreamed of being a college teacher in the early 1990s, I dreamed of breaking down the walls of the traditional classroom to connect to others learning around the world. I dreamed of a smaller world, a more open world, a world where distance from a physical university didn't matter. Through this MOOC, I just saw my dreams come true.

It's not as if I've previously been prevented from creating a global network—people have been doing it for decades. Technically, and technologically, I could have engaged years ago online and in open. But I didn't do it. I'm a committed life-long learner, but I did that learning privately or in local communities or through professional conferences with others I knew. A massive online learning experience centered on e-learning was the right reason for me to go massive and open and online all at once.

"I OPEN AT THE CLOSE"

Professionally, I've found a way to value the MOOC as a teacher and even as an administrator (I still regularly encourage other composition teachers in my program to explore MOOCs as possibilities for professional development beyond what our small program can offer). As a life-long learner, the culture of the MOOC will be what sustains my intellectual curiosity in ways nothing else has or could. I do not think MOOCs will replace higher education in which an expert guide works with a novice in small groups (not in my short lifetime). But could MOOCs work as ways to drive folks to higher education? Yes. Could they serve as means to prepare students for higher education who might need some extra experience learning? Yes. Could they be supplements for college courses? Yes. Could a MOOC serve as a professional development experience? Yes. Do MOOCs function to unite like-minded individuals in a learning environment in which they can: 1) learn; 2) connect; and 3) continue to learn? Absolutely.

MOOCs could be the next greatest change in higher education if the developers and professors can harness and manage a way to put the power of connecting, grading, assessing, reviewing into the hands of smaller groups. Make a freshman comp MOOC? Great. Do it. I actually loved the one Denise Comer and team did at Duke, and so did some of my students and teachers. I would have loved to "offer" the whole course to my students—make it a frame for a class I was teaching, so I could extend the thinking and writing assignments. Keep the peer review. Keep the massive everything. And keep the open, but let me learn and guide and manage the end experience for my students at my school for my program—perhaps even in conjunction with four or five other comp instructors. Now THAT would have been a fun thing to try. If only I'd thought of it before it was halfway over. Next time. Nothing says we can't all keep learning as professionals in this way through MOOCs and also help our students be open to learning alongside others all over the world.

Again, if I'd thought of it in time, could I have created a Facebook page for my own class as we started to get involved in the Duke Comp 1 MOOC? Yes. And could it have also incorporated students from other schools? Yes. And might that have been amazing? Yes.

I need to think about how to take the great from this grand experiment in freedom—both the EDC MOOC I took and the one on composition. I need to keep thinking about what the open part means, too. I, as a writing professor and administrator, can learn from, grow from this and from more of the same. I've always been dissatisfied with my limited reach in one or two classes I teach a year. Here's an opportunity to connect in ways I cannot totally fathom yet, but if I remember that this is about people connecting, not content digestion, about letting learning organically happen, then I have a chance to do something with MOOCs that may not have been intended (because what's there is sometimes not inspiring all the time—been-there-done-that-with-the-mostly-lecture-banking-model-of-education). But there's innovation happening, too. And I believe in the fundamental importance of evolution in higher education. Change is coming—I'm either going to be part of it, or I'm going to wither. Why not play with the new toy and bend it and twist it and see what we can make of it?

I will continue to be open to what's possible. I will enroll in more MOOCs—some that support my professional interests, some not so much. I will continue to hunt for courses that might work as supplements for what I'm teaching. At the close of my first MOOC, that's what I gained, and it's a lot more, and a lot better, than a certificate. I opened at the close, and I survived because of it, to MOOC another day.

Notes

1. The course, of course, needs to be well thought out and put together intelligently in order for it to work, even for the highly motivated student. This will not always be the case, and hasn't always been the case for higher education. But the lovely thing about MOOCs so far is that if the MOOC is not working for a student, they may gracefully extricate themselves with no fuss and no financial loss.

2. As of 5 November 2013 the group still exists and is mentioned by the course professors as an open for learning/communication in the second offering of the same course (in which I am again enrolled). I see many of the same folks taking the course again and active in the Facebook group, and as official course facilitators, which has grown by over 600 members since the first course began in January 2013.

3. Some Facebook group members were still uploading their artefacts [sic]—four months after the course was over.

4. The early adopters of the EDC MOOC #1, of which I am writing here, are still the leaders in the Facebook group for EDC MOOC #2—the newest version of the course that started November 4, 2013. They are back taking the lead and answering questions for those new to MOOCing, suggesting strategies for getting started, alleviating fears that include a massive intimidation factor—being part of a city-sized online group.

5. Emily Rose Purser, Angela Towndrow, and Ary Aranguiz. "Realising the potential of peer-to-peer learning: taming a MOOC with social media" eLearning Papers.33 (2013). Available at: http://works.bepress.com/emily_purser/10

6. The second time around, I am only going to engage on the official course site, the same Facebook as EDC MOOC #1, and follow the discussion via Twitter. I learned to downsize my commitment to manage my own learning and get what I need from this MOOC. This time, I'm not trying to swallow the sun.

7. I'm especially okay with it now because I'm signed up for EDC MOOC 2.0. I will likely not complete this one either, because fall semester promises to be extremely challenging, but I'll learn more this time, and something new, and make new friends and from them, be opened to other ways of thinking, seeing, being.

Here a MOOC, There a MOOC

Nick Carbone

It is possible that MOOCs will transform education in the way the creators and venture capitalists behind MOOCs such as Cousera and Udacity, to name the two most prominent at the moment, imagine, where instead of lecturing to a 100, the same professor can lecture to 100,000?* We might see a day where that course is purchased and offered by many colleges instead of just one, offered to residential campus students and not just online students. And so Coursera's May 2013 business plan (Kolowich)—to charge schools for course development and to get a fee per student who takes the course by creating courses where local faculty maybe lead discussions around the lectures of videoed star professor—might work. Who knows. But such a move would merely continue a trend well underway: reducing tenured faculty, increasing adjuncts, and probably hiring more administrators (Ginsburg).

This path merely makes MOOCs-as-a-business more of the same. That is, as for-profits, MOOCs aren't revolutionary. They're just another business venture seeking to promise educational efficiency—more students served—at lower per student costs. To the extent that MOOCs, while a new kind of online course (massive), aren't really breaking new ground, the debate about their role in remaking the education landscape takes attention away from more pressing issues. So MOOC enthusiasts such as Tom Friedman and Clay Shirky extoll the promise of MOOCs to alter higher education by delivering the best education from elite colleges to massive numbers of students for free

---

or at reduced costs. In direct reply to Friedman and Shirky, writers like John Warner, Carolyn Segal, and Andy Bady extol the virtures of the traditional college classroom, where a good teacher – by inference a full-time tenure tracked professor -- is at the helm of his or her course.

Yet the erosion of full-time and tenurable faculty, and increased use of underpaid adjuncts working with less academic freedom and control over the courses they teach is what MOOCs would be replacing. Adjuncts teach, at the most convervative analysis of data, 70% of college courses. While some programs in some campuses might admirably create more full time or even tenure track teaching positions, the trend nationally isn't shifting away from the use of adjuncts. MOOCs as a business seek mainly to promise that they can deliver courses and learning per student even more cheaply than hiring lots of adjuncts.

Thus it's not MOOCs that undermine the traditional college teaching model and role of faculty. It's a convergence of systemic issues and trends, which include, but aren't limited to, the following:

- university and college capital improvement programs that contribute to tuition increases (Edwards);
- cash strapped states that have cut investment in higher education; the amount of debt students and their parents take on to pay for college;
- the growth of campus administration and bureaucracy;
- too many tenure line faculty still treating adjuncts as outcasts; adjuncts who remain adjuncts by choice or trap despite poor pay, no insurance, and no job security;
- and the rise of testing and testing companies as outsized players in educational policy.

Skeptics of MOOCs claim, rightly, that learning in MOOCs is not as good as learning in a well-designed, well-taught course with a good teacher who can keep up with their scholarship and who earns a good wage. There are college presidents (Jaschik) saying not-just-yet to MOOCs because they are too new; there are faculty rejecting their administrations' MOOC deals. And that's good, but in the end, MOOCs will figure out what they need to make their business a go because we're already in a world where 70% or more of college courses are taught by adjuncts who often cannot design the courses they teach, lack time to stay current with scholarship, and are poorly paid.

Writing in MIT's *Technology Review*, Illah Nourbakhsh, in a piece called "It's Time to Talk about the Burgeoning Robot Middle Class," observes a truth that guides the drive to educational efficiency:

> Consider the automated checkout line at your local grocery store. It makes more mistakes than a human clerk, it is harder to use, and it is slower because of the rotating error light that loves to interrupt the whole process every few minutes. Is it better than a human? Of course not. It is simply good enough. And so begins the march of mediocre robots that can defensibly replace humans, not because they advantage the customer, but because they save money for a corporation. (No. Pag.)

Being nonprofit doesn't mean being noncorporate. Colleges are already experimenting and charging tuition for largely self-paced courses, layered with personal learning tools and some adaptive technology, where discussion boards might not even be used, and where teaching assistants or tutors instead of faculty might help out, where software gives most of the feedback on writing. Many of these experiments are for remedial courses, where, sadly, the courses are viewed as "simply good enough" for students enrolled. In many colleges, though students are charged tuition and fees for remedial courses, the credits do not count towards the degree. The goal is to get these students through the remedial program and ready to do college level work, but without giving students the time and attention of even adjunct faculty, let alone the dwindling pool of tenure line faculty.

As of this writing, San Jose State University's experiment with Udacity to offer a remedial math MOOC for only $150 is being analyzed. The spring iteration of the course showed a dismal pass rate (C or better)—only 23.8%—but a summer iteration showed an improved pass rate, 29.8% (Thrun). While both are below the 45.5% who passed the on-campus offering, the trend is up. But as Thrun himself notes, part of the reasons it's up is that the student population shifted:

> Among the student body, 53% reported that they already hold a post-secondary degree (5% Associate, 28% Bachelor's, 16% Master's, and 4% Doctorate). Only 12% of the students had a high school graduate diploma or equivalent, and 15% were active high school students. This is very different from the Spring Pilot, in which approximately 50% of the student body

were active high school students, and the other 50% were matriculated SJSU students.

In addition to having more students enrolled who are more and better prepared for college, Thrun and others rightly point to improvements in the MOOC's course design from spring to summer: better pacing, increased learning support, earlier warning systems about performance, and so on. But even with all that, including a better prepared student population, the pass rates are below the on campus courses. And those on campus courses very likely do not include anyone with a post-secondary degree.

So again, a MOOC might prove, over time, good for teaching people who already know how to learn, who might take a remedial math course not because they're the typical remedial student who needs support, help with study skills, time management, adjusting to college culture, and possibly taking other remedial courses in reading and writing, but are instead folks who want to brush up on math that they probably once had learned and forgotten. By Thrun's own analysis, the MOOC is good at teaching those easier to teach.

It remains to be seen how well a MOOC is for teaching those who struggle to learn in the best of circumstances, let alone in online courses still finding the right course design. At least the SJSU experiment lead to study and research, and the findings were published so they could be debated. Who knows. We may find that MOOCs succeed in teaching so many of the students primed to succeed in any learning setting, that more faculty are free to work more closely with weaker students in traditional classes, giving those students the deeper support and structure needed to not just pass the courses, but to really learn how to learn.

Somehow I doubt that will happen; I just fear that the mindset on remedial education in higher education is to do courses as cheaply as possible first, and as well as possible second. So what might be a good (Bousquet) use of MOOCs inside, or in cooperation with, a traditional college curriculum?

I joined a Coursera course, Writing II: Rhetorical Composing. The teachers and designers of the MOOC are from Ohio State University. Susan Delagrange, Cynthia Selfe, Kay Halasek, Ben McCorkle, Scott Lloyd DeWitt , teachers of record, are joined by Jennifer Michaels, Kaitlin Clinnin, and Michelle Cohen as co-designers. Writing II is one of four—along with Georgia Institute of Technology, Duke University, and Mt. San Jacinto Community College—writing MOOCs that received a Gates Foundation grant.

What I see is a course that, though it carries the same assignments as the campus-based OSU course, is radically different in promising ways. As a writing course, OSU's MOOC focuses on two pillars of good writing courses: students do lots of writing; and they give and get lots of feedback on writing by writing. Set aside whether every writer in the course could earn credit or would pay tuition, or whether their feedback comes from an expert teacher. Those are for-profit questions, higher-education-institutions-as-corporations questions. The better questions, the good question, for me is: what happens when you have lots of writers doing lots of writing as well as giving and getting lots of feedback? How does that change the teaching of writing?

Here are some changes I see happening. First, teachers are not the same kinds of centers-of-attention as they are in traditional courses. In traditional writing classes, with one instructor to 20 - 30 students, students expect:

- teachers to talk more during class (either lecturing, explaining assignments, calling out what students need to do better);
- teachers to give them assignments and to create incentives (grades) or structures for tracking their completion of assignments;
- to give most of the substantive feedback they will get on writing;
- and to give the student a grade in the course that records to their college transcript.

Teachers in a MOOC can still hold attention when they hold forth as video-talking-head, choose to comment in a discussion board, answer questions in video chat, or send email reminders about what's coming up next. But most of the attention to teachers in a MOOC is preset—videos are recorded in advance, or non-instructional—updates and reminders are administrative rather than educative. And so while there is a teacher presence in a MOOC, teacher video talk being in many cases the only talk students will hear aurally, most of the written talk, the discussion talk, will be with other students.

For writing MOOCs to really work, pedagogically, the key work in the course needs to be the student-to-student sharing and commenting on writing; MOOCs have to work, to echo a Peter Elbow title, as a variant of writing without teachers. So MOOC design really forces instructors to move out of the center mainly because the size of the course means the center cannot hold. A MOOC moves teachers further from center because the volume necessitates assessment and grad-ing have lower thresholds for marking successful completion.

That is, assessment in the traditional sense hasn't been solved, which is what makes MOOCs for traditional academic, at least in writing courses, so daunting. It's clear automated machine scoring, while it can be reliable, isn't valid for writing assessment. And the vol-ume of students makes traditional, teacher determiner of grades im-plausible. For example, OSU's MOOC had five instructors of record and two TA's. According to Coursera, 32,835 students signed up for the OSU MOOC, and 18,103 were active. If 10 percent of those active students completed the course for a grade, that would be 1,810 papers to grade in a way commesurate with a single teacher grading 25 papers in a traditional course.

But where meeting the corporate college need via a MOOC model to grant credit isn't an issue, a shift to some alternative assessment model is a good thing. Because the shift decreases focus on the teach-er, and continues to move writers' attentions to their own and others writing. On assessment, the idea posited by Duke University's MOOC makes sense to me: students do a lot of writing in the MOOC, and their work is verified, resulting in a portfolio that can then be assessed, separately, by a college which might choose to give students credit for a course. Services such as LearningCounts.org offer a variation of this, helping students who take their courses "create a learning portfolio to demonstrate your expertise for undergraduate college credit."

But what fascinated me about the OSU MOOC experience was the participation of students who were not in the course for credit; that's the shift that matters. This shift goes to motives for learning. In a traditional writing course, students enroll because getting their de-gree requires them to either take the course or allows them to use the course as part of their march to enough credits, properly distributed and earned, to graduate. Given increased cost and student loan debt incurred by students and their families, passing matters. And so while some students may enter genuinely motivated to examine and improve their writing or themselves as writers, and while some may be persuad-ed to those motivations, in traditional college settings, most take the course because it is required and they do the work mainly to meet that requirement. Students I saw in the OSU writing MOOC entered for different reasons: they're not in the course because a degree requires it; they're in because they care about their writing.

Many of the students weren't even especially interested in the Certificate of Completion the MOOC offers. MOOCs recognize varied student motivations. For example, the OSU MOOC's course directions said "if" you are going for completion, do this list of completion things. Even more telling about how a MOOC changes assumptions about learning is this: "A note to participants joining us after May 9, 2013: We welcome new course participants anytime, and we believe this course has much to offer participants regardless of whether you are pursuing a Statement of Accomplishment." I cannot imagine a college professor welcoming students to start a traditional course when it is almost a third over by saying just come on in, do what you can and don't worry, I know you cannot get credits, but you are welcome, and you will enjoy things.

This, I think, is the best thing about MOOCs—that people can do them for their own reasons and not just for reasons compelled by graduation requirements. And better yet, people can join the course at any time, stay for a little or all of it, and still get something out of it by watching videos or reading some text on the subject at hand, and even better, if they take it, give something back to it by sharing their writing, giving feedback to writers, working with feedback from writers, and joining discussions.

MOOCs let people in to learn what they want in the way they want. The volume of participants alone does not guarantee that a discussion post will be responded to or that writing will get feedback or that feedback given will be acknowledged, but with a bit of persistence and kindness in the giving of words, most writers I've seen find some feedback coming their way. So the size of MOOCs increases the likelihood that interactions will occur. As in a traditionally taught writing course, the quality of writing feedback and discussion in a MOOC will vary. But the energy and desire to participate behind the MOOC discussion and feedback cheered me. Those who participated genuinely sought to be helpful, and believed in the value of what they were doing, in ways that came intrinsically.

Again, not every MOOC participant behaves this way, and there are always some students in a traditional writing course who are good participants, naturally getting into the ethos and purpose of activities. Still, overall, a greater percentage of MOOC students than one sees in traditional college writing courses come ready to give the best feedback they can and come seeking feedback from fellow writing students. They do this because they understand that's the heart of the course and the course is a choice. It's incredible to participate with writers who want to write and give and get feedback on writing.

MOOCs are not ideal, of course, but there is real energy that, with time and patience, can be focused. As Karen Head noted in a comment on a draft of this essay, the Coursera MOOC OSU (and Head's colleagues at Georgia Tech, as well as Duke) used lacked good tools for giving peer review. OSU worked around this by using their own peer review program, the Writers Exchange (which they dubbed Wex-MOOC.). But even as good as WexMOOC is, it still isn't designed for the volume of feedback a MOOC produces. And too, the other issue to be solved is teaching people how to give useful feedback. Enthusiasm is one thing; being constructive another. But those challenges can be met.

So where are we now? MOOCs will not kill colleges and universities; those entities require and thrive from granting degrees and charging tuition and fees to earn those degrees. They confer degrees by establishing finely wrought curricular requirements, so fine that many students who enter programs of study have, if they're lucky to have any at all, room for maybe one or two electives. A key feature for making all that work is grading—the earning of GPA scores as measured by faculty designed and/or program-designed course assessments that are valid, honest, and reliable.

Wrestling MOOCs into entities that can meet assessment challenges is doable, but adds cost. For a writing course, one has to design an assessment measure that reflects the goals and outcomes of the course, and train and pay human readers (assuming a portfolio will be used and machine scoring will not be used) to score the writing. In a traditional course, the writing teacher who grades does this almost ineluctably and intrinsically. But large scale courses call for large scale assessments of the kind we see in placement testing, exit exams, or accreditation reviews. That is, composition and rhetoric knows how to do large assessments and knows that best practices cannot be done cheaply. The point is, assessment models exist, and they can be adapted to MOOCs.

Doing assessment well will necessarily add more costs to MOOCs, but that cost and the cost of the MOOC itself, could be covered by students at an overall lower cost to them of a traditional course with a teacher grading in the traditional way. One can imagine a fee to go to a testing center to take a proctored writing exam, or a fee to have a writing portfolio read, along the lines of getting experiential credit. There will be other ideas. MOOCs might simply become textbook alternatives and students pay a StraighterLine type of fee to enter them, and so campus students use a MOOC space instead of going to a bookstore.

If that happens, if MOOCs become part of them, colleges and universities risk killing MOOCs by shifting away from the "open" part of the acronym. In a college setting, a MOOC becomes a MOC—massive online course—offered as just another option to completing the march of credits required for a degree.

The best part of MOOCs are the parts that exist apart from what a college wants or needs or thinks or does, the part that's free and where the people taking the MOOC find ways to use the discussion boards to learn from each other and make some sense of what they are learning on their own, even if what they learn is not what the curriculum had in mind. And so I wonder, would it be possible to offer MOOCs that stay open and massive, that a college or university might sponsor to in fact attract more learners who are motivated for different reasons than the students attending the college or university might be?

Imagine a writing MOOC such as OSU's or any of the other Gates Foundation grantees exploring writing, where at those schools, local students, the one's paying tuition and fees and commuting to campus or living in dorms, also join, as part of their campus writing courses. That is MOOCs are free and open so they can be part of the curriculum. The value of MOOCs for the matriculated student would be a wider audience, meeting writers from around the world, getting their feedback and giving them feedback. A MOOC such as this might have a filter so that campus course professors can find and see what they're students are doing in the wider MOOC. In this way, the MOOC provides a new learning landscape. It could make every writing course a semester abroad of sorts without leaving campus. It would open students to people with different histories and cultures but who come to the same course they're in because they want to write. It would alter how ESL students are taught and supported. It would be a lot of fun to teach at such a campus, where as an instructor good practice would likely come to encourage not just asking students to participate in the MOOC, but also participating as well.

Think of the way having students see writers motivated to write in the course for different reasons might then alter class discussions on campus, might alter assignments, might alter all kinds of things that teachers seek often to alter?

If colleges do that, at least, keep MOOCs open and don't use them only to find efficiencies, they could use the what's good and best about MOOCs in ways that serve their mission.

WORKS CITED

Bady, Andy. "Questioning Clay Shirky." *Inside Higher Ed.* December 6, 2012. http://www.insidehighered.com/views/2012/12/06/essay-critiques-ideas-clay-shirky-and-others-advocating-higher-ed-disruption

Bousquet, Marc. "Good MOOC's, Bad MOOC's." *Brainstorm: The Chronicle of Higher Education.* July 25, 2012. http://chronicle.com/blogs/brainstorm/good-moocs-bad-moocs/50361

Edwards, Julia. "Stephen Trachtenberg is not Sorry." *National Journal Online.* October 1, 2012. http://www.nationaljournal.com/features/restoration-calls/stephen-trachtenberg-is-not-sorry-20120927

Friedman, Thomas. "The Professor's Big Stage." *New York Times Online.* March 5, 2013. http://www.nytimes.com/2013/03/06/opinion/friedman-the-professors-big-stage.html

Ginsberg, Benjamin. "Administrators Ate My Tuition." *Washington Monthly.* September/October 2011. http://www.washingtonmonthly.com/magazine/septemberoctober_2011/features/administrators_ate_my_tuition031641.php

Jaschik, Scott. "MOOC Skeptics at the Top." *Inside Higher Ed.* 2 May 2013. http://www.insidehighered.com/news/2013/05/02/survey-finds-presidents-are-skeptical-moocs

Kolowich, Steve. "In Deals with 10 Public Universities, Coursera Bids for Role in Credit Courses." *The Chronicle of Higher Education.* May 30, 2013. http://chronicle.com/article/In-Deals-With-10-Public/139533

LearningCounts. "College Credit for What You Know." September 17, 2013. http://learningcounts.org.

Nourbakhsh, Illah. "It's Time to Talk about the Burgeoning Robot Middle Class." *MIT Technology Review.* May 14, 2013. http://www.technologyreview.com/view/514861/its-time-to-talk-about-the-burgeoning-robot-middle-class/

Segal, Carolyn Foster. "MOOCs R Us." *Inside Higher Ed.* March 7, 2013. http://www.insidehighered.com/views/2013/03/07/thomas-friedman-wrong-about-moocs-essay

Shirky, Clay. "Napster, Udacity, and the Academy." *Clay Shirky Blog.* November 12, 2012. http://www.shirky.com/weblog/2012/11/napster-udacity-and-the-academy/

Thrun, Sebastian. "Update on our SJSU Plus Summer Pilot." *Udacity Blog.* August 28, 2013. http://blog.udacity.com/2013/08/sebastian-thrun-update-on-our-sjsu-plus.html

Warner, John. "An Ad Hominem Attack Against Thomas Friedman." *Inside Higher Ed.* March 6, 2013. http://www.insidehighered.com/blogs/just-visiting/ad-hominem-attack-against-thomas-friedman

Writing and Learning with Feedback Machines

Alexander Reid

One of the challenges in evaluating MOOCs is understanding what their goals and objectives might be, and because there are so many different initiatives that go by the MOOC name, there can be no uniform answer.* A MOOC that provides free and open education to individuals who would otherwise have little access or opportunity is very different from a MOOC whose aim is to offer a college credit-bearing alternative to individuals who are already enrolled as college students. The large-scale xMOOCs that have been offered through Coursera, edX, and Udacity are largely modeled on the pedagogies of large lecture or conventional online courses. That is, for the most part, the activities of an online course of 100 or more can scale to 100,000: lectures, interactive assignments, testing, and, to a lesser degree, student discussion forums. However, where a single professor might be able to handle the office-hour questions of a 100 students, this is clearly not possible with 100,000. From the student perspective, if the expectation is to watch lectures, read a textbook, take notes, do homework, and pass an exam, these activities can be as easily accomplished with 100,000 peers as with 100, though one may wonder if this is an effective pedagogical approach regardless of the number of students.

Of course pedagogy is not the only concern driving university investment in MOOCs. Elite research universities may be looking to expand their global brand; they are not likely concerned with

---

* This work is licensed under the Creative Commons Attribution-Noncommercial-ShareAlike 3.0 United States License. To view a copy of this license, visit http://creativecommons.org/licenses/by-nc-sa/3.0/us/ or send a letter to Creative Commons, 171 Second Street, Suite 300, San Francisco, California, 94105, USA. For any other use permissions, contact the original author.

using MOOCs to reach their own students. Large state university systems (like those in New York, Georgia, and Tennessee) have signed agreements with Coursera in efforts to expand online, credit-bearing courses. Elsewhere, institutions like San Jose State may feel the pressure to employ MOOC courses for credit to respond to overwhelming demands for courses it cannot deliver by conventional means. For institutions seeking brand recognition, offering a MOOC in first-year composition was not a likely first choice. However, following upon the Bill & Melinda Gates Foundation's decision to offer $50,000 for the development of MOOCs for introductory courses, three such courses appeared in Coursera (offered by Duke, Georgia Tech, and Ohio State). First-year composition, along with the rest of any general education curriculum, will be a necessary part of any state system online degree program, and it may certainly be among courses that are impacted by heavy demand for enrollment. However, this does not mean that first-year composition can be easily offered in a MOOC environment. At the very least, it is clear that the pedagogical assumptions that drive massive, online education do not match with those that have traditionally informed writing instruction.

Indeed, writing instruction has always operated at the other end of the scale from massiveness. NCTE guidelines suggest that first-year writing courses should be limited to 15 students, and while it is the rare institution that adheres to that limit, such courses generally enroll 20-25 students. Similar practices are found for other "writing-intensive" courses offered across the curriculum. Furthermore, such writing instruction is often supported by a writing center where the primary practice is one-to-one consulting. Why does writing require intensive, individual attention while other subjects from psychology and world civilization to astronomy and computer programming do not? There are several possible answers. One is that instruction in many disciplines might be improved with small class sizes. Another answer recognizes that instruction in practice, in "know-how," such as teaching students writing practices in first-year composition, requires very different methods than those required for curriculum that focuses on imparting discrete bodies of knowledge, or "know-that."

This would certainly appear to be the case when one examines the key pedagogical method of writing instruction: the offering of careful feedback on student drafts from instructors, writing center consultants, and peers. This labor-intensive work, more than anything else, establishes the limit on class size. 20 students writing 25 pages of final drafts (plus submitting at least one earlier draft of each assignment for instructor feedback as is conventional in a writing course) would result in an instructor responding to 1000 pages or more of student writing per class each semester. Obviously this is a practice that does not scale. One possible solution that has been offered rests upon the possibility of computers being programmed to simulate the feedback offered by human readers. While such efforts are ongoing, they have been met with strong resistance by writing instructors as evidenced by a petition against machine scoring with nearly 4000 signatories. As the petition states:

> Independent and industry studies show that by its nature computerized essay rating is
> - *trivial,* rating essays only on surface features such as word size, topic vocabulary, and essay length
> - *reductive,* handling extended prose written only at a grade-school level
> - *inaccurate,* missing much error in student writing and finding much error where it does not exist
> - *undiagnostic,* correlating hardly at all with subsequent writing performance
> - *unfair,* discriminating against minority groups and second-language writers
> - *secretive,* with testing companies blocking independent research into their products ("Human Readers")

It is not my intention to investigate the relative merits of current or possible future machine-grading systems as a potential replacement for human reader feedback. Instead, in my view, the more interesting question regards the process of feedback itself. One of the features of machine-grading systems is that they do not seek to offer "good" feedback but simply to predict how human readers would respond to a given text within the context of a large-scale evaluation of student writing. As such, machine-grading cannot directly offer the formative assessment that is so integral to composition pedagogy. Where machine-produced, summative feedback might tell us *that* a student is struggling in some way with writing, it cannot describe *how* those struggles have been produced. And this is what human, formative feedback has always attempted to do: to describe how students are writing and how they might write differently. However, while humans may be able to provide a kind of formative feedback that machines cannot, this does not mean that they do or that they do it well. How effective is instructor feedback on student writing? Or put differently, when faculty in rhetoric and composition defend traditional pedagogical approaches to teaching writing on the merits of instructor feedback and human readers, what exactly are those merits?

Obviously the quality of instructor feedback varies across the hundreds of thousands of sections taught each semester in the United States. Some sections are taught by wholly inexperienced graduate students with great enthusiasm but little knowledge; others are taught by adjuncts who have taken on more than 100 other composition students at several different institutions in an effort to make a living wage; still others might encounter senior faculty who are only there because some other course they planned to teach did not enroll. Instructor feedback on college student writing has been long-studied in the field of rhetoric and composition. The results indicate that while research in rhetoric and composition can describe best practices for providing feedback or that any one of us might imagine an ideal feedback scenario, this obviously does not mean that students are actually encountering those feedback practices. As such, if the argument against machine-grading and massive writing instruction rests upon the value of human feedback as it is provided in practice in composition classrooms, then that foundation is not as sturdy as one might hope. However, I do not believe that the argument for human readers and feedback finally rests upon any empirical evidence regarding the quality of comments that students actually receive. Instead, the argument reflects a broader set of values concerning the humanistic qualities of writing practice: specifically the belief that writing is an activity between two humans.

Perhaps this seems like a provocative claim. Even though the humanities certainly concerns itself with reading publics and with the cultural dimensions of literacy, the activities of interpretation and close reading emphasize individual acts and place little or no value on aggregated or collective reading experiences. A review of journal articles in rhetoric or literary studies would quickly demonstrate that such scholarship ultimately operates by individual scholars reading and interpreting texts. This is entirely understandable given the industrial era that gave rise to these disciplines and the communication technologies that were available during the period that our disciplinary paradigms developed. It is certainly the case that from the inception of writing technology a writer might communicate with many others, but even in the modern era of industrial publishing technologies only a small group of professional writers ever wrote for large audiences. Even the most noted of pre-Gutenberg era authors could not have imagined writing for the tens of thousands of potential readers that the typical student in a MOOC now addresses with each forum post. In the modern era, most writing was for very small audiences, often a single individual: a friend or lover, an employer or customer, a professor. The tutorial model of instructor feedback reflects this information and media ecology.

Needless to say, writing activities today are very different from those of a century ago. We may still write for audiences of one on occasion, but we also write for far larger audiences. In addition, we write for machines. Even the Human Readers site could not operate if it were not machine-readable. It relies upon servers, networks, personal computers and mobile devices to read its HTML code to make its pages viewable to human readers. It also needs Google and other search engines to read those pages and make them accessible via searches. This is not simply a matter of technical know-how; it is also a rhetorical practice, specifically a matter of delivery. Reaching an online audience means composing a text that is findable and accessible. Attracting an audience via Twitter requires mastering the rhetoric of 140 characters. Learning to write in a MOOC immerses students in this rhetorical situation. It requires students to develop a facility with networked rhetoric that simply cannot be learned in the one-to-one writing environment of the traditional classroom. As has been evidenced by current MOOCs, students struggle with this. Faculty struggle with this, which is all the more evidence that even a highly-developed print literacy does not prepare one very well for the challenges of networked communication. And it is, of course, networked communication that our students will most need to practice moving forward.

If the traditions of the tutorial model of individual feedback reflect a gone-by era of writing, what form of feedback would be appropriate for contemporary networked communication? In asking this question, let me make clear that I am not suggesting that the traditional feedback model has suddenly become ineffective or unnecessary, though I imagine that most of us can recall far more teachers and professors who bled red ink over our papers or, even more common, offered minimal and inscrutable feedback, than instructors whose feedback might have really made a difference to us as writers. That is, traditional feedback can be valuable, but I would caution against romanticizing its effects in an effort to resist entering new media ecologies. It might be helpful to begin by broadening the concept of feedback by thinking about it in cybernetic terms. Any information system will include feedback. In the conventional composing situation of the word processor, there is feedback in the sound and feel of the keys and the appearance of letters on the screen. There is feedback in the interaction between the writer and text she has composed. Indeed, the theory behind the tutorial feedback model is in part to help students internalize the advice they receive from us, to provide their own feedback. When a student posts her text to a MOOC, it enters a network with thousands of other writer-readers and texts. Hypothetically, it seems like it might be possible for a MOOC to analyze submitted texts and group students by common interests. From there it might be possible to work toward groups that are closer to the size of traditional classrooms where it becomes feasible for each participant to read the others' texts. Part of the problem with peer feedback is that, as faculty, we are uncertain of its quality. (Personally, I believe we have no less reason to be concerned about the quality of faculty feedback, but that's another matter.) Feedback systems like ELI Review developed at Michigan State might contribute to providing automated feedback *on feedback* and thus improve the quality of peer feedback.

The real value of traditional feedback in a composition classroom is that it reflects the writing situations students will enter later in their academic career (though they are unlike to receive the same volume of teacher feedback again). If students can learn how to seek and use good feedback in the composition classroom, then they are better-positioned to do so again in the future, especially in other college courses but perhaps in their professional lives as well. On the other hand, such tutorial models do little to prepare writers for understanding the feedback provided through networked environments. In a conventional classroom, one knows one is writing for a tiny audience (perhaps an audience of one), and thus individualized feedback, especially from that specific audience, is crucial. However in a MOOC and elsewhere online, one is writing for hundreds or thousands, and the responses of a small number of individuals are perhaps less useful. What is the function of writing in this environment? It is not so unfamiliar to those with blogs or YouTube channels or large numbers of Twitter followers. As a blogger, the comment offered by a single reader is welcome and helpful, but the evidence of pageviews, RSS subscriptions, and reTweets might tell one more about the reception of a post than the single comment. However, interpreting the latter kind of feedback is not straightforward.

MOOCs and these other social media spaces are closer to Burke's parlor[1] than the print writing situation of the traditional student, where response has to be required or paid for, though parlor may not be the right term. For a MOOC, auditorium or even stadium might be more apt. In large, physical crowds, groups organically form, limited by the distance a voice can carry if nothing else. In virtual crowds, establishing affinity groups can be more complicated, and at least in MOOCs so far, those mechanisms seem absent. One imagines that a well-designed survey and recommendation engine could help MOOC users find such affinities. In the end though, the activity is not so different from that of the parlor conversation: one must listen to the conversation and respond in kind. This is how one builds a blog readership: responding to other blogs. And this is how one develops a Twitter following: responding to other tweets. Of course one has to make a valuable contribution as well. Not surprisingly, one might discover that the features that make writing valuable in a classroom are quite different from those that are valued in a MOOC. This might be an argument in defense of the claim that we shouldn't use MOOCs as a substitute for composition courses that are designed to prepared students for academic writing. Conversely, it might also be an argument that MOOCs, or some hybrid of the current composition course with the MOOC, are better situated to prepare students for writing in digital media networks.

I agree with the authors of the Human Readers petition that machine scoring, at least in its current instantiation, is not a pedagogically effective substitute for human feedback. However, the argument does beg the question about the values behind human feedback itself. Within the contexts of the modern industrial world, writing instruction, if not the entirety of institutionalized education, came to be understood in specific material terms. Our pedagogies, our modes of evaluation, even our understanding of what learning is and what it looks like, have all been shaped by this history. Furthermore, our modern separation of the human and cultural from the natural and technological has envisioned writing as an activity that is uniquely human. These values underlie the premise that the feedback we see in traditional writing classrooms is pedagogically necessary. The emergence of digital media networks suggests that we must understand composing in a different way, however. They reveal that composing is a networked activity. While the current design of MOOCs may be charitably described as "under development," and one may certainly question the motives of the for-profit interests behind many of these ventures, neither of these criticisms suggests that it might not be possible to develop online learning networks where large numbers of students come to write and improve upon their communication skills. In my view, realizing that possibility is not a matter of simulating the experiences or outcomes of traditional composition instruction, including feedback. Instead, the challenge begins with understanding the very different compositional spaces of the web and developing pedagogies that fit into those contexts.

NOTE

1. In *The Philosophy of Literary Form: Studies in Symbolic Action*, Kenneth Burke employed the metaphor of joining a conversation at parlor party as a way of describing the activity of entering into an ongoing discussion. Burke's parlor has served as an enduring concept in the field of rhetoric and composition for explaining to students the way in which seemingly isolated texts are in fact in conversation with one another over an extended period of time.

WORKS CITED

Burke, Kenneth. *The Philosophy of Literary Form: Studies in Symbolic Action*. Baton Rouge: Louisiana State UP, 1967. Print.
"Human Readers." *Human Readers*. N.p., 2013. Web. 05 Nov. 2013.

Learning Many-to-Many: The Best Case for Writing in Digital Environments

Bill Hart-Davidson

FROM ONE-TO-MANY TO ONE-TO-ONE

In a chapter I contributed to a volume on assessment in technical communication in 2010, I had been asked to write a response to some work done by colleagues at UNLV to build a comprehensive electronic resource around their technical and professional writing service courses (Jablonski & Nagelhout, 171; Hart-Davidson, 189).* I saw in that argument something of a radical possibility that, for me, is the reason I took up "things digital" as a scholarly matter—way back before the World Wide Web existed. The possibility was for digital technologies to get us closer to supporting the way most humans actually learn to write. Before I go further with that thought, let me offer a couple of pictures of what that looks like.

So what's going on here? And what does it have to do with digital technology and learning to write? Peerlearning. A performance. A moment when one of our dancers is behind the move just a bit . . . and she sneaks a look down the chorus line to catch a glimpse of a fellow

---

dancer. Or maybe we are seeing a dancer subtly leading a learner who, for the moment at least, who is also a more capable peer.

   If behind, she is able in this brief moment, to re-calibrate. To mobilize what she "knows" and has practiced no doubt for many hours before this moment and execute on it. She corrects her course just slightly. And the moment that was introspective, self-reflexive "What am I doing?" becomes, once again, a performance for an audience: "Here's what we are doing."

   Some readers might recognize theoretical code words in this description: "more capable peer" and "calibration" to name a few. Those words belong to an idea by a Russian developmental psychologist named Lev Vygotsky—and his students, by the efforts of whom we know much of his work—and they are most famously associated with a theory of learning that goes by the name "peer scaffolding." When I first encountered it as an undergraduate education major studying to become an English teacher, the core idea of peer scaffolding was both breathtaking in its obviousness and startlingly counterintuitive: we learn most and most effectively from peers rather than adults or other figures (see Gosser, et. al. for an outstanding example of the way Vygotsky's theories inform pedagogy). Within peer networks, there is a dynamic that arises from the rich set of resources each individual learner has to draw upon that boosts the learning potential—and the performance level—of each individual. Vygotsky calls this the "Zone

of Proximal Development" (32-33). In the ZPD, we can all dance better than one of us alone because we are surrounded by resources—one
another—to scaffold our learning. What counts as "more capable" and
"peer" are in flux in the context of a performance like a dance. There
are moments of relative fluency and confusion. There may be no stable
individual 'experts' at any given moment, but among the group there
exists a collective ability for a successful performance.

WRITING & DANCE

Learning to write is a lot like learning to dance in a few important
ways. It is an art. That is, a civic practice that requires deliberate practice to get better (Young, 1980). It can be learned. There are ways to
build an individual repertoire of a few key moves, and to build mastery in those, but each performance may call for them to be done in
nearly infinite combinations, in different rhythm, with different levels
of formality, intensity. One can seemingly do it alone, though each
individual uses a shared vocabulary that must constantly reference the
Other lest it fail to be understood. One can do it with others, in which
case the coordination of effort becomes an additional set of challenges

for the performers and may call for another social role—a choreographer?—to handle the inventional, the ideational work.

I'm going to come back to several of the claims I've just made—the ones about learning and deliberate practice in particular—and present some evidence to support them. But before I do I promised to connect this with digital technology. I argued above that within peer networks, there is a dynamic that arises from the rich set of resources each individual learner has to draw upon that boosts the learning potential—and the performance level—of each individual. *It's that dynamic, that learning potential, the possibility of ubiquitous, near-constant connection with a peer network that is (has always been?) the best reason to think about digital technology in relation to writing, learning, and teaching.* Yes, it's the same potential that makes us horrified by overshared accounts of revelry on Facebook. But even there it is powerful.

What I began to suggest in the 2010 article what I will argue more emphatically here is that writing programs have not adequately used digital technology to anything like their full potential in this regard. In higher education, we have used them, largely, to support a different model of learning all together: learning one-to-many. This is largely the model that MOOCs by Coursera implement. This is a model that there is a fair amount of evidence to show works **less well** than peer learning in the zone of proximal development. MOOCs may, actually, provide us with the means to do just that. But we need, first, to understand the way learning involves *interaction*.

Learning & Interaction

The stunningly obvious but also counterintuitive idea of Vygotsky's regarding peer learning has some interesting corollaries. One that I won't talk so much about but which is worth a mention is that humans are amazing at learning from one another and from their environment. We do it all the time. You'll find it is a hard impulse to turn off. But if learning is autonomic, it is also true that learning depends on interaction. Maybe most significantly on interaction with other people. We know this too. But let's dig into it a little more.

Do the patterns here look familiar?

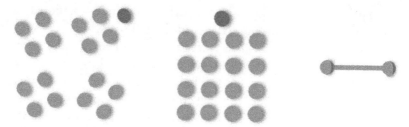

They represent, more or less, our thinking about what writing classrooms should look like. More to the point, they hint at the kinds of interactions we think best facilitate learning to write. The one in the middle is the traditional classroom, and we in composition studies have long since "flipped" or "activated" that model in ways that attempt to decenter it. In fact, in the preface to a new edition of his book on the contemporary history of Rhetoric & Composition titled *A Teaching Subject,* Joe Harris suggests that this may be our signature contribution to the academy: the disruption of the lecture model in favor of more engaged, peer-learning models in the undergraduate curriculum (Harris, xii). Whether we can take credit following several waves of writing across the curriculum, among other attempts at outreach, the flipped classroom and student-centered learning is hot.

Of course we—that is our colleagues in Rhetoric & Writing—are not quite sure what all the fuss is about. We try, after all, to have our classrooms look like the model on the left. And we supplement that model generously with the model on the far right: peer-to-peer. We even have a special place on most campuses where writers can go for that sort of one-to-one interaction. It is the key idea in Stephen North's 1984 essay "The Idea of a Writing Center" and the idea expanded and applied in Mickey Harris' 1986 book *Teaching One-to-One:* writer meets a reader, one-to-one, to talk about writing in the midst of the act. "Any writer, any time, any type of writing" was the tag line of the writing center in which I worked as a peer tutor as an undergrad at Bowling Green State University. Learning, one-to-one. High-bandwidth interaction with a more-capable peer.

And what about the interactions in the other models? One-to-many is the default lecture model. Though the one can be a student too—call that "presentation mode"—but no way around it, it's a low bandwidth, constrained interaction model. On most days in my own writing classrooms, I try to spend as little time in presentation mode and as much time as possible in studio mode—the one on the left in the figure above—where the interaction possibilities are both rich and fluid. Peer groups—few-to-few—share ideas and offer guidance. A coordinator (choreographer?) facilitates cross-group exchange, coordinates the large group with regard to shared goals and outcomes. It is an exciting way to teach and to learn. It is also expensive. It requires robust connectivity—and coordinated attention by all participants. It can take place with participants distributed in time and space—across the country or the globe, over time—but the coordinative work required to guide practice and to maintain attention on shared goals and activities becomes significant, if not overwhelming. And so it's no surprise that while the digital environment makes ever larger, ever more persistent peer networks possible...we still haven't figured this model out:

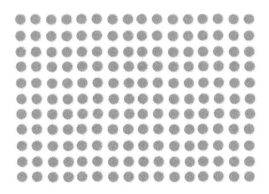

Or maybe it is more accurate to say, with MOOCs, we are just starting to try? It is not a trivial matter to devise infrastructure that supports these interaction models in a consistent way in built environments whether they be physical or virtual ones. With MOOCs, we are perhaps seeing initial attempts at building robust many-to-many learning infrastructures. It is easy to become excited about the upside of this model, in theory: learning many-to-many. It may represent the ultimate promise of digital networks: unlimited means to find and coordinate with those more capable peers in whatever endeavor we may undertake. Dancing? Writing?

But as I mentioned above, most of the MOOCs I have seen are getting the interaction part of this wrong. They are still one-to-many affairs by and large with an occasional and poorly supported attempt at many-to-many in crowded, noisy discussion forums that are NOT the main learning activity of the course. As Phill Alexander points out in his dissertation that examined the way collaboration happens in MMORPGs games like World of Warcraft, or even more impressive in my book—Minecraft—what gamers have right and MOOC providers mostly have wrong is the many-to-many part. Most MOOC environments simply do not prioritize learner-to-learner interaction in their pedagogical design or their delivery infrastructure.

We have only just started to explore what might be possible if we take the idea of learning writing many-to-many seriously. But there are some really, really good reasons to do so. I'd like to work through some of those and then come back to talking about what that might mean for the way we build programs—including technology & curriculum—to support learning many-to-many. This is an argument for building digital spaces for writing that may, or may not, include MOOCs.

The Evidence, Part I: Deliberate Practice
Produces Gains in Writing Performance

There is good news with regard to what is, in 2013, the commonly accepted wisdom about teaching writing. And, by the way, also about the use of peer networks, digital technologies and multimodal composing as interventions in learning. If you are a writing teacher who uses these methods, the evidence is more strongly in your favor than if you are using lectures, doing grammar worksheets or sentence combining, or constrained-choice exercises in general. In a 2009 article published in *Educational Psychologist,* Kellogg & Whiteford conduct a thorough review of the available evidence on effective methods in writing instruction. In doing so, they build a convincing case for something that is, for many of us, a welcome if not altogether surprising result: writing is best learned via deliberate practice (257). By deliberate practice Kellogg & Whiteford mean activity that is guided by an expert toward some end, but is actively and consciously undertaken by the learner as a means to improve performance (254).

And guided means just that: prompted and supported, but not overdetermined. Where feedback and conceptual knowledge is required—as it must be with writing—and most importantly where feedback about applying knowledge to practice is needed, those are best provided by—you guessed it—capable peers. More than when course-correction advice comes from an authority figure, when it comes from a peer, students will retain and use feedback to enhance their own performance.

The takeaway here is clear: Vygotsky's ZPD is real. And it may constitute the best reason to teach writing in digital environments, regardless of what kinds of texts (or movies, or presentation slideshows) are assigned. Peer networks. Connectivity. These provide quite possibly the ideal conditions for *deliberate practice*. Of course, not all online spaces afford peer networking. Most MOOCS absolutely do not. They operate on a different interaction model: one-to-many and dramatically under-resource learning many-to-many or even few-to-few. I'll have a bit more to say about that in a moment. But first, more good news, by which I mean good *evidence*.

The Evidence, Part II: Revision Based on Higher-Order Concerns Produces Strong, Reliable Gains in Writing Performance

In their 2007 meta-analysis that examines the effectiveness of various pedagogical approaches to teaching writing, Graham & Perin found that specific kinds of deliberate practice produces the most significant gains in writing performance. Across a variety of levels of education and institutions, writing improves most for students that spend time revising. In particular: planning and executing revisions in response to feedback on higher-order concerns such as tailoring appeals to a specific audience, strengthening evidence associated with claims, or illustrating concepts with detailed examples (466-67). More time spent doing this is generally better. And it is better when revisions are made with high-quality feedback—guided practice again—that steers the writer back toward higher-order concerns (467).

Where this kind of practice is infrequent or intermittent, or where it occurs with very little feedback to guide a subsequent revision, it tends to be not only ineffective but can be detrimental to future performance. Now...think about that for just a second. Think about the red-pen marked-up "final draft" with a comment that says "awk" and "C" on it for just a second. It has a focus on lower-order concerns, with a vague summative judgment that neither aims to guide revision nor is provided in time to do so. The evidence as presented by Graham & Perin says this does more harm than good (462).

When feedback is focused on higher-order concerns, Cho & McArthur (334) have shown that it is most effectively taken up and acted upon if it comes from peers. Cho & Cho have also shown that peers engaged in giving this sort of high-quality feedback learn from that too (640). They learn not only to be better reviewers, as we would expect. But to the extent they learn to give good feedback (that is, feedback that guides revision for higher-order concerns) their own writing performance also improves. I hope this is not news to most teachers of writing. But it is worth repeating when we contemplate writing MOOCs for a simple reason: a one-to-many learning interaction model is **NOT** the way this kind of learning happens!

LEARNING WRITING ACROSS THE LIFESPAN

I'd like to make one more point about the available evidence for learning in writing.

It is not about how, but when. People don't just learn to write when they are students in writing courses. Or when they are undergraduates, for that matter. They keep learning and growing as writers right along. They start long before we see them in first-year writing in post-secondary schools, and they continue on the job, in their personal and professional and civic lives for years after. And when they do this, they learn informally. Where this learning takes the form of deliberate practice—where it is undertaken explicitly for writing improvement—this informal learning has a familiar shape: review and revision.

Jason Swarts' 2008 book *Together with Technology* is outstanding in its documentation of the various forms this can take in workplace settings. Informal, but nonetheless rich and valuable, Swarts shows us how in moments of peer and supervisor review, together with technology, writers engage expert guidance and capable peers to improve their writing. It is a great study that opens up a bit more of what I like to call the "long arc of learning to write."

Building Digital Spaces to Support Evidence-Based Practice in Formal & Informal Writing Instruction

What should we be doing, based on the evidence, in formal settings like our institutions and programs and classrooms to enhance learning and boost writing performance? The evidence as I understand it is increasingly clear that we should do at least two things that I've covered here:

1. Make review and revision focal activities—teach both—because doing this helps writers improve. This means providing the means to foster the kinds of many-to-many, few-to-few, and one-to-one exchanges where meaningful review and dialogue about revision can take place regardless of whether the learning space is digital or face-to-face or a hybrid of both.

2. Wherever we can, we should introduce more cycles of expert guided, peer-scaffolded, deliberate practice: write-review-revise cycles focused on higher-order concerns. The more the better. Because, quite simply, this is what the evidence says works best.

The implication that follows from these two recommendations is, I believe, equally clear: writing programs should invest in, and invent where necessary, technology to help teachers & students use evidence to engage in deliberate practice. To do more cycles, to be more focused on higher-order concerns. This may mean experimenting with the many-to-many model so that deliberate practice in writing can happen across the lifespan. This may mean something like a MOOC. But it likely means something very unlike the way most MOOCs look today. Or perhaps it means something that looks like what Stephen Downes and George Siemens, among the first to talk about MOOCs, were thinking all along.

WORKS CITED

Alexander, Phill.. *Individual copycats: Memetics, identity, and collaboration in the World of Warcraft.* Unpublished Dissertation. East Lansing: Michigan State University, 2010.

Cho, Young Hoan, and Kwangsu Cho. "Peer reviewers learn from giving comments." *Instructional Science* 39.5 (2011): 629-643.

Cho, Kwangsu, and Charles MacArthur. "Student revision with peer and expert reviewing." *Learning and Instruction* 20.4 (2010): 328-338.

Downes, Stephen. "Connectivism and Connective Knowledge: essays on meaning and learning networks." *National Research Council Canada,* http://www.downes.ca/files/books/Connective_Knowledge-19May2012.pdf. 2012.

Graham, Steve, and Dolores Perin. "A meta-analysis of writing instruction for adolescent students." *Journal of Educational Psychology* 99.3 (2007): 445.

Harris, Joseph D. *A teaching subject: Composition since 1966.* Upper Saddle River, NJ: Prentice Hall, 1997.

Gosser, D. K., et al. *Peer-led team learning.* Upper Saddle River, NJ: Prentice Hall, 2001.

Harris, Muriel. *Teaching One-to-One: The Writing Conference.* Urbana, IL: National Council of Teachers of English, 1986.

Hart-Davidson, William. "Reconsidering the Idea of a Writing Program. In Hundleby, Margaret N., and Jo Allen, eds. *Assessment in technical and professional communication.* Baywood Publishing Company, 2010. 189-196.

Jablonski, Jeffrey, & Nagelhout, Ed. "Assessing Professional Writing Programs Using Technology as a Site of Praxis. Hundleby, Margaret N., and Jo Allen, eds. *Assessment in technical and professional communication.* Baywood Publishing Company, 2010. 171-188.

Kellogg, Ronald T., and Alison P. Whiteford. "Training advanced writing skills: The case for deliberate practice." *Educational Psychologist* 44.4 (2009): 250-266.

North, Stephen M. "The idea of a writing center." *College English* 46.5 (1984): 433-446.

Swarts, Jason. *Together with technology: writing review, enculturation, and technological mediation.* Baywood Pub., 2008.

Vygotsky, L. S. *Mind in society: The development of higher mental process.* Cambridge, MA: MIT Press, 1978.

Young, Richard E. "Arts, Crafts, Gifts, and Knacks: Some Disharmonies in the New Rhetoric." *Visible Language* 14.4 (1980): 341-50.

PHOTO CREDITS

After the Invasion: What's Next for MOOCs?

Steven D. Krause

When we first imagined this project in April 2013, MOOCs were riding high.* Just a year before that, March 2012, in a *Wired* magazine interview, Udacity founder Sebastian Thrun imagined a future where in 10 years, "job applicants will tout their Udacity degrees. In 50 years, he says, there will be only 10 institutions in the world delivering higher education and Udacity has a shot at being one of them."

In the year since that 2012 prediction, Udacity, Coursera, edX, and scores of other education entrepreneurs and start-ups, university presidents, politicians, and op-ed columnists gushed over MOOCs and pressed on as if Thrun's prediction was not only inevitable but perhaps too cautious. Laura Pappano's *New York Times* November 2012 article declared it "The Year of The MOOC" and recounted the breathless speed of MOOC growth—"faster than Facebook" boasted Coursera's Andrew Ng. True, there were the issues of the high drop-out rates and the problems with basic grading and feedback on student work, but it seemed only a matter of months before MOOC course credit would be accepted at most colleges and universities.

In other words, when the contributors to this collection were drafting and editing the essays in this volume during the summer and fall of 2013, the inevitability of MOOCs in higher education was palatable. Udacity's partnership with San Jose State University to offer a math MOOC for university credit (as described in more detail in the

contributions in this volume from Carbone and Decker) were well underway, and there was every reason to believe it would be successful.
The invasion of the MOOCs seemed inevitable: for better or worse,
massive online open courses in one form or another were going to be
a part of the future of higher education, and the question that most of
the writers in this collection consider is what is that inevitable future
likely to look like.

But as we go to press in 2014, that future is a little less certain.

The results of Udacity's partnership with San Jose did not match
up to Thrun's hopes, and in a November *Fast Company* profile, he all
but threw in the towel. "We were on the front pages of newspapers
and magazines, and at the same time, I was realizing, we don't educate people as others wished, or as I wished. We have a lousy product,"
Thrun said.

MOOC critics pounced, and it wasn't just Thrun's own feelings
that Udacity was not living up to his ideals. Here is how Steve Kolowich of *The Chronicle of Higher Education* in a blog post titled "Academics to Udacity Founder: Told Ya" describes it:

> Beyond schadenfreude, Mr. Thrun's humbling has left some
> academics wondering who MOOCs are good for, if not un-
> derprivileged students in California. Researchers at the Uni-
> versity of Pennsylvania recently noted that the students taking
> MOOCs from Penn on Coursera, another major MOOC
> platform, tend to be well educated already. "The individuals
> the MOOC revolution is supposed to help the most—those
> without access to higher education in developing countries—
> are underrepresented among the early adopters," wrote the re-
> searchers.

Even the *New York Times* described the San Jose State Udacity classes
as "a flop" in December 2013.

"The invasion" of MOOCs might be over and their inevitable march to revamp higher education as we know might have been
stopped, but this does not mean MOOCs specifically and innovation
in online education in general are over. For one thing, while Thrun
(not to mention his competitors at Coursera and edX) and the pundits
might have envisioned a future with only ten or so institutions educat-
ing the world, not many who actually work in higher education shared
that vision. At least that's not the vision of any of the contributors

here: none of these authors are suggesting that MOOCs could replace college courses or degrees as we now know them, and that includes contributors who wrote favorably about their experiences as MOOC instructors. MOOCs, what comes after MOOCs, and online pedagogy are going to continue to be part of the mix for delivering higher education in the U.S. and beyond for some time to come, but only a part.

As we came to the final stages of proofreading and preparing the manuscript for publication, I emailed contributors and asked if they had anything to add in light of Udacity's "failed" experiment and the other MOOC developments since this project began. Their responses all pointed out the importance of perspective in understanding MOOCs as another in a series of technological innovations in education. For example, Aaron Barlow wrote:

> Africa is littered with dinosaur bones—the remains of grandiose development projects that once were going to save the continent. They are constant reminders that progress is made by local people working together and not by great designs conceived at a distance. Just so, the history of education is the study of failed projects also of revolutionary design. Real progress comes when students and teachers interact face-to-face, as the programmed-instruction gurus of the fifties had all learned by the end of the sixties. Perhaps the proponents of MOOCs, in light of the stalling of their great new vehicle, are also, though belatedly, learning this ages-old lesson.

Alexander Reid similarly put the "newness" of MOOCs in perspective in his response:

> Those who are busy writing MOOC obituaries today are probably no more accurate than those predicting the MOOC revolution a year ago. Current MOOC platforms may fold, as technology start-ups often do, but conceptually the potential for people to learn in a massive, distributed way remains. The ongoing churn of technological development and contemporary news cycles might condition us to believe that changes will happen rapidly, over months. It might be helpful to think about these changes on the scale of decades instead. The Internet has been around for 20 years or so. We are only at the beginning of the shifts that digital media and networks will bring to education.

In other words, this latest "failure" of MOOCs isn't so much an end to the "invasion" as it is an opportunity to rethink how to make better use of the innovations and to put it in perspective. Despite the dreams and wishes of startups like Udacity, Coursera, and edX, successful and meaningful innovation in higher education is not easy and it takes time. Alan Levine offered this would-be caution to the view of MOOCs as the "easy" solution:

> If anything has come from this experience is a putting into serious discussion nearly at every institution what should be their stake in online education. But perhaps going forward this will take place without such a seemingly glib solutionism approach. Perhaps as well here in North America there might be more awareness of the vast potential yet different cultures of education around the world, and that our models may not be the one the rest of the world needs.
>
> Perhaps there will be realization that education is not a mass manufactured experience and that there is more to an education than a letter of completion.

Finally, while the MOOCs may have lost some of the mainstream steam and attention they had a year ago, it's not as if the MOOC invasion has stopped. All of the major providers (including Udacity) continue to roll out new MOOCs, there are more MOOC providers in Europe and Australia, and the innovations with how MOOCs are constructed continue everywhere. Jeremy Knox and his colleagues successfully ran their EDC MOOC ran again just this past November, and Kay Kalasek and her colleagues are preparing for a new version of their Rhetorical Composing MOOC for Fall 2014. In her email to me, she reflected on that and on the lessons learned about teaching MOOCs and teaching in traditional settings:

> The work of designing OSU's Rhetorical Composing MOOC, for instance, has proven so different from any curricular efforts we had previously undertaken that it throws into sharp relief the ideological belief systems undergirding our normal face-to-face classroom teaching habits: teachers as expert graders; a fixed curriculum that all students completed; and students who shared common cultural, linguistic, and geographical understandings. For us, the new work of teaching

in MOOCs demanded that we re-consider approaches previously accepted as regular features of our classes. This routinization of instruction, we were reminded, can blind us to the changing demands of teaching and learning—especially in digital global eduscapes that change so rapidly and are so very different from brick-and-mortar classrooms.

And of course, all kinds of people—including some of our contributors—continue to sign up for MOOCs. The vision of MOOCs competing with more traditional degree programs at colleges and universities might be over, but the value of MOOCs for personal enrichment and for the pleasure of learning continues unabated. Elizabeth Woodworth summed up the spirit and I suspect the motivation of many MOOC students:

> I continue to sign-up for and explore MOOCs with the express intention of getting something amazing from each one if I can. I mostly gravitate toward arts-oriented MOOCs, but I search for leadership MOOCs, too, and those on higher education to explore as well as something totally out of my wheelhouse: like astronomy or architecture. It's there for the investigation—why not see what I can learn that I could then bring back to my classroom? It's like having a huge playground for my teaching self where all the toys are free to take home.

Ultimately, the most lasting impact of the rise of MOOCs will be for us as educators to once again step out of the routine and static practices of "traditional" classrooms to acknowledge the different ways students and teachers can encounter and work together in online settings, in face to face classrooms, and in everything in-between. The invasion of the MOOCs hasn't stopped; it's just slowed, changed directions, and begun to morph into the next big thing.

WORKS CITED

Chafkin, Max. "Udavity's Sebastian Thrun, Godfather of Free Online Education, Changes Course." *Fast Company.* 14 November 2013. Web. 20 December 2013. <http://www.fastcompany.com/3021473/udacity-sebastian-thrun-uphill-climb>

Leckart, Steven. "The Stanford Education Experiment Could Change Higher Learning Forever." *Wired Magazine.* 20 March 2012. Web. 20 December 2013. <http://www.wired.com/wired-science/2012/03/ff_aiclass/all/>

Lewin, Tamar. "After Setbacks, Online Courses are Rethought." *New York Times.* 10 December 2013. Web. 19 December 2013. <http://www.nytimes.com/2013/12/11/us/after-setbacks-online-courses-are-rethought.html>

Pappano, Laura. "The Year of the MOOC." *New York Times.* 2 November 2012. Web. 20 December 2013. <http://www.nytimes.com/2012/11/04/education/edlife/massive-open-online-courses-are-multiplying-at-a-rapid-pace.html?smid=pl-share>

Contributors

Aaron Barlow's most recent book is *The Cult of Individualism: A History of an Enduring American Myth*. In addition to teaching at New York City College of Technology (CUNY), he is Faculty Editor of *Academe*, the magazine of the American Association of University Professors.

Siân Bayne is a Senior Lecturer in the School of Education, and Associate Dean (digital scholarship) in the College of Humanities and Social Science at the University of Edinburgh. Her research is focused on the many ways in which the digital changes and challenges education, with a focus on open, distance and higher education.

Kaitlin Clinnin is a PhD student in Rhetoric, Composition, and Literacy Studies at the Ohio State University. Her research interests center on the intersection of composition pedagogy, learning communities, and modes of education delivery.

Nick Carbone began teaching online in 1988, has published several articles and presented hundreds of workshops about teaching online. Currently the Director of Digital Teaching and Learning for Bedford/ St. Martin's, he frequently consults with departments on online course design, professional development, and issues in teaching online.

Denise Comer is an Assistant Professor of the Practice of Writing Studies and Director of First-Year Writing at Duke University. She teaches theme-based first-year writing seminars on such areas of inquiry as illness narratives, civic engagement, and travel writing. She taught her first MOOC in 2013. Her scholarship, which has been published in such journals as *Pedagogy, Writing Program Administrators Journal,* and *Composition Forum*, explores writing pedagogy, writing program administration, and the intersections between technology and the teaching of writing. She has two books forthcoming from Fountainhead Press in 2014: *Writing in Transit: A Reader* (ed.) and *It's Just a Dissertation: The Irreverent Guide to Transforming Your Dissertation from Daunting to Doable to*

Done (co-written with Barbara Gina Garrett). She lives in Raleigh, North Carolina, with her husband and their three children.

Glenna Decker is an instructional designer at Grand Valley State University as well as a senior adjunct instructor in Adult and Higher Education. She is currently working on her dissertation towards a Ph.D. in Higher Education Leadership. In addition to traditional in-seat teaching, she has taught online courses since the late 1990's.

Susan H. Delagrange is an Associate Professor of English at the Ohio State University at Mansfield, where she teaches courses on rhetoric, digital media, and professional writing. She has published print and digital articles in various journals and edited collections, including *Kairos, College Composition and Communication,* and *Digital Writing Assessment and Evaluation.* Her digital book project, *Technologies of Wonder: Rhetorical Practice in a Digital World,* was published by Computers & Composition Digital Press/Utah State University Press and won the CCCC Outstanding Book Award in 2013.

Scott Lloyd DeWitt is an Associate Professor of English at The Ohio State University at Columbus, where he teaches composition, composition pedagogy, and digital media production and is the Vice Chair of Rhetoric, Composition, and Literacy. An OSU Alumni Association Distinguished Teaching Award recipient, he is the author of *Writing Inventions: Identites, Technologies, Pedagogies* (SUNY), which was awarded the "Computers and Composition Distinguished Book Award" in 2003. He recently published *Stories That Speak To Us* with H. Louis Ulman and Cynthia Selfe, a scholarly collection of curated exhibits from the Digital Archive of Literacy Narratives (Computers and Composition Digital Press, 2013).

Laura Gibbs has been on the faculty at the University of Oklahoma since 1999, and she has been teaching fully online courses (Mythology and Folklore, Indian Epics, World Literature) since 2002. You can see her online course materials at MythFolklore.net.

Jeff Grabill is Chair of the Department of Writing, Rhetoric, and American Cultures at Michigan State University and also a Senior Researcher with Writing in Digital Environments (WIDE) Research. Grabill studies how digital writing is associated with citizenship and learning. He has published two books on community literacy and articles in journals like *College Composition and Communication, Technical Communication Quarterly, Computers and Composition,* and *English Education.*

Kay Halasek is Associate Professor of English and director of Second-year Writing at Ohio State. Author of *A Pedagogy of Possibility, Writing Lives, and Landmark Essays on Basic Writing,* she has also contributed essays to *College English, Written Communication, Rhetoric Society Quarterly,* and other journals in education, composition, and rhetoric. She currently serves as book review editor for T*he Journal of Teaching Writing.*

William Hart-Davidson is Associate Dean for Graduate Studies and a Senior Researcher at WIDE Research at Michigan State University.

Karen Head is an Assistant Professor in Georgia Tech's School of Literature, Media, and Communication and Director of the Institute-wide Communication Center. Her research focuses on communication theory and pedagogical practice, especially the implementation and development of writing centers, writing program administration, and multidisciplinary communication. An award winning teacher, Head's courses center on analyzing, critiquing, evaluating, and creating a variety of texts that demonstrate an understanding of audience and adaptation of multimodal rhetorical strategies and tools. In 2012-13, she became the lead instructor on a team awarded a Gates Foundation Grant to develop one of the first MOOCs focused on college composition.

Jacqueline Kauza received her B.A. in English (with Honors) and Anthropological Archaeology from the University of Michigan in 2011. She is currently pursuing a Master's degree in Written Communication with a focus on the Teaching of Writing from Eastern Michigan University.

Jeremy Knox is an ESRC funded PhD student with the Moray House School of Education at the University of Edinburgh and a tutor on the MSc in Digital Education. He is currently researching Massive Open Online Courses and the open education movement with an interest in critical posthumanism and new materialist theory.

Steven D. Krause is a Professor in the Department of English Language and Literature at Eastern Michigan University. Most of his teaching at the undergraduate and graduate levels focuses on the relationship between writing and technology. Some of his recent scholarship has appeared in *College Composition and Communication, Kairos,* and *Computers and Composition*, and he has published commentaries in *AFT On Campus* and *The Chronicle of Higher Education*. His blog at stevendkrause.com won the John Lovas Memorial Weblog award from Kairos in 2011. Besides this collection and other scholarly projects on MOOCs, Krause was also both a graduate and dropout of several MOOCs, and he plans on enrolling in more.

Alan Levine is widely recognized for expertise in the application of new technologies to education, As an early pioneer on the web and early proponent of blogs and RSS, he shares his ideas and discoveries at CogDog-Blog.

Charles Lowe is an Associate Professor of Writing at Grand Valley State University where he teaches web design, professional writing, business communication, document design, and first-year writing. He is a long time open educational resource advocate, and the co-editor of *Writing Spaces Volumes 1 and 2*.

Hamish Macleod has a background in psychology and biology, and is now a Senior Lecturer in the School of Education at the University of Edinburgh. He has spent a number of years as a member of the University's Centre for Teaching, Learning & Assessment, but is now primarily involved teaching on the University's MSc in Digital Education. He has long standing interests in the uses of information technology, particularly computer-mediated communications, social technologies, and digital games and simulations, in teaching and learning.

Ben McCorkle is an Associate Professor of English at the Ohio State University at Marion, where he teaches courses on composition, the history and theory of rhetoric, and digital media production. He is the author of the book *Rhetorical Delivery as Technological Discourse: A Cross-Historical Study*, published by Southern Illinois University Press. He has also published essays in various journals and edited collections, including *Computers and Composition Online*, *Rhetoric Society Quarterly*, and *Composition Studies*.

Jennifer Michaels is a PhD candidate in English at The Ohio State University, where she teaches courses on composition, digital media, and technical communication. Her dissertation research examines how scholars use social media to support their composing processes and suggests ways to apply social media to undergraduate composition pedagogy.

James E. Porter is a Professor at Miami University with a joint appointment in English and in the Armstrong Institute for Interactive Media Studies. He also directs the program in American Culture & English, Miami's English language program for international students. His current research investigates questions of design and economics for online writing and communication courses.

Alex Reid is an Associate Professor of English and Director of Composition and Teaching Fellows at the University at Buffalo where he studies digital rhetoric. He is the author of *The Two Virtuals: New Media and Composition* and the co-editor of *Design Discourse: Composing and Revising Professional Writing Programs.* He blogs at Digital Digs (alex-reid.net).

Jeff Rice is Martha B. Reynolds Professor of Writing, Rhetoric, and Digital Studies at the University of Kentucky. He is the author of *The Rhetoric of Cool: Composition Studies and New Media and Digital Detroit: Rhetoric and Space in the Age of the Network,* as well as numerous articles and chapters on pedagogy, writing, rhetoric and new media.

Jen Ross is the programme director of the MSc in Digital Education at the University of Edinburgh. She researches and teaches on topics including MOOCs, digital futures for learning, museum and gallery education, and online distance approaches to teaching and learning. She is co-author of the Manifesto for Teaching Online, and co-creator of the E-learning and Digital Cultures and Warhol MOOCs at the University of Edinburgh.

Bob Samuels is President of UC-AFT and teaches writing at UCSB. He is the author of the blog Changing Universities and the forthcoming book, *Why Public Higher Education Should Be Free.*

Cynthia L. Selfe is a Humanities Distinguished Professor at the Ohio State University, where she coordinates the Visiting Scholars in Digital Media and Composition program. Selfe is the first woman and the first English teacher ever to receive the EDUCOM Medal for innovative computer use in higher education. She has authored or edited a number of works on digital technology, both alone and in collaboration with colleagues. Along with Scott DeWitt, she is the Director of Ohio State's annual Digital Media and Composition (DMAC) summer institute.

Christine Sinclair is a lecturer on the MSc in Digital Education at the University of Edinburgh and is also a graduate from the programme. She has worked in four very different Scottish universities and is particularly interested in language and literacy issues related to student and teacher experiences, now focusing on digital environments.

Melissa Syapin is a graduate student at Eastern Michigan University completing a Master's in Written Communication, with a focus on Professional Writing. She has explored concepts of multimedia writing, rhetoric, and media ecology, and will graduate in spring 2014. Melissa earned a Bachelor of Arts in English and Communication Studies from the University of Michigan.

Elizabeth Woodworth, PhD, is the director of composition and associate professor of English at Auburn University at Montgomery where she teaches courses in writing studies, composition/rhetoric pedagogy, Victorian literature, and seminars for an interdisciplinary honors program. She was born and raised in LA and loves writing, the Victorians, and baseball. (In that order.)

Edward M. White is a visiting scholar in English at the University of Arizona and professor emeritus of English at California State University, San Bernardino, where he served prolonged periods as English department chair and coordinator of the upper-division university writing program. He is the author or editor of 14 books and more than 100 articles and book chapters on literature and the teaching of writing, including five English Composition textbooks, most recently *Inquiry* (2004) and *The Promise of America* (2006). His work has recently been recognized by the publication of *Writing Assessment in the 21st Century: Essays in Honor of Edward M. White* (Hampton, 2012), and by the 2011 Exemplar Award from the CCCC. His newest book (with Norbert Elliot and Irvin Peckham) on the assessment of writing programs is scheduled for publication by Utah State University Press in 2015.

Heather Noel Young is a graduate student of Rhetoric and Composition. Her research interests include MOOCs, online writing education, and the intersections between writing pedagogy and technical and professional communication studies.

Index